Random Scribblings

Junk I've Littered the Internet With for Two Decades

Also by mcgrew:
Yesterday's Tomorrows
Mars, Ho!
Nobots
The Paxil Diaries

Cover photos: mcgrew
Hardcover ISBN 978-0-9910531-6-2
Printed in the United States of America

Table of Contents

Random Scribblings

I've written for most of my life, but nothing was made public until I was able to get on the internet in 1997. None of what I wrote before then has been published, and most likely won't be. Most are lost, paper notebooks left behind in moves.

I was online in 1983, but there was no World Wide Web. I was on bulletin boards later, which got close to the web but wasn't quite it.

I was pretty poor back in 1997, but got a huge promotion and raise a couple of years later. But in 1997 I had no established credit; when my then-wife and I tried to buy a car, we were informed we were "ghosts". We weren't in the system.

A local video store chain, Family Video, opened its internet-connected servers for $12.95 a month dialup service, and unlike every other ISP you needed no credit card. You could use one, but cash and checks were perfectly acceptable as well.

They offered "unlimited access" for the $12.95, and from what I could tell they were true to their word. Part of the access was banner-free personal web space, which appeared to only forbid posting commercial pages.

The first Saturday I was online I wrote *Steve's School of Fine Art*, a parody of an art class and a history class I took in college.

I had been an avid video gamer since the first coin-fed video games in the late 1970s. I bought a small, cheap computer in 1982, mostly to play games on. There were very few games for that model. In fact, there was little software of any kind for it, so I learned programming and wrote my own.

By the time I got on the internet there were plenty of excellent games. Two of my favorites, Screamer and Road Rash, had a paucity of information on the internet, so I collected what I could and put it famvid's servers.

Later in 1997 I wrote *The Life and Times of a Dumpster Cat.* There were others, but unfortunately have succumbed to "bit rot" and were lost.

The next Spring, someone who had seen my "Screamer" and "Road Rash" pages suggested that I start a Quake page. It seemed pointless to me, since there seemed to be an unlimited supply of pages about that game.

However, I noticed that most were poorly designed and usually contained little, if any, content, so I decided to make a site about that game that would actually be well-designed and full of useful and interesting topics. Much of it was humorous. I built a huge collection of tested console and server commands, cheats, tips for newbies, jokes... it was full of solid content. It became popular and I gained fans.

Most of it you would not have any interest in whatever, but if I'd made a book of what I have of that old site on my hard drive, it would probably be well over a couple thousand pages long. I've included parts I think are funny or interesting in some way, but probably only added a tenth of it or less to this tome.

I got tired of it by 2002, a few months before my wife abandoned our two teenaged daughters, her cats, and me. The kids and I sought therapy, and after listening to all three of us separately and together, said that he of course couldn't be sure but he suspected that the wife was afflicted with Dissociative Identity Disorder.

A few months after she left, I discovered kuro5hin.org, a nerd site where "community members" would write and submit articles and keep diaries. It helped keep my mind off of my troubles, both financial and emotional.

My diaries and articles were even more popular at what was known as "K5" than the old Springfield Fragfest. Only a small number of submitted articles, which were voted on by logged in K5 members, made it to front page. Three quarters of mine were accepted and placed on K5's front page, seventeen in all. Unfortunately, a lot of them I don't remember, and they're too old to be easily found at K5.

After I submitted my first article, some were discussing whether or not I was some famous writer just "slumming" at K5. I was greatly amused!

After a few years of the diaries, people were requesting that I turn them into a book, which I finally got around to earlier this year. It's called "The Paxil Diaries" and is available in bookstores right now.

After a few happy years at K5, Rusty Foster, the site owner and a fan, spent all his time at his new left-leaning political site that was becoming insanely popular, and pretty much handed K5 to his admins. After an online argument with one of them, I left in a huff. Most everybody else did, too, probably because of that one admin.

I discovered that slashdot.org had instituted journals, so I started posting there. I'd had an account since the previous century.

Like the Quake site, only a small fraction of what I wrote at K5 and slashdot is included here. The first crude drafts of my books *Nobots* and *Mars, Ho!* were posted there before editing and book publication. *Mars, Ho!* crude drafts were also posted at a new site, Soylent News, at soylentnews.org.

Here are the articles I chose, in the order that they were written.

Oct 22, 2014

Steve's School of Fine Art

The Faculty

A bunch of people who were dumb enough to study art and smart enough to get a Master's Degree in it, plus a few who went on to obtain their doctorates, thus condemning themselves to teaching Art History for the rest of their lives. For the ultimate college art teacher, rent *The Eiger Sanction*.

The job you get after you graduate

You might become a high school art teacher and teach a bunch of talentless miscreants and hoodlums who won't listen to a word you say to go out and vandalize box cars with spray paint. A job in advertising, you say? HAH! Forget it. Marry someone whose dad owns an ad agency instead. Advertising is a field where they want to know who you know, not what you know. They don't care if you graduated Kindergarten. Can't you tell from looking at ads? The only talented person ever in the advertising field was Andy Warhol, and he hated it. You want to be an artisté and have your crap hanging in fine galleries? Marry a gallery owner or an art critic. You want to make a lot of money? "Look at Van Gogh", you say, "his paintings sell for millions!" As your will learn in Art History, poor Vincent only sold one painting in his entire life, to his brother, for about five dollars in today's money.

Lesson 1: The Critique

The ultimate in masochism. Your grade depends on the critique. In the critique, everyone in class exhibits their work, and comments on all of it. How good yours looks depends on how bad theirs looks. Each work is scrutinized and ruthlessly shredded by your competitors, whose grades depend on how good their work looks compared to yours. These people are mostly talentless losers, not unlike yourself, who desperately want their work placed somewhere where someone might see it, just like you and Vincent.

To survive this ordeal, keep your work covered until nearly everyone has their work displayed. Place yours prominently next to the worst piece of crap in the room. While everyone is ripping each other to shreds with pompous, empty, multi-syllable phrases, translate what they say into plain English, which will demonstrate to the instructor that you, unlike they, actually understand this gobbledygook. Praise everyone's work with backhanded compliments in such a way that the teacher knows that you know it's crap, while the other students think you're complimenting their work.

Beat everyone to the punch by being merciless about your own work, especially if you've outdone yourself and have actually produced something that doesn't suck. The teacher knows what you've done right; show him/her/it that you know what you've done wrong.

Smile smugly when you're ripped. Let your face say "HA! It worked! They HATE it!" (See *Insulting an Art Student* and *Art History*, below)

Lastly, be an attractive woman with large breasts. The heterosexual men and the lesbians will all be trying to get in your pants and won't be hard on your work, the homosexual men will be afraid of being thought of as misogynistic, and the heterosexual women will dismiss you completely as a total, talentless airhead. This is the only place they won't think of you as a threat.

Insults for the art student (see *The Critique*, above)

"Gee, that's really *nice!*" "Nice" is the worst insult you can give to an artist (See *Art History*, below).

Call a sculpture a "statue". Besides "nice", "statue" is the worst thing you can call a sculptor's work. The only person who hates "statue" worse than a sculptor is an actor.

Call a painting a "picture". Go ahead, show your ignorance!

Call the work "pretty". This is an insult to every artist except Audrey Flack.

Those of you who are art students or have been art students understand this. Those who aren't have probably hit the "back" button (or the "get me the *hell out* of here *right now*" button) already. For those of you non-art students who've stayed with me (i.e., so stoned out of your mind that even this is entertaining even though you don't understand a bit of it), although the original purpose of art was decoration, it no longer is. "Decorative art" is considered by those who know and understand art to be an oxymoron. Art stimulates the mind, the brain, the senses, or better yet, all three at once. If it doesn't make you think and/or feel, it isn't art. See See *Art History*, below.

Art History, or "Who the hell is this Vincent guy, anyway?"

In the beginning, some ignorant savage discovered that a burned stick made marks. After he discovered that spoiled grapes and some kinds of poisonous plants made him feel really funny without actually killing him, he discovered that sometimes those marks could look like more than marks.

Somewhere around the same time, some other ignorant savage discovered that the spoiled berries she was gathering also made marks, and these were in *color!* WOW, *look at the colors!* These two got together, smoked some poisonous plants and drank some spoiled berry juice and procreated some more ignorant savages. These two ignorant savages became "medicine men" and "witch doctors", known to us who live tens of thousands of years later as politicians. Bill never inhaled. Oxygen deprivation does weird things to the brain.

Later, the biggest and baddest of each group of ignorant savages beat the bejeebers out of everyone else, took their stuff and declared that everything they could see for as far as they could walk was theirs and if anybody had anything bad to say about this they were going to take a real long nap under the dirt. Nobody complained much, at last nobody with much sense. These jerks were known as "kings", and some of the less unenlightened ones let those who could make marks that looked like something other than marks make marks instead of working. Note that the German currency is known as the "mark".

Some four to ten thousand years (the figure is disputed by those who don't know for sure, meaning everybody) before a guy got nailed to a cross for not stealing an ass (go figure), one of these incestuous Egyptian kings decided that he wanted a really nice grave. Prehistorians (or "archaeologists") claim that it really had something to do with the economy instead of the fact that the guy was stupid and crazy because his father was also his uncle. Anyway, this prehistoric era is known as the dawn of post-prehistoric art.

After this civilization (run by people who called their dad both Dad and Uncle) perished (see the *Old Testament* for details; hey, it's documented, if you don't believe witnesses you probably think Elvis is alive and the moon landing was a hoax), the Greeks (Sodom wasn't in Greece but don't tell that to a Greek) built a civilization of their own. These folks (Aristotle, for one) kind of figured stuff out without the benefit of modern science, much like our present day politicians. They brought art to a high not seen since the Egyptians, even without all that gold. About the time their civilization bit the dust, the Romans rose (at least the male Romans), famous for their drunken orgies. The poor Jews still weren't over what the Egyptians had done to them.

During the early part of the Greek civilization there was another culture, the Minoans, who produced stunning works of beauty and grace, and are thought to have been wiped out by an explosive volcano. It is also believed that this same explosion caused a tidal wave that caused the parting of the Red Sea, just in time for the Jews to get across and drown a bunch of mean guys that were chasing them with big knives.

Meanwhile, my ancestors were painting themselves blue and worshiping trees. Funny what spoiled berries will do! When they were a little more sober, if not completely sane, they were building the world's first PC, known to us as "Stonehenge". The hardware was fairly simple, but programming it wiped out their culture completely (the YzeroK problem; they were too stupid, cheap and shortsighted to use more than one digit for date calculations).

Of course, after the Romans built their famous roads, Visigoths used those roads to come for a visit. Civilization as we know it came to an end. A thousand bloody and pestilence filled years or so later, give or take a couple of centuries, after the Visigoths paid their nice visit to the Romans, the Renaissance began. Art and Science started to be reborn, and we actually know some of the artists' names. Artists were known as artisans; well, not really, since English as we know it wasn't spoken, but that's what the art historians teach so I'll repeat it here. They weren't superstars like the artists of the twentieth century, such as Pablo Picasso, Andy Warhol, or O.J. Simpson. They didn't get paid much (Except that brown noser Leonardo), even the ones who were well known in their time.

The people of this time had discovered the ancient Romans and Greeks and said "Wow, this crap is pretty good! How the hell did they do that?"

Some of them got pretty good themselves. Michelangelo Buonarroti nearly went blind painting some pictures on the Pope's ceiling (wasn't that Pope guy really nice?) and carved a bunch of statues of naked men with small penises (the Greek influence) out of big rocks. Jan Vermeer invented oil paint, making art theft much easier. Leonardo Da Vinci made a few bucks painting pictures while trying real hard to be Orville Wright.

Then, as now, only the rich or boring had access to fine art.

A "Library" was any building with a book in it. Books were chained to the walls of these buildings. So were people (usually not in libraries, though). Not content with ruining things in Europe, the Europeans sent their worst politically connected criminals to Australia.

While all this was going on, the Asians and Americans were building civilizations, inventing computers (The Mayan's computer, like our own, stops at the end of the 20th century, but it didn't matter nearly as much to them as to us, since they're all dead) and gunpowder, and, of course, destroying their own civilizations again and again in the process. Aren't computers

9

and gunpowder fun?

A couple of hundred years later, the peasants were revolting. "I could have told you that", the aristocracy said; but they were pretty stupid, and didn't know that what was meant was that revolution was brewing, not that the peasants weren't pleasant. The Queen of France, when she heard that the peasants had no bread, said "let them eat cake." The King of England, when he heard that the colonists were unhappy with taxes, raised the taxes on tea and passed a law making it illegal not to drink tea. In France, then considered the "art capital of the world", Neoclassicism (meaning that painters and sculptors were still in awe of the Romans and Greeks) was all the rage. The French revolution was blamed by some art historians on some of this neoclassical art (see the image above). In the English colonies, nothing was blamed on art, since all the homegrown stuff was really crap, and they were too busy growing hemp and plotting revolution, much like the hippies of the 1960s. They had long hair, too.

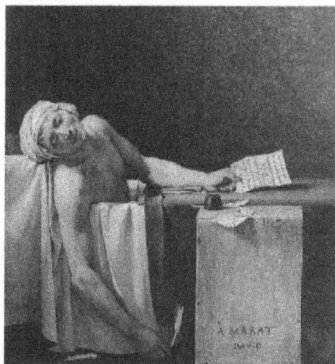

I have completely glossed over the Victorians, like Renoir, Titian (honest, that was really his name), etc., who liked to paint obscene pictures of fat naked women swinging on swing sets, laying on couches, and doing other silly things, and some of the art from Holland, including whats-his-name, who painted dark, gloomy pictures of ugly and/or dead people.

In the late nineteenth century, the galleries were filled with some real sucky crap that is considered crap even today. You won't see any of them in any museum, and may be unlucky enough to see one or two in an art history class as a good example of what art isn't. The painters that you will recognize weren't being hung; they were too busy getting big red "R"s for "rejected from this art show" stamped on the back of their paintings so nobody would dare offend the art establishment by trying to sell one. We will go into some of them in detail here.

Art as we know it was being born in this period; art for art's sake (yeah, like they would have been offended if you offered them money) which explored light, color, form, abstraction, and all of the elements that make the average layman say really lame things like "my five year old could do better than that" and "but what *is* it?"

There were several different "schools", meaning kinds of painting, not where they learned to do it. The first were the impressionists, such as Renoir, who I lied about earlier. Well, it was the Victorian era but he was known as an impressionist, with such greats as "child with a whip", "Head of a dog", and "Bather arranging her hair". Manet painted such memorable works as "The queer musician" and "Fruit on a table". Edward Degas painted "After the bath" and "Woman Drying Herself". Claud Monet painted the "Luncheon on the Grass" picture, famous for its big red "R" stamped on the back, "Lady in the Garden at Sainte-Adresse", a nice picture, it's really pretty, and "Poppy Field", which may give you an idea of where some of their inspiration came from.

The impressionists were trying to "catch the light", the way a scene looked like in an instant that the light was unusual, which explains why so many of their paintings look fuzzy and/or sketchy. Pretty avant-garde for the time, but if you try to do it they'll say it's real lame.

Then there were the post impressionists, who painted pictures of posts. Well, okay, that's a lie, too. They were Post

Impressionists because by the time they found out they weren't ever going to be hung in the fancy high priced galleries Impressionism was already starting to be passé, so they painted pretty much the same way and gave it a new name. Two of the most infamous were Vincent Van Gogh (So *that's* who Vincent was) and Paul Cezanne. They were "roommates" at one time, and Cezanne hated Van Gogh's guts. Nobody except a few other artists ever heard of Van Gogh at the time, and all of them thought his stuff sucked.

Gaughan is known for some of his primitive looking pictures of unclad and scantily clad ugly women, one of whom was his wife. Gaughan used bright, garish, clashing colors, much like I was criticized for in critiques, which are now widely used in advertising by dimwits who don't know any better or care.

Van Gogh was a real nut case, a homosexual alcoholic drug abuser who cut off his ear and mailed it to Gaughan as an indication of his affection. Limp-wristed Vincent only sold one painting in his entire life, to his brother, for a pittance, as payback for some money he owed his brother. This loser painted some incredibly stunning paintings that must be seen in the flesh to be appreciated. Actually, all of the paintings mentioned here must be seen to be appreciated. Most of them are really huge, and there's no way the detail and color can be reproduced in an obscenely expensive art book, which this isn't, let alone on a computer screen. One of Van Gogh's paintings is of a branch of a blooming dogwood tree. Up close, it is completely abstract, and you can't tell what it's a picture of. From across a very large room it stands out in stunning detail, and appears to be a real branch with real flowers standing out about three feet from the canvas.

His last three works were of the same corn field. The first was very detailed, using a very small brush and must have taken forever to paint. The second was much sloppier and painted with the kind of brush most people use to paint window trim with. The last is a finger painting. After he painted the third version, he sat down in the cornfield he had just painted and shot himself.

The opening of the twentieth century brought even weirder stuff. The cubists attempted to portray four dimensional images on a two dimensional surface. The most well known of these was Pablo Picasso, whose early work wasn't cubistic at all, but quite realistic. Laymen who see Picasso's early work say *"That's* Picasso? When did *he* learn to paint?"

The Surrealists Attempted to make sense of their dreams, or what they would like you to think were their dreams. Surrealism was first invented by German writers, and visual artists, always looking for something different, stole the idea.

The most famous Surrealist was Salvador Dali, a Spanish guy who was nearly as nutty as Van Gogh, although he had better reason to be out of his tiny little mind. Dali's older brother was also named Salvador (Hi, I'm Larry, this is my brother Darryl, and this is my other brother Darryl). Salvador is Spanish for "savior", as in "Our lord and savior Jesus Christ". After the older brother died, Dali was born, and his parents, obviously at least as nutty as their offspring, named the second

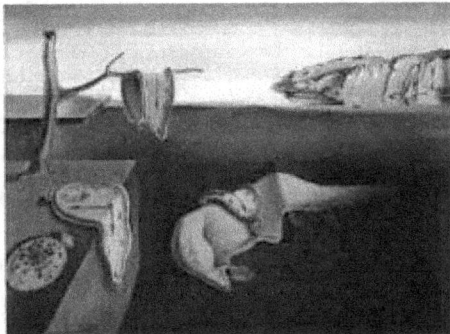

baby Salvador also, thinking the second baby was the reincarnation of the first baby. Salvador was led to believe that he was Christ, or at least the Anti-Christ. This loony tunes is most famous for the picture illustrated above, the one with the melted clocks. Another of his paintings has some very photorealistic images of dead flies on it... no, wait, they're *real* flies stuck on the canvas! Dali had himself hung from a flying airplane by his mustache. Even Van Gogh wasn't crazy enough to do something like that.

Some of Dali's works are disturbing, hell they're *all* nutzo. This guy was downright *weird*. This guy, who you definitely wouldn't want your daughter (let alone your son) to date, painted some beautiful stuff, none of which makes any sense to anybody except another lunatic. Terrified of dying, he found religion in his later years and painted huge religious pictures that are as crazy, weird and beautiful as the early stuff. When you go to Florida to see Mickey Mouse and try and get a job making cartoons for the kiddies, be sure to go to Tampa and see the Dali museum.

In the 1920s another school of artists sprung up, and this bunch was also rejected by the art establishment. If you're starting to get a clue, well, good for you. This art is known as "Dada" (Note that there is an art museum in Chicago known as MOMA). Dada was anti art art (Huh??), a total rejection of the art establishment. Marcel Duchamp hung a urinal from the wall as a statement about the art establishment, and critics praised it for its color and form. A dada exhibit featuring a woman reading poetry wearing nothing but a hat was busted by the local constables. There is some dada to the left.

By the end of the twentieth century, things were changing at such a rapid pace that I would get way too bored to get into all of them with even the most cursory examination, but some of the folks that may or may not be remembered by art historians include

Andy Warhol, the shoe salesman turned pop culture icon, Jackson Pollack, who made nice pictures; well, actually he did it by splashing paint on canvasses from usually about six feet away, Audrey Flack, Robert Rauschenberg, Lets see, that guy that made that one picture, you know the one...

Painting
Color
There are only three of them. They are not the same three you see on your monitor. In painting, the only three colors there are are red, yellow, and blue. At least, they are the only colors that matter, since you can theoretically make all the colors from those three. Theory is often wrong in art.

Your Eyeball
There are theoretically an infinite number if colors, some of which you can actually see. Light bounces off of things right into your eyeball through the part that isn't opaque, called the cornea. A lens focuses the light through this aperture where it lands on what is known as "that movie screen thing on the back of the inside of the eye", or

TMSTOTBOTE, also known as a retina.

The retina has microscopic rods that can detect brightness, and microscopic cones that detect certain wavelengths, roughly corresponding to magenta, cyan, and yellow. These cones send signals through nerves to the brain, where you actually do all the seeing. Nobody has the faintest idea of how the brain works.

There are an infinite number of colors, but you can only see about four thousand of them. You can make all four thousand of them with just red, blue, and yellow. At least, if you also use black and white. And use warm and cool versions of each of your three colors.

Your first assignment is to make a color wheel using only black and red. And you have to be blindfolded.

Design

There are three kinds of design: Good design, bad design, and design that everybody argues whether or not it's good or bad design. You should strive for the third. You will not accomplish it unless you understand both the principles of good design and bad design. For an example of bad design, see "The *very worst* page on the web" and "webpagesthat-suck.com".

Learn the "Golden mean". It was good enough for Leonardo and Michelangelo, it's good enough for you. Unfortunately, it's a mathematical concept which is way too boring for art students. Infoseek lists 902 pages discussing it, if you want to get *really* bored, look it up. Hey, you have a computer, use it!

After learning how to use burned sticks and spoiled berries, my attention turned to more modern (and postmodern, and postpostpostmodern) media, such as acrylic polymers, airbrush, and pixels. Art is art. Since the newest art form is electrically stimulated glowing phosphors, further discussion of design will use (yawn) HTML.

Here are a few less uninteresting design principles:

If it's boring, it sucks.

Heavy things fall and light things float. Somehow, the untrained seldom realize this.

Keep your audience's eye on the media (see "the golden mean" and "If it's boring it sucks", above).

Yellow on white is very hard to read. Use it if you wish to induce insanity. Yellow on black is readable, but not until the background loads.

Yellow on black is ugly, unless your ancestors came from Mars or Stroggos.

If you go far enough back in prehistory, everybody's ancestors came from Africa. At least, that's the prevailing theory. They may even be from Mars.

Frames usually make paintings suck less. Frames usually make web pages suck more.

Tables are often useful in sculpture. They are also often useful in HTML.

Never, EVER, make a web page as long as this one.

In painting, Java is often useful to make a nice brown color, or to stay awake. In HTML design, Java can be used to drive viewers away from your page. Never EVER make that "There is a possible security risk" window come up unless you don't want anybody except the violently insane to see your page.

To plagiarize, uh, I mean "quote" one of my instructors (John Adkins Richardson) from his book "The Complete book of CarTOONing", which we had to buy or flunk, so I'm finally going to get my money's worth:

"I do not for one minute believe that Milton Caniff laid out the composition by any procedure as organized as this, but he might have" and "The way in which such relationships actually develop on paper is made clearer when they are seen in working drawings. Gil Kane's preliminary layout for his book *Blackmark* is uncommonly coherent..." (page 169)

Next: Perspective, color, and a bunch of other junk

nobody will read.

1997, reprinted around 2005 at Kuro5hin

The Life and Times of a Dumpster Cat

I never liked cats. Perhaps it was because my parents didn't like cats, maybe it was because one scratched me badly when I was two years old. Whatever the reason, I never liked cats.

It was six years after I married Becky, and a year after we had moved into a new apartment, that I first met the cat.

I was putting a new battery into the car, and threw the old one into the dumpster. A loud shriek came out, followed by the gray blur of the cat yeowling into the afternoon.

A week or so later, Becky and I were sitting outside when the cat came up and rubbed against Becky's leg. "Oh, she's so cute!" exclaimed my wife.

"There are no cute cats," I told her. "They're evil malicious creatures that haunt the night."

"Well, I don't think so," she said haughtily. "I think she's cute."

"NO!" I said. "You're not getting a pet, and especially not a cat. I hate cats." The death of our poodle, Moondog, four years earlier, and how Becky grieved when Moon was run over, was still fresh in my mind. I *didn't* want to go through that again.

"Don't worry", she said, "I'm not getting any more pets. She belongs to someone, anyway. She's wearing a collar. It's okay if I just pet her, isn't it?"

It didn't matter to her if it was okay with me or not.

A few days later, Becky broke the news that the cat's owner had moved away from the apartment and abandoned her. She was a "dumpster cat", one of fifty or so that roamed around the apartments, haunting the dumpsters and eating the lizards (which was another reason I added to my list of why not to like cats, since the lizards ate mosquitoes).

"No! We're not getting a pet, and especially not a cat,

and especially not a wild one!"

"Don't worry," she said.

The next day there was a bowl of milk on the porch.

"The poor thing's hungry. I can give it a little milk, can't I? Don't worry, I'm not going to get attached to her."

Becky lies a lot, especially to herself.

The next day, the cat came around, of course. This time she jumped in to my lap and started purring. "She likes you," Becky said.

"I don't like her," I replied.

"Then why are you petting her?"

A week later there was cat food on the porch. "You *said* it was okay to feed her. I can't let the poor thing starve."

I was adamant. "You're *not* getting a pet, especially not a cat."

"Don't worry."

In central Florida in the summer it rains every afternoon. Sometimes it rains *hard*. Sometimes there are tropical storms, even hurricanes. Two weeks after she had put the cat food out, and by doing so fed all of the fifty cats around the apartment, it rained *really* hard. We hadn't seen the cat in a week.

It was only three in the afternoon, but it was dark and the sky was an evil greenish tint. An ear splitting **meow** shattered the relative silence of Ted Nugent blasting from the stereo. The cat was hanging on the window screen, dripping wet and baring her teeth, looking completely miserable. She, of course, wanted in out of the rain. Becky, of course, wanted to let her in out of the rain. "Come on, you wouldn't let the poor thing freeze in the rain," she said, despite the fact that it was summer in Florida. I reluctantly let her let the cat in, with admonitions to keep her eye on her because "you know how cats tear things up." The neighbor's cat had just destroyed his six hundred dollar speakers shortly before visiting the Humane Society.

I admit, even though I don't like cats, and didn't want

my furniture to suffer the same fate as the neighbor's, I don't like to see anything suffer. "Just 'til the rain stops."

Two weeks later we had a litter box in the kitchen.

By then, "Kibbles" had a name. I was even the one to name her. "You know, like the dog food." I was thinking "Kibbles and bitch" but didn't say it.

"Really funny," she replied dourly, but the name stuck.

So did Kibbles. She was a really sweet animal, and contrary to my beliefs and expectations, showed great affection, especially to me. She really seemed to like me. Despite my fears, the furniture remained intact. I grew to really like this cat, even though "It's not coming into the house" had turned in to "It's your cat, your responsibility. I'm not feeding the damned thing."

One day I came home from work, and Kibbles had a nasty gash just above her right eye. Becky explained what had happened to her. She hadn't seen it, but Dan, the neighbor across the way, who now had a big red dog since getting rid of the destructive cat, had. Kibbles had been sitting on the porch when the dog decided to make Kibbles live up to her name, and tried to bite her head off. Kibbles pulled her head back and sunk her razor sharp claws into the dog's sensitive nose. The dog pulled its head back, swinging Kibbles, who was holding on to the dog's nose for dear life, over its head. Dan reported that Kibbles then rode the dog like a man rides a horse, spurring the dog's hindquarters with the claws on her left rear leg. When Kibbles decided that the dog, who had shed copious amounts of blood, fur, skin, meat, and screams, had enough, she hopped off and strutted back to the porch. The dog walked with a limp for a month, and never bothered Kibbles again.

Except for the fleas.

All kinds of bugs are problems in Florida. Flies, gnats, mosquitoes, cockroaches, even flying cockroaches sometimes infest the best of houses. Where there are dogs, there are usually fleas, especially in Florida. The dog had its revenge by giving Kibbles fleas.

Kibbles got them bad.

What's worse, she was allergic to them. Pretty soon she was "Kibbles the Bald Cat". The only hair left was on her head.

Several cans of flea spray and a trip to the vet later, we finally got rid of them. Kibbles reacted badly to the vet's shot, and wouldn't eat, tried to bite us, and didn't even try to find her litter box. She had gone completely insane. Fortunately, it was only a reaction to the drug, and she was back to her old self a week or so later.

I have read that animals can't see the picture on a TV. I know for a fact that this is incorrect.

Shortly after Kibbles adopted us, Becky and I were watching a nature show on PBS. Kibbles was laying, as usual, on the couch between us. There were prairie dogs on the TV, doing whatever it is that prairie dogs do. One of them stuck its head out of its hole and squeaked. Kibbles' head shot up, ears high, staring intently at the TV. The prairie dog stood there for a minute, kibbles staring intently. It then turned around and saw the camera, and ran off away from the camera.

Kibbles leaped off the couch and around the TV, trying to catch the prairie dog. She sheepishly came out from behind the TV and watched up close for a minute, then embarrassedly slunk back to the couch. We laughed in uproarious hilarity. Kibbles shot us dirty looks, as she hated to be laughed at.

Kibbles watched TV from then on. Her favorite shows were the news, baseball, and nature shows, especially ones about birds or big cats.

By this time, believe it or not, Becky was teaching Kibbles dog tricks. Kibbles would stand up and beg, shake hands, even roll over. She seemed to understand nearly everything a human said, and would talk back if she thought she was being scolded unfairly. Of course, you couldn't understand what she was saying, but it was obvious that she was arguing.

By now I had come to realize that this was a very special animal. She had never destroyed anything or made a mess, except for her period of drug induced insanity, and was a very loving creature. She wasn't loving like a dog, who will "kiss" anybody kind enough to pet it, but only those she knew and loved. If she didn't know you, she wouldn't let you come near her. What's more she would do nearly everything we told her to do. She would come when called, and if we told her to "go lay down", she would go lay down.

This doesn't mean that she was never catlike. She had her cat instincts, like (fortunately) using a litter box. If she was angry at you, she would get what Becky called a "cattitude" and have nothing to do with you except give you dirty looks.

The one catlike behavior that annoyed Becky to no end was lizard chasing. She had honed her hunting skills to perfection in her dumpster cat days when she lived on garbage and lizards, and still enjoyed the hunt, even though she now had real cat food. Becky and I would be sitting outside the apartment, and Kibbles would prance up with a lizard tail hanging out of her mouth, twitching around like an evil green tongue. Becky would always scold her, and this would give Kibbles a cattitude.

Another reason I hadn't wanted Becky to let Kibbles in, besides the fact that I hadn't liked cats, and didn't want to go through the grief of losing another pet, was that we were not supposed to have pets. I had capitulated on this point, since this was a rule that was never enforced. It was probably a liability issue, the apartment owners not wanting to be sued for a dog bite and being covered with this unenforced rule in effect. At any rate, despite the fact that nearly half the people in the complex had pets, we didn't want to advertise the fact that we had one.

Cats like to perch, especially in windows.

Becky and Kibbles would argue with each other for hours about this point. They finally reached a compromise, whereby Kibbles could perch in the upstairs window, where she couldn't easily be seen.

It was her favorite window, anyway.

Windows weren't the only place she liked to perch.

One morning I got in our big '74 Pontiac go to the store. When I turned the key, an awful grinding noise came from under the hood. I had visions of expensive repairs. Starter? All the oil had drained out? Maybe I'll be lucky (ha!) and it will be a belt hitting the fan.

I opened the hood, and the familiar gray blur streaked out. By nightfall, we were sure we would never see her again.

As I mentioned earlier, Kibbles always came when she was called. She never roamed like other cats, either, but she was nowhere around. We thought she had slunk off and died from whatever injuries she had received under the hood. From where all the blood was, it was obvious that she had been caught in the fan, and she wouldn't have been the first cat to die from napping under the hood of that car.

Becky called and called, and looked and looked. Kibbles was nowhere to be found. I thought I saw her once that night, but couldn't be sure it wasn't a different cat. Becky thought I was telling sweet lies. Later, she thought she saw her, too, but wasn't sure if her eyes were telling her sweet lies.

The next morning I *did* see her in the weeds of a vacant lot. I knew it was her, but she wouldn't come, and disappeared in the weeds when I tried to go get her.

She had run off, and it was obvious that she wasn't coming back. That night was even sadder than the previous night.

The next night, I heard a "meow" outside. "Kibbles!" I exclaimed.

"No, it isn't", Becky said. "That's not her, it's another cat. She's not coming back, I know it. She's probably dead by now, poor thing," and started crying.

I opened the door. It was Kibbles.

Most of her, anyway.

She limped in, most of the fur and some of the skin on her left rear leg missing, along with fully a quarter of her tail. She had a look on her face that said she was really sorry she

24

had run off, and could she have a bowl of milk?

She had been gone for two days. Becky had been so sure Kibbles wasn't coming back she had taken up her water and food, and emptied the litter box. Kibbles drank the milk, and went to look for her food and water just as Becky was putting them back down.

"Don't worry, Kibbles, I have your litter box, too; I was just cleaning it out," Becky said. "I knew you'd come back."

One day at work I got a call from Becky. She was in the company hospital – her knee had collapsed at work. I went to retrieve her to take her home. The company doctor had put it in a brace which extended from her ankle nearly to her thigh. He put her on "light duty", which was meaningless, since Disney World, where we worked, didn't allow tattoos, jewelry, mustaches, sideburns, or visible casts or braces (a really family-friendly, handicapped-friendly place) on employees.

Two weeks later the company doctor told her she would need surgery, and referred her to another company preferred orthopedist. His diagnosis was calcium spurs under the kneecap, like the elderly (such as my grandmother or the not yet thirty year old Becky) often get.

Becky went in for surgery. The doctor slit open her knee and stuck in a fiber optic lens to look at the spur. There was no spur, but he scraped off the inside of the kneecap anyway. Becky was in the hospital for a week, and I broke my promise to not feed or water Kibbles.

It was very painful for Becky to have me help her to the bathroom. She took a clue from Kibbles and used her litter box. Kibbles didn't seem to mind.

Six weeks after the surgery I took her to another doctor, this time one not connected to Mickey Mouse at all. His diagnosis was a birth defect, an underdeveloped muscle that holds the kneecap in place. Her kneecap had simply slipped out of place when it first collapsed on her, and the brace and the surgery had both made the situation worse. He prescribed a different kind of brace designed to keep the knee in place, and therapy to strengthen the muscle. Under threat of a lawsuit, Disney paid for the doctor and the therapy.

One afternoon in 1984 I came home to find Becky crying. I was afraid something had happened to Kibbles. By this time, I had grown quite attached to the lovable little creature, who liked to play catch and keep away, and sit in my lap and purr. She had always kept me company in the bathroom when I took my morning stool. She acted as a back up to the alarm clock, waking us if there was a power failure during the night, which was quite frequent, as Orlando's power company wasn't too reliable. I would have hated for anything to happen to her.

"Kibbles is fine. She's upstairs, sleeping on the water-bed."

"Then what's wrong?"

"I'm pregnant!"

I didn't understand why she was crying. I thought it was wonderful news. Becky, always the optimist, was afraid I would leave her for being pregnant, since I had seemed to be happy with just the two of us for the past eight years!

Her tears of sadness turned to tears of joy.

As Becky's belly swelled from the baby within, Kibbles took to sneaking up on Becky's belly when she was asleep. The vet, when Kibbles had the flea problem, had informed us that Kibbles would never be a mother, as she had been "fixed" when she lived with the people who had abandoned her.

Becky's pregnancy was Kibbles' substitute for her own pregnancy that could never be. She was never as contented, or purred as loudly, as when she was laying on Becky's bloated belly. When the baby kicked, Kibbles purred even more loudly.

On The morning of the birth, Becky woke me at three. "It's time." Of course, I was groggy, it being three in the morning. "Time for what? Do I have to go to work today?"

"I mean it's *TIME*. I'm having contrac ... OH! OOH!"

"Oh," I replied stupidly. I don't think I ever got dressed as quickly.

"Make some coffee," she said. "We have time to get to the hospital."

I made the coffee. We didn't have time to drink it. By this time, we had traded the huge Pontiac for a somewhat less huge Volkswagen Rabbit. We called the doctor and went out in the pouring rain and thunder to go to the hospital.

The nurse said they were false contractions, and that we should go home. The doctor checked her out. "This baby has to come out now, its 'distressed'," which is polite doctor talk for "the patient is trying to die on me."

Becky's pelvis had been broken in an auto accident nearly a decade earlier, so could not have a normal birth. Since it was a cesarean, the medical team didn't want me there. Becky would have no part of that. "I'm not going in unless he can." The doctor was concerned that I might faint, or throw up. I assured him that I had cleaned more than one game animal in my time, and Becky's insides couldn't look much different than a rabbit's insides, only bigger. He reluctantly agreed, being afraid that arguing with Becky would take too much time.

It was the best medical decision he had ever made.

I was scrubbed and gowned to hold Becky's hand as she was cut open. I peeked over the sheet just in time to see the baby's head appear. She was born with the most surprised look I have ever seen on anyone's face, before or since. I know nothing will ever surprise that girl as much as being born did.

The "distress" was that the umbilical cord had wrapped around the baby's neck, and the baby had dropped a stool and gotten it into her lungs. The medical team got the baby out and on a table trying to make her breathe. No one but me was paying any attention to Becky. "I don't feel good all of a sudden," she exclaimed, and became pale. The numbers on one of the machines started dropping. "OOoh!" Becky exclaimed. The numbers dropped faster. Becky passed out. The numbers dropped even faster.

"Nurse!", I called. "NURSE!" One of the nurses,

watching the doctors work on the baby, looked in my direction. "That gauge," I said pointing.

"Oh my God!", she replied. "DOCTOR!"

The doctor looked, ran over, and did something. The numbers started rising again, and Becky woke up.

The doctors finished cleaning up the baby, and invited me over to meet her. They had her breathing and crying. Her astonishment at being born had turned to loneliness, anguish, and discomfort. I took her hand and she stopped crying and looked at me with her big blue eyes. It was love at first sight.

Later, I called my parents and in-laws and grandmother with the news. We named her Leila Marie, after my Grandmother, whose maiden name was Zelma Leila Lennon, and Becky's mother, whose maiden name was Florence Marie Holmes.

I went back upstairs to look for Becky and the baby. Becky was still in surgical recovery. Leila was in a bassinet in the hallway by herself, crying. I went to her and held her hand. Again, she stopped crying.

A nurse came out and told me I could hold her. Of course, I was terrified I would hold her wrong, or drop her, or something. The nurse assured me that it would be okay, and I held my daughter for the first time.

They finally took her for her first real bath and a bottle, even though she would be mostly breast fed from then on. I went in to visit Becky. She was crying. She was sure that Leila wouldn't like her!

Of course, this was silly. Leila got along with her just fine, especially after her first taste of breast milk. The first time Becky held her, I handed her to her.

Kibbles and I spent a lonely week together, just like it had been when Becky had her knee surgery. When I first got home, she greeted me, then stood by the door, waiting for Becky. I opened the door to let her out. She looked out, and turned around, came back in, and looked at me.

"They're still at the hospital," I told her. She laid down

with her chin on her front paws. I sat down, and she jumped in my lap, but she wasn't purring. She missed Becky.

A week later, I brought Becky and Leila home. My father had bought a baby bed for her. My mother bought a car seat and chest of drawers. I bought her a little lay-down baby chair, diapers, and all of the other paraphernalia one needs when a new baby comes home.

Kibbles was really happy to see Becky, and happy, anxious, and a little nervous at meeting Leila. Leila was delighted with Kibbles, and laughed like Kibbles was the funniest thing she had ever seen. Of course, Kibbles *was* the funniest thing she had ever seen, not having ever seen anything but the hospital and the inside of the car.

"You know, you're going to have to get rid of that cat," my dad said. "Why?" I asked.

There is an old wives' tale that says that cats will be jealous of new babies, and will jump into their cribs and smother them, murdering them to regain the baby's parents' affection. My dad, indeed, none of the older folks, thought that this was false, and believed it as the gospel, although no one could ever tell me of a single instance of this ever happening. After knowing Kibbles, and hearing of Sudden Infant Death Syndrome (which *wasn't* believed in until fairly recently), I can see how this tale would have started. The cat, instead of being jealous of the baby, is protective of it. If the baby dies of SIDS, the cat jumps into the bassinet to try to wake it, and is blamed for the death, and usually killed itself.

"It's not my cat," I told him. "It's Becky's cat."

"It's your baby."

"it's Becky's baby, too. If you're worried about Leila, you'd better talk to Becky. I didn't want to get a cat in the first place, and there's no way I could talk her into getting rid of her." A coward's way out, I know, but sometimes discretion is the better part of valor, to coin a cliché.

Kibbles stayed. I was glad. I had grown to love "Fuzzybutt", as Becky sometimes called her after her brush with the radiator fan.

Aside from being a backup alarm clock, she started earning her keep in another way. She would guard the baby.

The apartment was a very small, two bedroom townhouse, with the living room and a small kitchen downstairs, and a large bedroom and a tiny bedroom I used as a studio upstairs. Leila's bed stayed in our room.

When Leila was napping, Kibbles would lay under her bed and keep watch. When Leila woke up, Kibbles would come halfway down the stairs and stand on the rail and meow and make as much noise as she could, until somebody came upstairs and got the baby.

Kibbles not only watched over her when she slept, but watched TV with her (at arm's length), especially baseball.

When Leila was an infant, she would lay in her little chair and watch an entire game without complaining about anything. When the game was over, she would want to be fed and changed, but was perfectly content while the game was on, regardless of how wet her diapers were.

Kibbles would watch the whole game with her.

Leila loves baseball to this day.

When Leila was six months old, we moved back to Illinois. My parents had divorced shortly before I got married, and my mother was the only relative for a thousand miles. Everyone else lived in Missouri or Illinois. So we moved to Illinois.

Lacking jobs, we spent a month in Becky's sister's attic, and another month in my father's back room. The month was January, the air was cold, the snow was deep, and, since my stepmother was so afraid that Kibbles would shed or tear something up, despite the fact that Kibbles had never hurt anything and they had a poodle, Kibbles, who had spent her life in Florida, spent that month on a leash in the garage.

Besides being one of the sheddingest animals on the face of the Earth, poodles are also the stupidest animals on the face of the Earth.

When someone tells you that their poodle died of "natural causes," they mean natural for a poodle – it was hit by a car. All poodles get hit by cars. If you see a poodle older than five years old, it is not a full blooded poodle, or it would have been hit by a car.

If you never let the poodle out of the house, a car will crash through your wall and hit the dog.

Shortly after we moved into our own house, the poodle was, of course, hit by a car.

The new house was tiny, and it was a dump. It had two bedrooms and was smaller than a double wide trailer. It was fifteen feet from a railroad track and was infested with mice and roaches. The stove was so filthy it was completely unusable until I completely disassembled it and cleaned each part with steel wool and strong detergent. To Kibbles, it was like heaven.

It took two years to get rid of the roaches. The mice were no problem.

Being next to the railroad track, the mice would move in every fall. Moving in in February, they were already there. There were several dead ones, and several open boxes of mouse poison under the sinks, in the basement, in the cupboards. We had a lot of cleaning up to do before we could move in. Having to pay a security deposit on this dump was a cruel, evil joke.

The first morning after we moved in, we awoke to the sound of strange thumps in the hallway. It was Kibbles playing with a half-dead mouse. I took the mouse, to Kibbles' chagrin, and Becky repaid her with a can of tuna fish.

The next morning, there was a dead mouse next to my chair, stretched out like a trophy. Kibbles was happy; she was on the hunt again. To Kibbles surprise, not only did Becky not scold her for hunting, but even rewarded her with her favorite treat, the one she used to teach her the dog tricks with. Kibbles was happier than she had ever been.

The next summer was a drought year. People think of

Florida as hot and humid, being in the tropics, but in the five years we lived there, the weather service never admitted a temperature higher than ninety eight degrees. If the humidity went over seventy percent it rained.

In southern and central Illinois, the humidity can be ninety percent and not a cloud in the sky, especially when the temperature reaches or exceeds a hundred. That year, it did just that, and often.

The only air conditioner was in the back bedroom, and there were no other windows that an air conditioner could fit. We moved Leila's bed and the couch and TV into the back bedroom, and moved our bed in the living room.

Leila's first Christmas was the winter before the drought summer. She had her first birthday in June, in over ninety degree weather. Kibbles didn't mind; she was a Florida cat. She spent part of the summer roaming around the yard, looking for the nonexistent lizards.

After Leila was born, I soon learned which cry meant "change me," which cry meant "hold me," which cry meant "feed me", which cry meant "Turn on the TV, I want to watch the ball game," and which cry meant "Boy, I'm tired and crabby and you're not going to get any rest until I do," just as I had learned which meow meant "Feed me" or "Water me" or "let MEOWt."

Humans in the Western World think that speech is their unique, private domain, shared by no other animal. This is despite the fact that every one of them has had a dog tell them, at one time or another, "Get the hell away from my territory before I kill you and eat you." In fact, all animals that make noise talk. Granted, it isn't English, but the Koreans don't speak English, either. Also, animals have very limited vocabularies; in the case of dogs, it is only three words, "I'm hurt", "I'm lonesome", and "Go away before I eat you." Anyone who realizes this can become an instant "Dr. Dolittle"; just don't expect much in the way of really intelligent conversation with an animal. And don't expect any jokes from one, as humor and laughter are what really differentiates us from the other creatures.

In Thailand, their "Garden of Eden" story is a little different from the Judeo-Christian version. In their version, when people lived in Paradise, they were happy because they didn't know how to talk, and therefore had nothing to argue about. Then the evil cats taught them to talk, and they have been arguing and fighting and going to war and killing each other ever since.

What is interesting about this legend is that there are absolutely no noises that a cat makes that isn't a real Thai word. In fact, "Meow" is Thai for "I want". If you are ordering fried rice in a Thai restaurant, you say "Meow Cow Pot". Two women arguing in Thai sound exactly like two cats fighting. The term "cat fight", referring to two women fighting, probably originally comes from Thailand.

Kibbles was the first animal I knew that learned to talk in English. Unlike a parakeet, she knew what she was saying. When Leila started calling Becky "Mom", so did Kibbles. Kibbles also said "out" when she wanted out, "rat" when she wanted food, and her favorite word, "No".

I suspect that this is not too uncommon with some cats, as I met a cat later that could say "hello" and "Help". As far as I know, Jeff's cat only knew these two words, but they were clear and unmistakable. One time when we were visiting Jeff, his cat, who lived outside, woke me up with several "Help!"s. I thought it was a ten year old child. I opened the door, and the cat walked in and said "Hello!"

Leila's toddling around was not pleasant for Kibbles. Kibbles was Leila's favorite toy, and Leila pestered her constantly. One thing she loved to do was to sneak up on Kibbles when Kibbles was sleeping on the couch, then slam her little hands down next to kibbles and yell "CAT!". Kibbles would jump a foot in the air and take off running. Leila would laugh as loud as she could, and Kibbles always hated to be laughed at.

After Kibbles slapped her the first time, Leila treated Kibbles with a lot more respect.

Kibbles took to laying on Becky's belly again, so Becky went to the doctor for a pregnancy test. Of course, it was positive.

One cold, overcast, windy, snowy morning, it was time. I didn't have a car, so my dad loaned me his pickup truck. I took him to work and Leila to my grandmother's, then went back home to take Becky to the hospital.

I didn't have as much trouble getting in to the operating room this time, especially since Becky had told her doctor about Leila's birth. This time, things were much easier, and there were no problems.

The new baby's birth was nothing like Leila's. The baby wasn't surprised, she was furious. She came out screaming her little head off. When the nurse brought her around to show me, she screamed even more loudly. It was pretty obvious that this little girl didn't like me a bit.

We named her Patricia Jean, after my middle name, and my mother's middle name.

After phoning everyone with the news, I went to see Patty again. She had quit crying by then.

The nurse handed her to me, and she started screaming again.

By the time I left the hospital, the sun was shining and it was seventy degrees.

Kibbles, Leila, and I spent another lonely week. Becky hadn't tried to potty train Leila yet, so I did that week. I was very lonely that week, especially at night. Leila seemed to do okay, except at night. Kibbles slept a lot. I stayed home so Leila and I could go see Becky and Patty every day. Because of the hospital's incredibly stupid rules, Leila met Patty only once that week, which made her even more angry than it made me.

The second day we went to visit Patty and Becky, Leila had been in potty training for two days. The weather was nice, so we walked the two miles to the hospital. Well, I walked –

Leila rode in her stroller.

Halfway there she started crying. "What's wrong", I asked. "I gotta go potty!" she wailed. I told her it was okay and comforted her, but she cried the rest of the way there. She wanted to be a "big girl", especially since she had a baby sister. Becky wanted to know why she was crying. When I told her, she didn't believe me. She hadn't thought Leila was old enough to potty train, especially in three days! Actually, it only took a day.

About a week after Becky and Patty came home, Patty started liking me a little. Feeding her and changing her diapers helped. Kibbles had a new baby to watch over, and was very happy. If she couldn't have kittens, well, kids would do.

By the time Patty was four, we were able to take a vacation back to Florida to visit my mother and Mickey Mouse. Kibbles, of course, went with us.

Becky bought a covered litter box for kibbles, since Kibbles often kicked litter out of her old box, and we were pretty sure my Mom wasn't going to like that very much. We put a couple of suitcases and Kibbles' litter box in the back of the little car, with a towel in the bottom for her to lay in. The kids had their pillows in the back seat with them, and the car was packed – literally.

During the three day trip, kibbles didn't go "potty" once, even though Becky took her outside often.

My mother wasn't too happy about having a cat in her house. She was afraid Kibbles wasn't potty trained, or would tear up the furniture or something.

I was afraid Kibbles would get outside and get lost.

Of course, neither happened. By the time we left, Mom was starting to like Kibbles. I even caught her petting Kibbles once.

From then on, when I would talk to her, she always asked "do you still have that silly old cat?"

A few years later, the house across the street became vacant, and Becky snatched it up. It was much larger, with a larger basement, an attic, and a very large back yard. I spent weeks mowing the waist high grass.

The girls had mixed feelings. They liked the big yard – they hadn't been allowed in the tiny yard without supervision at the old house, since there was a railroad track and no fence, and their bigger bedroom, but it was strange to them. Patty had never lived anywhere else, and Leila hadn't since she was six months old.

Besides that, we didn't get cable hooked up at the new house. They were pretty mad about not getting to watch Nickleodean.

We weren't sure what Kibbles thought about the move. She did, however, go across the street once in a while, and seemed to look longingly at the old place.

She missed the mice.

Kibbles slept more and more, and played less and less. She had windows she could lay in, and porches to sun herself on. On weekends, Patty would get up early and watch television. Kibbles would watch with her.

Some people with a big dog moved in next door. Kibbles got fleas again. The fleas took quite a toll on Kibbles and her allergy to flea bites. The people next door moved out, and we finally got rid of the fleas by late winter.

One springtime Saturday morning that year a wasp got in the house. We found out about the wasp from Kibbles' frantic yelp – she was sunning herself in the pantry window when it stung her on the cheek. We got the wasp out, finally. I don't know who was more afraid of the wasp, Kibbles or the girls.

By that night, her cheek was swollen up to the size of a marble.

Becky took her to the vet, who lanced the swollen, infected cheek. Her cheek would quit draining, then she would scratch it open and it would drain some more.

One Sunday afternoon, Becky came in, shaken. "I think my cat is dead!", she said. I went out on the porch to look. She was limp and didn't seem to be breathing. I lifted her head, and she opened her eyes. She seemed disoriented and could barely walk.

By the next weekend she was strong enough to climb up in Patty's bed, but not strong enough to jump off. She tried anyway, and landed with a thud. She was going downhill again. The sore on her cheek still hadn't healed. She couldn't walk at all.

Again, she got stronger. She got to the point she could again get in a window, and kept falling out. It seemed she would get better, the sore on her cheek even healing.

She took a turn for the worse a few weeks later. In a few days, she went from jumping up in the window to walking with a stagger. That Monday night, we were awakened by a plaintive, pained "Mom!", and thought it was one of the children having a bad dream. Becky went to comfort whoever it was. It was Kibbles.

The next morning we all knew was her last. She couldn't walk, could barely lift her head. I asked her, concernedly, "Kibbles, are you going to be all right?"

"No," she said.

Patty, the one who loved school, didn't want to go to school.

When I came home for lunch, Kibbles was laying in the bathroom, where she had been spending most of her time the last week. I went in to pet her, and when I went to the kitchen, she tried to follow me, but couldn't. I picked her up and carried her in with me. Becky petted her while I ate. Kibbles tried to get down off of her lap, so Becky laid her down on a towel. She lifted her head one last time, choked, and was gone.

Becky didn't want to face the children alone when they were to arrive home, so I took the afternoon off from work, and dug a hole in Kibbles' favorite spot in the back yard. She had always liked sleeping in cardboard boxes, so we wrapped her in a towel and laid her in one, and put her cat toys in with her, and waited for the end of school.

When the children came home from school, they knew something was up. "What's wrong, Mom? Oh NO! KIBBLES!"

We all went in to the kitchen, where Kibbles was in her box, to pay our last respects. There were tears all around. We closed the box, and I carried it to the back yard for the funeral.

Everyone threw a handful of dirt on the box, and I shoveled the rest in. Leila gave the sweetest eulogy I have ever heard for anyone, animal or human.

"Yesterday we were the richest people in the world. Now we're really poor."
1997

The Springfield Fragfest

As mentioned in the book's preface, my Quake site at famvid was started in Spring of 1998. The first entries weren't dated, so they may be out of order.

Here are a few notes about the game and people the web site was about. Without them, some of it will be almost incomprehensible.

The headlines were designed to look like "messages" that flashed across the top of the screen when you were playing the game. I did deviate once in a while.

Quake was a game where you ran around a virtual nightmare while shooting evil scary people and things. Quake II was science fiction, and took place on a planet named "Stroggos". The inhabitants of Stroggos were called "Stroggs". It's been too long since I've played it to remember what the US Marines were doing there.

The Stroggs were mostly humanoid, although there were dangerous animal Stroggs. One was the "shambler", brought forward from the first Quake. Another was a vaguely dog-like animal with a very long, deadly tongue. These were called "Parasites". Both were highlighted in a few of the Fragfest posts.

Most people playing online, where everyone but you was a Strogg, were modem users. High speed internet was very expensive, but college students in dorms and the wealthier Quake players who could afford fast connections had a huge advantage over modem users. These folks were called "LPBs", LPB being an acronym of "Low Ping Bastard" with "ping" a technical term for the length of time to send a signal to another computer and receive a signal back.

One LPB's name was Gestalt. His real name was John, and I've forgotten what his last name was. He was a rich young Quake player who rented a T-1 to play Quake on, registered

PlanetQuake.com and started Planet Quake, which eventually made the rich Gestalt even richer.

A camper was someone who waited for another player to come running, and had an easy shot. The very worst camped by the respawn point, where you would reappear after being killed, and shoot you as you materialized. It wasn't long before servers would kick you off for camping.

This book's characters' actions were made up, of course, but they were alter-egos of real people who ran sites like mine.

John Romero was a co-founder of Id Software, the company that produced Quake. Todd Porter was head of the rival Ion Storm.

John Romero held a contest in 1997, an online deathmatch, with his Ferrari 328 as the prize. Dennis Fong, an excellent player to begin with who went under the name "Thresh" rented a T-1, about the fastest internet connection there was at the time, which gave him a huge advantage. He won the car and went on to be a professional Quake player, then an entrepreneur.

Nobody I knew online was anonymous to me, except one fellow, "Flamethrower".

He had good reason to be secretive; Todd Porter's lawyers were trying to serve him papers for a libel suit. Porter nor anyone else ever found out his real identity. All anyone knew was that he was British.

Joost Shuur ran "Slipgate Central", a search engine for quake sites. It closed down a month before my site opened. Its page was replaced with a light yellow background with a Strogg holding a sign that read "Haste does not bring success."

It never reopened. Joost was hired later by Planet Quake, and built a new engine there.

Someone wrote an editorial called "So you want to be a webmaster?" on Planet Quake, which mainly tried to dissuade would-be webmasters from starting a page. Everyone who had a page posted angry rebuttals on their sites – except me. I sent my editorial, "So you want to be a webmaster, too?" to Planet

Quake, who posted it that week.

It was very well received. My traffic went up quite a bit and I got a lot of mail about it, all of it positive. One piece of mail was from the fellow who wrote the article my article was about, and his note was an apology!

The "webmaster" editorial is referenced here, but alas, the article itself is gone. I can find it neither on my hard drive nor archive.org.

In December 1998 I posted the Quake Christmas page, which went viral. My British friend Neil Harriot (AKA "Yello There") asked me to do a weekly column at his Arcadia site, which I did. Neil had health and money problems, and the site closed after I had posted six articles there.

Nacho's real name was also Neil; a different Neil. Nacho was American, Yello was British.

What follows is from *The Springfield Fragfest* as well as the six Arcadia articles, plus a seventh that has previously not been published.

Oct. 23, 2014

Springfield

International

thefragfest.com

Ne s

News of Quake 2? Start here!

Music
Real Audio Fragfest for the illiterate

Old Strogg's Home

Cheats

Tested and valid
Console Commands

Server Commands

Search

Get Quake
Demos and Patches

Strogg Humor

wtf?

email
Send Nooze!

Links

Frame escape

"Those who would give up, um, yada yada yada" -Anonymous Coward

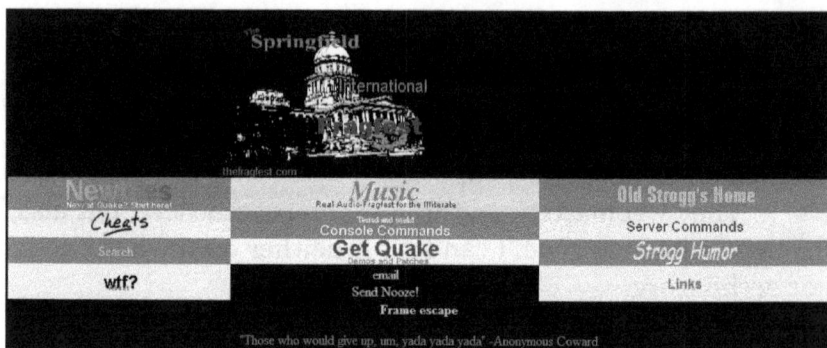

Fragfest can't escape Prozac's super shotgun

The Fragfest is bouncing off those rubber walls this week; Tikki sent me the transcript of the Slipgate party, posted here.

There is a bit of blue language, kiddies. Don't go unless you're over 18. At least, don't let your Grandma see it.

Speaking of the Quake Asylum, one of the inmates has escaped! Yes, Assassin has cleaned up his act. The site is still full of Quake cartoons, and is still funny as hell. The "sik jokes" section is still there, but he took that *really* sick one out. So, Assassin's Payge is now in the regular U.S. Column.

And in his links section... HEY! WTF! Where's the Fragfest?? Ah, well, most of his visitors get there from here anyway.

Assassin's rubber room isn't empty, though. After the changes to Flamethrower's page, he's gained a spot in the links section. The ALT tag to his logo alone puts him in the Quake Asylum. He's there because, hey, I like what he did to it. Good job, Flamey!

Quake2Bunker is trying to get out, too. Looks like they may make it.

Clans frag each other

I just came back from Tikki's new and improved redesigned page, where he's added the "Stupid [expletive] of the week award". This week he's fragging people "who write in

42

guestbooks only to say the site sucks for no reason, and suggest adding pr0n as a way to make it good." As an example, he cites his clan's guestbook. I surfed over there with every intention of fragging the site for no reason and suggesting c0rn, but got sidetracked by the webring on the door. There are a TON of clans listed, more clans than you can shake a shotgun at, and some of the clan's names are fragging *hilarious*.

I'm in a weird mood tonight so I went and signed the guestbook. I wrote "The site sucks for no reason, I suggest adding p0rn as a way to make it good. No, not your site, mine."

I *really* don't get it, though. I *solicit* flames (once had an email tag that read "tell me why this page sucks") and never had a single one; the closest was Assassin, who pointed out an error in in the commands page, but I couldn't call it flame. My mail reads like, "Cool page"; "Cool page, dood"; "I like your page"; "Come see my page"; "How can I fly in Quake 2?" (yes, it can be done); "Thank you for sunbitting your site to our search engine, you are listed on page nine million"; "Cool page"; "wow, kewl payj"; "As a radio professional we are sending you this spam to try to sucker you into buying our crappy service"...

There is, as of today, only one entry in my guestbook, and it's drug related! Krapp!! Anyway, back to the clans, I got a kick out of the names of the clans. Yes, I have excluded clan ONLY sites from my links page, but I'm thinking of adding a "clans" page to the "Links" page. If thirty of you send in your clan's names and URLs, I'll do it.

And would somebody please drop through the gift shop and write something really offensive in the guest book? Thanks, I need a good ass chewing. Be sure not to buy anything.

BTW, Tikki, I know you're reading this, I don't mind your dropping my link for 2 reasons. (1) You dropped everybody's, including Flamethrowers, and (2) neither of the two links you have left (blues & PQ) work! I still like your Beach house, even if you *did* board up all but two doors and took the hinges off those. I like the new paint job!

Update: Nacho just broke into the Beach House and added links to the Fragfest and to Flamethrower. Thanks, Nacho!

Nobody frags anybody

Evil Avatar's on vacation. Tikki, Flamethrower, and Quaker's refuge are having that "who can go the longest without updating" contest (Zaphod's winning; Lag City hasn't been updated in so long that... oh, wait, he's just lagged). Planet Quake is on their week long birthday party. Bet it has one hell of a planet sized hangover next week. Planet Crap was revisiting old crap yesterday, probably because nobody else is at home. SO, Instead of talking about Quake news, I updated the humor page; two new Stupid Strogg jokes. If you have any Quake jokes, SEND 'EM IN. They don't even have to be Quake jokes; most of the worst of "ethnik jokss" cease to be offensive when you turn 'em into Strogg jokes and are even funnier than the originals, although some can't be turned in to Strogg jokes easily (what's a seven course meal for a Strogg... no, wait, that one won't translate).

Remember, folks, If it ain't fun, it ain't Quake. So go away, Newt. And take that sucky Monica with you.

Update (before it's even posted): Tikki loses, he's been busy fragging a football, and will be updating his page this weekend.

Posts frag contest

The no-post contest is over. The loser is Zaphod from Lag City, who started uploading before the contest started, but he's lagged; its still uploading. Next was Devirginizer, who got back from vacation and updated Quaker's Refuge after 5assedmonkey got its act together. Evil Avatar was only away for a week.

Flamethrower posted a game review over at Avatar's Weakly Web yesterday (see yesterday's posting about the posting below), so the winner is (drumroll): Tikki God, who won a beer. I drank it for him last night.

The contest's over, Tikki, you can update your page now. If you want to see the updated pages, they're all in the Links section.

Speaking of Tikki, his clan's still the only one listed on the Fragfest Clan Links page. Are the rest of you clans scared the Arsonists are going to kick your sorry asses when they find you? Come on, send me your URL!

Flamethrower joined the game

The jj-joneses... man, I look everywhere. "Ya got any FLAMETHROWER, man?"

"Na, it's DRY as a bone. There ain't any Flamethrower ANYWHERE, man. I was hoping you knew where *I* could get some."

"No, you want to ride along?"

..."Ya got any FLAMETHROWER, man?"

"Sorry, dude, there was a big bust up in Canada, nobody's got any. You don't look too good, slick. Want some Hulka?"

"I dunno, man, I heard that stuff causes brain damage. How about some Immortal? Ya got any of that?"

"Yeah, but it's been cut, it's kind of weak. Here, have a hit."

FINALLY, over at Evil Avatar's 7-11 parking lot, I run across this really scary looking dude, who's got some skimpy overpriced nickels. So if you're jonesing for some Flame-thrower, go on over there and see a non-real audio review. It isn't Quake, but it IS Flamethrower, who promises at the end of the article, "The show hasn't been updated for a while, but it will be, soonish."

And before your Mom writes another nasty letter, the above dialog came from an old Miami Vice rerun. The pusher gets shot and the junkie gets rehabilitated. The end.

Assassin trips over, uh, trips, uh... what was I going to say, man?

Assassin (AKA Necron99) is letting the Fragfest use his Quake cartoons for the humor section. This week is *The many facial expressions of the Quake guy*. My favorite is the Quake guy's impersonation of Bob Dole.

I asked if he was coming to the party, and he wrote, "anyways, id like to come, but im not good with dates.....so dont expect me there unless someone sends me a last minute ICQ or e-mail...."

Uh, it's when those little kids knock on your door demanding candy. I'll send an email.

He doesn't remember ever dying, but, well, memory is a funny thing...

Planet Quake frags Springfield Fragfest

Gestalt (who has seen the Fragfest) has renamed part of the Planet Quake Mailbag's "Shut the F* up" section "The Asylum".

The sincerest form of flattery! John, I'm honored!

And there's ANOTHER "noo" site called "UGN 3D" that's got an asylum, too. I'm NOT honored. Hey, Planet Quake let me use one of the "shut the f* up" letters; published something I sent them; and Flamethrower, hosted by them, pimped the Fragfest on his RA show. Besides that, PQ is an old, very good, respectable and well respected site. UGN3D is an upstart, and have ripped off trademarked and copyrighted cartoons from Fox and South Park. It's obvious from the writing style that they've been here before (hint – listen to your English teacher, not me). UGN guys, I'm glad you've been to the Fragfest, now acknowledge it.

In return, I'm ripping off some of their bandwidth. That illegal Eric picture is sitting on *their* server. :p

Everybody melted

Hey, I scooped everybody but Planet Crap (where

Flamey made the announcement) on the Flamethrower news. I even scooped Evil Avatar, whose site is hosting Flamethrower.

Meanwhile, Planet Quake is hosting a new site, "3", who quotes Monty Python on their opening page. They also Quote my quote of the Bible from the humor section, "And on the 3rd day..."

Now you know where all the other webmasters get their stuff from.

Irvine frags more
Bong frags less

I wrote Bong for a link button, since he's linked the Fragfest. He says, "Attached. It's small and not animated. Your page is already too graphics-intensive:)"

Meanwhile, Irvine Imagination's killer link says, "...mainly a text based site with so much information that by the time you're done readin' it, you'll have Quake II leakin' out yer ears!"

So I guess I must have the balance pretty good. Besides, word for word, Bong has more graphics.

Webmeisters disconnected

Flamethrower is still "twisting in the wind" (Chubby Checker after beans?) Tikki God's Quake Beach House has been out of tequila since November, and Quaker Refuge hasn't updated since earlier this month; its webmaster, in the U.S. Navy, is probably lugging a BFG to Iraq to kick Saddam's ass with.

This means the "no post" contest is *back on.* Last one to post wins. The winner receives – First prize: A vacation to beautiful downtown *nowhere.* No expenses are spared – or paid. Second prize: A brand new cherry red 1999 convertible *swift kick in the ass!* Third prize: a rasperry ;p. Fourth prize, provided we get another entry: Absolutely *nothing!*

Crash, Slipgate, and other permanently dead sites are ineligible. Void where prohibited or otherwise inconvenient.

Taxes, shipping, and all other costs are the responsibilities of the winners. Keep out of reach of children. Close cover before striking. Contents under pressure.

So root for your favorite non-posted site today; you may win a pound of fresh *content!*

If you own one of the above mentioned sites, tomorrow's poll is "how often should the Fragfest be updated"; 'cause I'm thinking about sitting on *my* ass for awhile; why should *you* have all the fun?

Update: Quaker Refuge updated 12/18. So far Tikki's winning; no update in over a fraggin' *month*. And – Nacho couldn't get the RA going, so that new RA show won't be. There are a few other new shows linked, though.

Flamethrower frags update

So the winner of the no-update contest is (drum roll) – *Tikki*, who has an (ahem) excuse. Seems not only is his browser software screwed, but the Arsonists' FTP is screwed, too.

He wins the no-expense paid round trip to... *Nowhere!*

Flamethrower's update, about Romero's team, was worth waiting for. More of Flamethrower's famous flames than we've seen for a long time (and an apology to a previously flamed individual). Go see the article (must be 18 or at least see it when your Mom is gone).

UPDATE: Nope, the contest is still on; Pile's page puts him back in the running. Gimme them tickets back, Tikki, the contest's still on.

Tikki joined the game [observer mode]

News from Tikki – Seems the page wasn't updated

because of a little problem at the Beach House. Somebody mistakenly put up one of those thirteen month calendars with January, 2000 on it, and all the electrical equipment in the place went haywire. First the computers acted up, making rude noises and demanding parts. Then the coffeepot started dancing and whistling some obscene 16th century sailing tune. The audio equipment then burst into flames. Luckily, Tikki has three large shamblers with good kidneys to get the blaze under control. And, thirteen truckloads of rum are supposed to be delivered next week.

Okay, that's not what really happened, but he says he'll have an update soon.

UPDATE: No he won't, either – the Arsonist server is playing games with them. Enjoy your vacation, Tikki!

Yello didn't see Blue's Grenade
Tikki Disconnected

I got an email from Yello last night, he's in a bit of a "funk" (not sure if "funk" means the same thing in Britain as here... actually, I'm not sure Yello is British............................. ;)

The "fecker" traded Granny's mule for a voodoo 3 card and she's slapping him around? Id ignored him? Don't feel bad, Id ignores me, too. G.I.N. or Bouncy Pointy Breast Lady didn't renew his banner ad? Not sure what the trouble is, but drop by his page and send him an email telling him how cool his page is, that usually gets *me* out of a funk. Tell him John Carmak sent ya.

Mail from Tikki: he *really* needs a host. Drop by his page, if you have a hosting service and like his page send him an email.

And in other mail, we have another newbie to frag! That's right, folks, he *and all his friends* had a few questions about patches and servers. Lets welcome these poor fraggers into the community by *blowing the hell out of 'em*, just like they did you when *you* were a newbie! And after their gibs have rotted on the floor for a while, let them know how to respawn ;) so you can kill 'em again. Remember, there are two kinds of Quake p1ayers, ones who are typing and ones who are breathing. And remember your manners, boyz and gurlz; when someone shoots you, there are two things you can do. Planet Quake advocates praising their sk1LLz; Planet Ho Slap advocates accusing them of cheating. Get enough fraggers arguing about whether camping is cheating and you can kill *all* of 'em!

Of course, the height of fun is catching two newbies next to a wall shooting each other with pistols at close range, and bouncing a rocket off the wall between them. Sure wakes 'em up in a hurry!

Hulka frags uh, something or other that has nothing at all to do with Quake or gaming...

Ever notice you never see Ross Perot and Quark from Deep Space Nine in the same room at the same time?

This just in: Hulka still thinks the Fragfest sucks, but most of his army likes it. He's on Zyban, I'm on Nicoderm; the Quake patches never made me want to quit playing Quake any more than the cigarette patches make me not want a cigarette. They're hard as hell to light, too.

Too bad he doesn't like the Fragfest, his link button is cool as hell, I'd love to put it on my links page. Write and tell him if he listed the Fragfest he might get a few more hits, 'cause his link is kinda lost in the middle of the rest of all those other Fragfest links.

HULKA! Major Futcup wants you in his office ASAP.

Community Died

"Oh my God! You killed Community! You bastards!"

Yello says he's both in better spirits and British. He didn't say what was bugging him, but I realized what the problem was when I saw his page yesterday – "dust and ashes", about the Christmas wake/funeral/murder trial over at Planet Crap. I should have known, since I was there, too. My apologies, but I was too jubilant over the birth of a ton of newbies (I think Quake 2 outsold Ferbies at Christmas) and was having too much fun drinking and talking with the murder victim to realize he was dead, and that Yello was distraught over Community's death.

This was the strangest trial in the history of trials. It seems the Quake community was brutally murdered sometime in the last three years, but the forensic specialists were all too drunk to determine time of death any more closely or whether the victim was, in fact, dead. There were between 50 and 200 jurors, even though there was only one juror, the murder victim. There was no judge, unless you count Morn and Andy, and they weren't being nearly as judgmental as the jury. The sketch artists were Salvador Dali and Andy Warhol. Since both are dead and neither showed up, there were no pictures.

The only witness called was the murder victim, who spoke at great length about the travesty and injustice of his murder, although he wasn't sure when he died or what he died from. The corpse cried out not only for justice, but plain assed revenge. Actually, most of the trial centered on whether the victim was actually dead.

There was more than one suspect. The first suspect called to the stand was Planet Quake, who was accused of poisoning the victim with the deadly drug, commercialism. Planet testified that not only was the victim not dead, they were only out getting high and no malice was intended; that if the victim overdosed, it was accidental. Blue, who didn't show up at the trial, was charged as a co-conspirator in the poisoning.

Flamethrower, on trial in another courtroom for arson (he was acquitted after his hanging), showed up to condemn Planet for his choice of what drug he was pushing, and said you could get a better high from the Fragfest or Spew (who also testified) anyway, and not have to worry about overdosing. He then excused himself, saying something about "petrol", which I believe may be some sort of flammable substance the British use for motor fuel, very similar to American gasoline only more expensive.

More witnesses were called, who accused Id of killing Community by forcing him to conceive and give birth to himself, and gave the time of death as December, 1997. Id did not appear at the trial, but instead sent his lawyer Activision from the firm Activision, Amazon, Barnes and Noble, who argued that not only was Community not dead, he had been born twice. Some witnesses for the prosecution (the prosecutor was also the defense attorney and victim) testified, "I knew Community would die when Quake 2 came out, and if he's not dead, he might as well be because he *just hasn't been himself lately.*"

Another witness added "Yeh, thar's jest no *spirit* in the ol' boy any more. Why, I remember when I wuz yer age we had to *walk* to our deathmatches, draggin' a 486, in the snow, uphill, both ways. These young whippersnappers jest don't know what the ol' boy was like when he wuz young. Why, he'd take all you young punks blindfolded. He'd even prolly do purty good if you took off yer blindfolds."

Yello testified, "Look at him......................He's breath-ing..................look how *big* he's gotten........................" Yello was pretty choked up about Community's death, as you could see.

For my testimony, I did a little cut-and-paste from a posting I made here at the Fragfest last October from my deposition in the Slipgate Central murder trial held at the Beach House. Speaking of the Beach House, Tikki still needs a host or he'll be back in that cardboard box at Tripod again. Seems he's locked himself out or his roommate didn't pay the rent or something, and his shamblers are getting surly from being left out in the rain. I'd let him stay here for a while, but there's just not much room in this little shack.

Of course, he could do what crash did, just walk away and start living at Planet Crap. But I digress...

Any way, back to the murder trial. More witnesses were

called accusing Newbies of killing Community. Newbies didn't appear, since he not only didn't know the victim very well, he didn't know the trial was even being held. There has been a warrant issued for Newbies' arrest. Newbies was accused of aggravating Community's heart condition with his use of incivility, causing Community to die of a coronary. The rocket launcher and BFG that Community always carried around was not accused. Newbies was quoted as saying "L00z3rz, kewl", but the testimony was thrown out as being hearsay or heresy or something.

Newbies not only is wanted for the murder of Community, he's also wanted for swimming in the lava when the "no swimming" sign is clearly posted, vagrancy (camping without a permit), and cratering.

Sgt. Hulka showed up and demanded that the victim "gimme twenty", and seemed somehow to implicate Bill Clinton and Monica Lewinsky in the murder.

Planet Quake was accused again of killing community by kidnapping Joost Shuur, whose trial was at the Beach House last September (Joost was acquitted of Slipgate Central's still unsolved murder). Another witness (heh, it might have been me) testified that Community had a new foster parent, Quakeport, and was old enough to be out on his own, anyway.

In the end, Community was convicted of his own murder and sentenced to death. So now you know why Yello was so blue. He thanks you all for the kind card and letter.

To nearly quote Samuel Clemons (also dead), "the reports of Community's death have been greatly exaggerated."

Overheard in a different courtroom at the Planet Crap bar and jail: "You couldn't get a Clue if you were standing naked in a field of Clues during Clue mating season, rubbing Clue musk oil on your body while whistling the Clue mating call and dancing the Clue mating dance."

12/31/1998

53

Fragfest frags the illiterate reader

Planet Quake gets all the good letters, like the one they let me repost in the Humor section.

Yeah, people write "this is a dumb question" and "you're going to laugh but..." but it's then followed by a perfectly intelligent question, usually one that should have been addressed in Quake's manual but wasn't. Planet Quake seems to get all the morons. I want some, too.

So, I got a Real Audio encoder. Saturday (I hope) I'll have a Real Audio show, "Quake for the Illiterate" posted. This will be, as far as I know, the only Quake-only real audio show on the internet. Since I've been getting some good internet connections lately, I've bribed my daughter to do the first show while I play a little Quake. Besides, if it sucks, I can blame her! This one's more of a "test show", with just a little "nooze" for the illiterate, and some Quake music.

The bribe was that I'd help her with a Jazz Jackrabbit page for kids. So she's getting the best of the deal.

It doesn't usually take much to do a daily update of the page (unless I'm covering a murder trial or something), but I get the feeling a Real Audio show may take a little more work, so I can't say how often the RA shows will be. I'm thinking weekly but shooting for monthly.

Rudolph the parasite doesn't get along with shamblers very well (but you know they're like cats and dogs, anyway), but Tikki asked if he could keep his last shambler in the Fragfest Garage until he gets his cardboard box at Tripod prettied up. If that damned shambler pees on the car I'm feeding him to Rudolph. The car's fifteen years old, a little shambler pee would probably melt it. Tikki's also sending a review of some game that isn't Quake I told him I'd let him post on the garage wall. Hell, if Rock House can stay in the garage, there's no reason Tikki and his shambler can't, at least for a little while. If he sends the post as a .wav file, I'll stick it in the Real Audio show.

The show's being done for a 28.8 modem, so the quality

may be really crappy, but it's guaranteed to work on any PC that will play Quake 2 over the internet, as long as you have a real audio player.

You can count on next year's Christmas carols to be done in Real Audio format, along with the printed lyrics and midis you had a few weeks ago.

1/4/1999

Garage can't escape Shambler's BFG

What a mess! Not only did we get two feet of snow and the temperature is twenty below zero (that's so cold it's the same temperature in both Celsius and Fahrenheit), but there's a pregnant shambler camping in the garage. Of course, Rudolph and the shambler look at each other like you look at a piece of Grandma's pie, both making noises like "camper", "100z3r", and "usuk". If Major Futcup shows up he'll write me up for sure. Anyway, Tikki sent a review of Half-Life, presumably in honor of the pregnant shambler. No word on how the renovations in the cardboard box at Tripod are coming. However, it looks like when the beach house exploded, it took the Arsonists with it. Let this be a lesson, kids: Shambler pee and gunpowder don't mix.

If you haven't been to Flamethrower's Place, He's been on petrol in the Ion Storm warz. Sorry, I can't resist a really bad intercontinental pun.

1/5/1999

Defrag Died

Also over at the Weakly Web, Defrag is conspicuous by his absence in the "hosted sites" column. Wha' happened, dude? Oh, and it seems Pile wins the ticket to nowhere; he still hasn't updated. Careful, Tikki got a little shambler pee on it before I wrestled it back.

1/6/1999

Friends rail internet

Tons o' mail today. An online friend who will remain

nameless for now is starting a new Quake page. More news when Mr. Nameless lets me post.

Another online friend, the Omnipotent Tikki God, found a rune in the ashes of the Quake Beach house that allowed the beach house's ashes to reconstruct themselves into the old Beach House, which Tikki says he'll update as soon as he gets his FTP working right.

Also, believe it or not, a *newbie* alerted me that I missed a real important server command; I went to look for it in the Server page and it (blush) wasn't there. This will be fixed, like, right NOW!

As well as more than the usual number of suggestions and compliments. Anybody who says the Quake community is dead needs to put that hash pipe away for a while.

1/7/1999

Fragfest can't escape Game Complex's shotgun

It looks like I'll be joining the web Gypsies. Seems the Game Complex wants a unique Quake page, and have had their eyes on this one, according to Nacho, who wants me to move over there. It would be nice not having a "url from hell", as Flamethrower put it. There are one or two negatives; there are all those folks with links to here ("WHAT? I'm still linked to that damned Fragfest? WTF, I'm fixing that RIGHT NOW"). All in all, it seems like a good deal. I'll keep a "doorway" here for you folks who have it bookmarked so I won't just drop off the face of the internet like Captain Immy, Lag City, and the other web Gypsies did when they moved. Here's a thanks to Nacho and the Game Complex for wanting the Fragfest!

1/12/1999

Evil died

The Weakly Web will be down for a while while Mr. Avatar "works out a small personal issue" (like improving yer golf swing, dude?)

Kudos for the Evil one for telling us instead of just letting his page rot. SO, I guess there's a new "Ticket to nowhere" contest on!

crash, Immy, and all the other permanently dead sites are ineligible. Let your page go without an update longer than Evil Avatar and you may win a no expense paid ticket to *absolutely nowhere!*

BitchX is ineligible for two reasons. First, "she" almost never updates anyway, and second, well, she's a bitch.

Stay tooned.

Meanwhile, Evil's hosted sites (Flamethrower and LamingInsider) are still open for business. In fact, Flamey updated today.

1/25/1999

UPDATE: Spew hasn't updated, but I'm sure Desiato will in time to lose the contest. Meanwhile, Yello did. Something. I think. Hey, Kneel, where'd ya hide that damned Fragfest link? Ya want me ta bust yer starvatron again?

1/26/1999

Evil and Desiato gib ticket

Evil Avatar and Desatio, fighting like a cat and dog to keep from winning the ticket, have tied for the ticket to nowhere. Desatio (I'm speling that wrong, ain't I? damn!) *Desiato* is in Chicago. Being in Illinois, he's already in Nowhere (Springfield is the capital of Nowhere). God knows where Mystery Man Evil is.

Anyway, they tore the ticket to shreds trying to get the hell way from it; both have posted. So I guess I'll have to get a new ticket.

Desiato has two new shows, one talking about banner ads. He got rid of his (it was a pop-up geocities thing) about the time I got mine. Oh, you haven't seen it? It's WAY down at the bottom of the page. Go ahead and click it, I won't make (or lose) any money on it. I get a gig of space for having it there. Pretty good deal, I think.

OOPS, gimme back those ticket pieces, boys; Planet Ho Slap wins the no-expense paid *ticket to Nowhere*. Along with their fabulous no-expense vacation, they also receive *absolutely*

57

nothing. Sleek, modern transportation provided by *the contest winners.* Congratulations, ya hos!
1/27/1999

UPDATE: Desiato did yet ANOTHER new show last night, and mentioned the fragfest AGAIN! Next time I get to Chicago I'm gonna hafta buy him a beer! For now, I think I'll just post a GREAT BIG Spew logo.
1/28/1999

Gameplex frags new gamer's page

For the last month I've peen privy to a new page that looks good, and have had to keep under my hat. Last night I was informed via icq that I could *mention* it, but not give out the url yet (because the real url doesn't work yet). It may be up by tomorrow. If it is, I'll give out the url then.

Speaking of icq, I was on it quite a bit last night; something has gone wrong with an unknown driver and Quake is hosed on my machine. While I was there, Neil (Yello) popped by and told me to have a look at the front page of his Katalystic Media page, so I did. Thanks, Neil!

Unfortunately, it seems to be down right now. Neil told me last night that the internet was messed up all over England. It seems to be a world-wide thing, since some Canadian sites were down yesterday as well.

I suspect it's Yello's Granny's fault – I think she got him the wrong tube for that starvatron and it's overloading the CIA's big pukatron machine over here in the U.S.
1/29/1999

Ho Slap does a back flip into the lava

You guys tryin' to start another contest?
2/3/1999

Beach house can't escape Arsonist's Flamethrower

No, not Flamethrower, who updated today (and you'll be tripping on your own grenade if you don't see it *now*), *A* flamethrower.

Word has reached the Fragfest that an unidentified group of arsonists have hatched a plot to destroy Tikki God's Quake Beach House. The beach house, rumored vacant since November, houses a large store of cordite, TNT, plastique, dynamite, one or two small nuclear devices, and a shambler.

The authorities have suspected the beach house of harboring fugitives, but word at the beach house is "Joost hasn't been here since September."

The mayor has been trying to have the house condemned since its appearance, but can't get the housing inspector past the BFG and shambler. When informed of the plot, the police whipped out a large urn of coffee and several hundred donuts and threw a party.

I dropped by to ask if the beach house was indeed going to be torched, and why.
[beach house] Who is it, man?
[Fragfest] It's Steve
[beach house] Steve's not here
[fragfest] No, I'm Steve
[beach house] Steve's not here either.
[Fragfest] Hey, Tikki, open up!
[beach house] Tikki's not here.
[Fragfest] Dammit, Nacho, open the fraggin' door!
[beach house] Shambler, get the door, man

So I think I'll drop by tomorrow and use the window instead.
2/4/1999

Nacho can't escape Granny's Shotgun

I met a strange old woman as I was trying to get in to Tikki's beach house (see yesterday's post), a charming elderly British lady who informed me "Those feckers can really burn 'em down. Blimey, I wish me Neil would buy that bloody much!", and I have no idea who she was or what she was talking about. I assume she was selling ordinance, since she said something about how many shot guns Nacho took.

I didn't see the shot guns, Nacho must have had them in the gun rack already. The smell of lamp oil, candle wax, gunpowder, Incense, and something I couldn't put my finger on hung in the air. I opened a beer.

It seems the beach house isn't "scheduled" for "demolition" after all. Instead, it will be the 1999 Slipgate Central. On March 9th, a sign will be hung outside proclaiming "Haste does not bring success", and a fireworks display will be set off – inside the beach house. In the ordinance room. Thousands of Quake sites will have a "search for Quake" combo box that will lead to Tikki's "Haste does not bring success" sign.

Three trucks loaded with frankfurters and marshmallows are scheduled to arrive at the beach house by next month, as well as tankers carrying rum, tequila, and beer.

Tikki will be moving in to "Nacho Extreme (because all the other pages have extreme in the title)" as a reviewer. Nacho Extreme is the mystery page I referred to, housed in the penthouse of the Game Complex. It's still not done. Nacho says, "Okay, the site will be up eventually. But, being the lazy ass I am, 90% of my time is being taken up by this: If you want, let people know I'm lazy, but have a treat in store for them. Btw, I think tikki is gonna set the beach house on fire.

"Also, the game I'm playing is getting better. So, I won't be stopping till I finish. =)"

Volume 3 of the Fragfest Real Audio show has been finished since last weekend. I've kept from putting it up since (a) I mention Nacho's page which was supposed to be done last weekend and (b) Spew is supposed to have show 100 tonight. Desiato (whose bodyguard is heard in the Fragfest's show) said last week show 100 would be something special – and Hulka, his host, has been down all week. So we haven't seen show 99 yet, and 100 may be delayed. But I'm posting show 3 anyway. As the old English lady would say, "feck it".

Update: Hulka's is back up, and it looks like Desiato got the Wednesday show up, #99. 100 should be up tonight. Go hear Spew tonight.

2/5/1999

I made an animated graphic of Tikki God's Quake house that didn't do anything until the visitor clicked a link, which triggered a massive video explosion that left Joost Shuur's "Slipgate Central" as it looked when it came down. I emailed it to Tikki, who posted it on March 9th.

Oct 23, 2014

Yello frags grannies

I received this ransom note yesterday: "Yet another delightfully strange update............

"I'm keeping your granny.........

"Neil........."

And on the subject of Yello grannies, Desiato says he doesn't have a bodyguard, and may have show 100 done by Monday.

2/6/1999

Gameplex died

The Game Complex has been missing since last week. This ransom note was finally posted:

"Please stand by as Gameplex undergoes reconstruction.

"In the weeks to come, we will be able to offer the latest from the gaming industry, accompanied by exclusive previews and reviews."

Yello frags Neil

Yello, questioned about the disappearance of Neil Katalysmic, denied responsibility. Actually, it was his granny that did the denying, saying "Tsk tsk, that boy's totally irresponsible."

And regarding disappearances, Tikki was heard to say "Hey, what's with Gameplex, you heard anything?"

Harry Houdini was dug up for questioning and later released. Police are now looking for a gentleman named "David

Copperfield". It is not known if Mr. Copperfield is a suspect in the disappearances.
2/9/1999

Internet Disconnected

The Game Complex, Kneel, Nacho Extreme, Spew's show 100, and clan sites that registered with gamespyder are all still missing. Yello, in possession of some sort of Timewarp substance, amulet, or device, claims he is not responsible.
10/1999

Fragfest disconnected

AAAAAAGH! I can't upload! Somebody must be time-warping at gameplex; updates will be at *[a site that no longer exists]* until it's back up.
2/11/1999

Windows trips on his own grenade

I've spent the entire day trying to get Windows fixed. The Gameplex problem has been resolved. Sorry for any trouble.
2/12/1999

Fragfest Disconnected

...oops, it's not resolved. My apologies to all of you.

Gameplex's net admin informs me he's got a bit of a mess over there; he has my sympathies. Meanwhile, any nooze I find will be at the famvid address for a while.
2/13/1999

Fragfest joins the game

I'll bet you thought I was going to use that ticket myself! Gameplex has been having some technical problems, so if you don't see an update, go to the old address at *[old address]*.

Meanwhile, Desiato and Kneel are trying to wrestle the ticket away from me. Desiato is busy (according to his page) getting his ass kicked by his new job. Yello still denies

responsibility for Kneel's disappearance, but has kidnapped yet another granny, Desiato's. When questioned, Desiato's bodyguard replied, "Look, mate, I'm responsible for guarding his body and I'm NOT responsible for yours."
2/15/1999

Yello frags Kneel

In addition to Grannies, Yello admitted today to kidnapping Kneel Katalystic, and says he may release him. He has also kidnapped *YOUR* T-shirt, and demands that a ransom of (I think) $25 U.S. for delivery of your shirt be sent to:
Gimme Back my Yello shirt!
26 Claverham Park
Claverham
N.Somerset
BS49 4LR
UK

Yello plans to buy out Planet Quake with the proceeds.

He also accurately misquotes PQ's "So you wanna be a web guy, huh??? Well think again loser boy!!" article (twice), has some quack 3 screen shots you don't want to miss, and has a GIANT interview.
2/17/1999

Kneel frags Yello

In a stunning move, Kneel escaped from Yello's clutches, wrestled his weapon (a banana, I think) away, and kidnapped Yello. Yello had a backup weapon (a moldy dish rag), and each is keeping the other at bay, arguing about who is kidnapping who (or is that "whom"? Whom cares, anyway?)

At any rate, the new Kat page may be back as soon as this weekend. Regular contributors are Yello, Kneel, Tron (3d Gamer's Edge), Morgan Parry (TenFour), Desiato (Spew), and Tom Cooney (I think "the Grin Reaper", but I'm not sure). I may contribute something once in a while if I can get my muse to stand still. Kat's new page is big and unfinished, and I have no idea how they're going to pull it off by this weekend. Maybe they'll use Yello's overcooked Puntyum 3 timewarp processor and force hundreds of alternate Ben Siskos to do the work.

The new page will have, among other stuff: Editorials, Articles, Interviews, Game Reviews, Girl Gamers, Top Ten, Audiocadia (real audio? dunno, the link led to "AOL", er, "404 file not found". I *said* it wasn't done), Mod Reviews, Cheat Codes (blood 2 was up), Files, free Advertising for us po' folk that can't afford Planet Quake, Links, Give aways, Stumble Throughs, and a weekly column by the captive Yello, who Kneel now has trapped in a bottle.

2/19/1999

Flamethrower joins the game

Flamethrower, in danger of starting another "ticket to nowhere" contest, updated today, saying "There simply hasn't been ANYTHING that I could give a rats chuff about going on." He also says, "MIDWAY vs GT – If anyone (ANYONE) at Midway or GT would PLEASE write in about the spat I'd LOVE to hear from you. SHIT, if *anyone* has *any* rumours or interesting news, please let me *[Flamethrower]* know!!!"

He also has a cool new link button.

2/20/1999

Illinois State Government frags Y2K problem

It seems the State of Illinois has reached Y2K compliance. This email forwarded from a friend in government reached my desk this morning:

"Y2K Date Change Project Status

"Our staff has completed the 18 months of work on time and on budget. We have gone through every line of code in every program in every system. We have analyzed all databases, all data files, including backups and historic archives, and modified all data to reflect the change. We are proud to report that we have completed the 'Y2K' date change mission, and have now implemented all changes to all programs and all data to reflect your new standards:

"Januark, Februark, March, April, Mak, June, Julk,

64

August, September, October, November, December as well as: Sundak, Mondak, Tuesdak, Wednesdak, Thursdak, Fridak, Saturdak.

"I trust that this is satisfactory, because to be honest, none of this Y to K problem has made any sense to me. But I understand it is a global problem, and our team is glad to help in any way possible. And what does the year 2000 have to do with it? Speaking of which, what do you think we ought to do later this year when the two digit year rolls over from 99 to 00? We'll await your direction."

2/24/1999

Fragfest frags Arcadia

When I got home from work last night, a rather large blanket was thrown over my head and I found myself in a large burlap bag, bouncing around as if in a truck. I could hear a pair of giggling, cackling old women, but couldn't make out what they were saying. I feared the bag was on fire, as I smelled something similar to burning burlap, only sweeter. Eventually the jostling stopped, the bag was removed, and there was a blinding light in my eyes. An obviously fake German accent (actually it sounded like a Brit impersonating a Spaniard) spoke. I feared it was Todd Porter looking for Flamethrower. "Nya ha ha, we have you now, *Meester* Frogfast.......... There is no escape............. you WEEEELL tell us what you *know*.........."

I tried to tell the voice that I didn't know who Flamethrower really was, but was silenced. I hadn't expected the Spanish Inquisition.

"*Nobody* expects the SSSSSSpanish inquisitionn-nnn................"

After being being shown the torture chamber with its devious devices, including a "soft pillow" and a "comfy chair", I relented. And tried to think up some convincing lies, since I didn't have a clue as to the truth.

It wasn't Porter after all, and he couldn't care less who Flamethrower really was. It was actually Kneel on a "recruiting" mission. Since I have a low tolerance for soft pillows and couldn't bear the thought of the comfy chair, I agreed to his "request". Especially since he was armed with a bowl of raspberries.

So now you'll see me in a weekly column titled "The Electric Gamer's Weak End Hell Hole" at Arcadia. The first edition of the column may be up by Thursdak (which would be about four days early).

2/24/1999

The following is the first of the articles, which wasn't posted at my site, but at Arcadia. More Fragfest follows this article.
Dec 12, 2014

The Electric Gamer's Weak End Hell Hole

Hi folks, thanks for stopping by the hole.

In this first installment I'd like to thank some folks and kind of explain what I intend to accomplish here.

First, I want to thank Neil and the rest of the Kat crew for the opportunity to spout off, and everyone else for giving me a reason to. I especially want to thank Micro$oft for writing the OS everyone hates and everyone is forced to use. I want to thank my daughter for grudgingly giving up the computer so I can write this meaningless little piece of drivel, my other daughter for not stealing all the cookies, and my wife for not kicking my ass. And the cats for not pissing on the floor and scratching the furniture. And the elderly people next door for not calling the police.

The purpose of this page is nothing short of changing the world. Okay, scratch the last five words of the previous sentence.

Where in the hell am I going to come up with some content to entertain you folks? Simple: I'll just steal it, or ramble on about nothing and we'll just pretend it's content. I mean, come on, you're not paying and I'm not paid. Hell, you read that "Dear Minx" thing, which is even more meaningless than this, and she (I think he's a she) gets paid for it!

Since you haven't hit the "back" button (or the "get me the hell out of here" button) yet, you're probably wondering who the hell I am and why you've gotten so loaded that this is entertaining. The second question I can't answer.

As to the first, I'm Steve McGrew from the Springfield Quake 2 International Fragfest, which isn't a lan party, just another Quake page. I played my first computer game in 1964 -- and broke the computer (they were easier to break then). I put lots of quarters in Pong, Space Invaders, Pac Man, and other primitive games. I put enough quarters in Pac Man games to realize that those little dots the pac man eats are quarters. I still have Duke Nukem 2D volumes 1, 2, and 3. My gaming philosophy is "Realism? Screw that, if I want real I'll shut the computer off." Those Nascar games where you have to check the damned tires and get speeding tickets coming out of the pits bore me; gimme a motorcycle, a chain, and some cops to whop ass on and I'm happy. Give me a BFG and some newbies to splatter and I'm even happier.

My first computer was a Timex, which I wrote a version of Battlezone for in hand-coded assembly. I never tried to sell it, I just liked the game and there weren't any games for that computer. The new games are too complex for any one person to write in less than ten years, so I just buy them now.

I'm not in the gaming business, except as a consumer.

Life is too silly, and with too many stupid coincidences for me to believe that there is no God, or that He has no sense of humor. The other day when Kat opened and Planet Quake published my "So you want to be a webmaster, too" editorial (same day), I was ICQing Neil, and I made one of those lame "15 minutes of fame" jokes. About fifteen minutes later, I got a message from a fellow telling me how much the writer liked "my" old "White Trash" page.

It wasn't my page. There are at least six other Steve McGrews on the internet, and the one with the "White Trash World of Steve McGrew" page actually has had his "fifteen minutes", at least in a minor sort of way; he's a stand up comedian who lives in California, works in Vegas, and has been on Cable TV (comedy channel and a few others). Of course, that's not quite as bad as my friend Robert Blake, who also shares a name with someone who has had considerably more than fifteen minutes (and drinks a bit more than the Robert Blake on TV).

Here's a clue – if you see a pig on the page, it's not mine. If you see me on TV, it's not me. If you see a Strogg squishing Sonic the Hedgehog, uh, okay, I guess I have to admit to that.

If you want to file a lawsuit, file it against the other guy. He has money.

And no, Todd, I'm NOT Flamethrower. I'm not even British. Go talk to Queen Elizabeth, she lives in the same country as him (Aha! A clue!)

In closing, here's the "tip of the week": How to keep from being a loser.

Find a time machine (Yello might loan you his overcooked pimpyum III) and go back in time nine months before you were born, hand your father a condom and your mother a box of birth control pills. That ought to fix things.

Se ya at Tokay's Towers.

Asylum frags Old Man Murray

You might not have noticed this newish site buried in the links section. Maybe it would be more prominent in the Quake Asylum where it probably belongs (still too clean. Cuss a little, Marvin).

Murray claims his site to be the "official game site of the US Postal Service" and says, "Think about it: gun toting maniacs navigating the same tired route over and over again picking up and dropping off items. Have I just described quake players or mailmen?"

Right now (but maybe not tomorrow, this *is* the internet) he has a comparison between John Romero and Oscar Romero.

BTW, Murray says, "How do you like us now that we're pretty much in charge of the post office, Blues? Ignore us now and you get no mail, baby. You and your little friend Redwood."

I know I'm scared! Uh, wait a minute, I have direct deposit and the bills and junk mail come by... HEY, MURRAY! Ya know what yer momma told me?
2/23/1999

Update: Murray says via email, "We're working to increase the amount of swearing." Since he also says he's working on a links page, he won't have to, since he'll have a button.
2/24/1999

'nother Update: That boy's *fast*. In his news section today, he not only used every cussword in existence, he even made up a new one! You will now find the old fart in the Quake Asylum, complete with straitjacket. And when he finishes his links page, he gets a front page button.
2/25/1999

Fragfest can't escape Kneel's... comfy chair?

The (ouch) interrogation has been (ooh that hurts) completed, and I was allowed to go about my "business". Why anyone would want to read an interview with me is beyond my comprehension, but if you do, there's one over at Arcadia (or will be very soon).

Also, if you can't get enough of my drivel here, Kneel has posted the first of my weekly "Weak End Gamer's Hell Hole" columns (also at Arcadia), where I actually get to write about something besides Quake and Quake people, places, and things, and don't quite manage to.
2/26/1999

Gameplex died

When I got home today, I found Gameplex completely *gone!* And so was the Fragfest! Until I rebuild the structure over here, the internal links at the top of the page won't work.

I haven't got a single email from anyone at Gameplex, and everyone on my ICQ list connected with Gameplex is offline.
2/28/1999

Host gibs Fragfest

I was about to write, "It appears that gameplex is *gone*, as in 'won't be back'," when I received an ICQ informing me that ugn3d (gameplex's host) got a new, unnamed owner. The new owner dumped gameplex and all the sites that gameplex hosted. Gameplex will be moving to a new server and will get their own server later.

So, I don't think the Fragfest will be moving from this address unless I die or change ISPs. I've had too much of being hosted; the short URL isn't worth it.
3/1/1999

Fragfest joins the game

My apologies to all the folks who have been trying to access the archives (Old Strogg's Home earlier than mid January), and who have run across dead links and broken graphics in the other Fragfest pages.

I apologize also to my link buddies for putting up with a site change to gameplex and back.

I also want to apologize to Neil, who is still waiting for that "Silicone Drive" banner I promised. Considering how long it's taking, I'd better make it extra pretty. Guess I'd need to have the Quake Guy wear a little lipstick.

Speaking of Neil, he *really* wants the Fragfest over at katalystic.com, so *[dead site]* will soon get you here. The "url from hell" will remain working from now on, though.

And thanks to Flamethrower, for changing the link back to the "URL from hell" before I even knew gameplex was shitbombed!
3/2/1999

Shinola frags Steve

"Psst, buddy, wanna shoeshine?"

"Uh, I'm wearing tennis shoes." He flashed a goneplex logo.

I put my tennis shoe on the, uh, whatever you call that thing you put your shoe on to get it shined. I slipped him a five. "Whaddya know?"

He looked at the five. "Not Much. You're not going to like it."

I slipped him a ten.

Twenty dollars later I was still wondering whether or not to believe it.

It seems that someone had planned some sort of party for later this month, and had so much alcohol and explosives for the fireworks display, most of it had to be stored somewhere else.

A spark from a stray smoker caused the demise of an entire city block.

"So where does gameplex fit it?"

"Gameplex? Who's *gameplex?*"

If you know anyone who would like a nice, shiny pair of sneakers, I'm giving these away.

UPDATE: Two emails from two guys, the first reading "Don't jump to conclusions", and the second saying "that shoeshine guy is lying, and btw he gives you a crappy shine."
3/6/1999

Slipgate died

One year ago today, the "haste does not bring success" sign went up. In honor of the occasion, I am not going to post today. Huh? I did? Oh, never mind. BTW, you missed the fireworks. Oh, and I think there's a new *Weak End Hell Hole* posted at Arcadia.
3/9/1999
The following is that article.

71

The British are coming! The British are coming! (Quick, hide the gin)

My perception of those folks "on the other side of the pond" is even more skewed than that of most Yanks (Yes, Billy Bob, to an Englishman you're a "Yankee". So put that shotgun down). You see, I've actually met hundreds of British people while I was doing time at Walt Disney World, where I spent five years helping empty the world's pockets and bank accounts.

The rub is, the only British folks I met were filthy rich. It costs a shipload of money to jet across the Atlantic just to ride some stupid carnival rides. I never met any of the ruffians that riot at European soccer games, because they can't afford to go jetting across the ocean just to see an imaginary rodent. Probably wouldn't want to unless there was a soccer game (or "football", as everyone in the world but us calls it).

Most Americans (this includes Mexicans and Canadians) get their impressions of the British on TV. That means Monty Python and a few other British comedies, including CNN, where you see the British Parliament and their silly wigs and costumes. How anyone in British government can keep a straight face is beyond me.

Until I "met" British folk playing Quake (everyone in Europe must be gamers. Over here, we're a tiny minority), my impression of the British was that they were absolutely the *politest* people on the face of the Earth (and the Japanese, renowned for their manners, are the *rudest*). From what I saw, Eric Idle's portrayal of an Englishman in *National Lampoon's European Vacation* not only was accurate, but understated. If you would have walked up to any one of the British gentlemen ("gentlemen" is also an understatement) I met in Florida and deliberately stomped on his foot, he would have apologized profusely. This is *not* the tiniest exaggeration!

I always wondered how in hell the British ever won a war, let alone took over the world ("sun never sets..."). My picture of an Englishman in combat: "Oh, my, terribly sorry, old chap, I seem to have put my blade right through your kipper. I think I have a handkercheif... So sorry... Oh, I seem to have speared your friend as well. *Terribly* sorry. Here, let me help you into that chair. Oh, my, you seem to have stopped breathing, are you unwell, sir?"

Or more like, "Oh, terribly sorry, I seem to have gotten in the way of your sword, how clumsy of me. Oh my, oh, my, I seem to have gotten your carpet bloody. Oh, please pardon my language. I must apologize, I feel slightly..... *thump*"

I never met a Basil Fawlty until I started playing Quake, years after leaving Disney. You would probably think he's American until he uses a British manner of speech. "Basil" will often rudely chide you for being, in his opinion, rude. He will then say something using nearly identical language in another level. And here I thought Basil was fiction! I never thought I'd see the day when I'd see the words "bloody fucking bot using camper, you suck! You bloody wanker American asshole, blow me, you whore."

Yes, the real paradigm shift came in Quake, where you simply cannot tell an American from a Canadian from an Englishman (or woman). That is, unless he/she says "eh", "bloody" (more obscene than "motherf****" in Britain, a slur on the Queen), or "y'all".

I miss Flamethrower's real audio show. "Basil's" comments were typed; Flamethrower is the only Brit I've ever heard (audibly) using foul language, and I really got a kick out of it. For all I know, Basil could be an American (or Chinese) masquerading as an Englishman, whereas Flamethrower's accent is unmistakably British.

Blimey, it's late, eh? Y'all have fun. Adios, por este dia. See ya at Tokay's International Tower.

Jazz Jackrabbit can't escape Dad's shotgun

"Hey Dad, did you know you were famous?"

Daughter Patty ran across some of you guys playing Jazz Jackrabbit 2 yesterday. Talk was about her Quake-crazy dad, and the fellows asked for a name. When she said "Steve" they said "mcgrew? From the Springfield Fragfest? No wonder you're so good!"

Actually, Patty's butt-kicking sk1llz are her own, and if I ever played that rabbit game I'd probably get my sorry old butt stomped pdq. My own Quake sk1llz are waning, what with all the work, having the flu, getting used to the new config, campers, bots... let's see, what other lame excuse can I come up with for sucking...

Yesterday, in addition to being the one year down day for Slipgate, was Patty's birthday. So, thanks for giving her a cheap thrill.

Hey, thanks for coming by! Now, where'd I put that shotgun?

3/10/1999

Counter sank

I'm sure you don't mind a bit, but yesterday was this year's *record low* visitor count (so far... shudder). Not even half a gross (and I hate days when the Fragfest isn't totally grossed out).

I sent an email to Old Man Murray asking him if he's seen my missing visitors. No response from the Postal Terror, so I think *he's* got 'em. I'll have to send Nacho over there with a few sticks of dynamite.

When I went to GamePlex, a few of you got lost. When gameplex suddenly disappeared from the face of the net, the counter dropped like a rock. It was up to half normal earlier in the week when Planet Quake and Yello gave a link (thanx, guys!), but it's just me and you loyalists now. Do me a favor, write Blue asking "hey, whatever happened to the Springfield Fragfest?"

I'm about ready to put your picture on a milk carton.

3/11/1999

Nacho joined the game

Nacho, fellow victim of the evil IGN and their destruction of gameplex, told me last night that Nacho Extreme is almost ready to post. Gameplex has a server, but still doesn't have their domain, so Nacho is posting at his old Arsonist haunts.

I'll give you the URL as soon as he has it up.

3/11/1999

Quake 2 mod sank like a rock

The newest Quake 2 mod, "Unpronounceable Sword Thang" (as Yello puts it), weighing in at 35 megs (Canadians are laughing and thumbing their noses at Yanks and Brits) was released last night, and soundly trashed by the reviewers at Planet Crap.

To quote my daughter, "Nya Nya Nya Nya Nya, I know what the logo means in Japanese and you don't." Actually, I'd tell you, but "I can't post because it's not perfect yet" Nacho went to a lot of effort to figure it out, and he'll need a few visitors when he opens.

A big thank you to Neil for the p1mpage on yesterday's Yello page (which is where the "sword thang" link takes you). Judging from the counter, quite a few folks said "hey! A *real* link!"

UPDATE: Nacho Extreme is open!

3/13/1999

W2K frags Q3A

Micro$oft president Steve Balmer told PC Week (vol 16 #11) that the beta of windoze 2000, code named "Godot" (but not by Microsoft) will be out in April, and the final release will be "when it's done". Id executives did not comment on the use of their trademarked lie.

Speaking of which, Balmer also told PC Week "Microsoft has always... acted both legally and ethically". The article did not disclose if he then went to his plastic surgeon to have his nose shortened to its normal length.

Windoze 2000, AKA "Win Zero", is not the same program as Q3Arena, also code named "Godot".

Microshaft is also scheduled to release a new version of

its slow as molasses internet exploiter web browser tomorrow. Netscape released its Netscrape Navigrater browser last week, which crashes as often as previous versions. Sources say Netscape only crashes under certain circumstances, like when it's running. The new Netscape fixes the "windows spoofing" security bug (see 2/19/1999 post), and its price was slashed 50% to $0. Rumor has it Microsoft's free browser's price will be slashed 50% as well, to remain competitive.

Both browsers are still overpriced.

Microsoft is releasing its Windows CE OS for cell phones in Germany, meaning you Germans will have telephones that crash with blue screens and have to be rebooted frequently. They defended their use of the OS in autos, saying autos were crashing long before computers were. NASA officials were not asked if they would risk their astronauts' lives by powering shuttle computers with windoze. They did not answer "No way, are you stupid or something?"

3/17/1999

Team frags Murray

Nacho was out of dynamite, so I assembled a crack Quake team... wait a minute, an *expert* Quake team (wipe that grin off yer face) to go over and play CTV (capture the visitors) with that evil old man and his two insane boys (three if you count Marvin). Yello brought his overcooked p1mpyum spacetime distorter. Desiato brought his bodyguard. Hulka brought his whole fraggin' army. Tikki was going to bring a Flamethrower, but some guy wearing a t-shirt that said "I'm Todd, I'm Godd, worship and ph33r" on it kept pestering us, saying "who are you? who are you?"

Gestalt wasn't home, but thanks to Joost we found him at the Planet Crap Bar and Grill, and he brought his assimilation equipment.

Blue and sCary refused to take sides, saying the fight would be too unbalanced. Of course, some of us are a little unbalanced already.

The HoSlap and the X-Bitch were, as usual, nowhere to be found, the wooses. Levelord was too loaded to walk, so stayed behind. Good thing for us, too, since he's in cahoots with the old man. He also keeps trying to squirt water at our Flamethrower, screaming "Snot funny! Snot funny! Bad bad bad!"

We could have used more firepower. The place was a fraggin' fortress and was hard as hell to get in. Good thing for us hell is easy to get into.

In the end, we got some visitors back. Unfortunately, many of them had died or gone insane in some weird experiment involving an oak sword, a bald Native American, a Mexican, and a mental hospital. Not only that, but most of our equipment was jammed up with thousands of postage stamps, which are Murray's primary weapon.

So now you understand why Yello skipped a post or two – he was busy trying to get his p1mpyum back in order. That stamp glue is hell!

BTW, if you stop by Murray's, tell 'em where you surfed in from. And tell him to get that links page up!

I would like to thank the above mentioned linked folks (my apologies if I've missed you) for helping get back some of the missing visitors, especially Yello (who posted a plea for you all to come back) and Flamethrower (who had the link changed before I knew goneplex was history). There is still a very large shortage of visitors, since so many died or went insane, so please send any extra you have by.
3/17/1999

Yello joined the game
Tikki joined the game

Yello, who took the brunt of the damage in the visitor rescue, has enlisted the help of a house cat, a pocket knife, and certain chemicals, and has nearly freed himself from all the stamps. Word is he will have a new post tomorrow.

Tikki, who lost the keys to the beach house again (last

fraggin' *November*), has made 3 updates but was unable to post. He's trying to pick the lock with his ticket, so will soon have an update, *maybe* tomorrow.
3/18/1999

Quick updates frag Sunday

First, a thanks to my link buddies who have changed their links. The couple who haven't yet, I understand, it's a P.I.A. and I apologize for being a web gypsy for a while. I'm staying put now.

Also, Neil has posted the latest *Gamer's Weak End Hell Hole* over at Arcadia. I want to thank Yello for going to great lengths to get my traffic back up.

Oh, Yello, when I was feeding the grannies, one of them bit me. Has Tim's had her shots?
3/21/1999

The following is the "Weak End Hell Hole article.

So you want to be a webmaster, too, part three or so...
How to have people actually come and see your page

Actually, "How to have people actually come and see your page" isn't exactly what this week's topic is about, but I needed a title. I plan to ramble on about close to nothing, as usual.

Since you're here, I'm going to take a wild assed guess that you're a gamer. Since you're a gamer, your page is probably a game page. Since you have a game page, that makes you part of the "hard core gaming underground" (phrase stolen from the Flamethrower interview. Don't you just love that phrase? Makes you think of the Weathermen or somebody).

So if your page is about floral arrangement or something... well, this might still apply, but wtf are you doing here in the first place?

The first thing you need to do is steal Yello's overcooked pimpyum 3 for a little time warping. Go back in time a few years, kill Blue and Joost, and open "Blue's Quake

78

Rag" and "Slipgate Central". You can then fly around the world (or at least California) and go to all the geek conventions (live animals... yum); lan parties; and beatdowns, beatups, and beatoffs. Since you'll be Joost, you won't have to post "boycott Planet Quake" at Planet Crap every other week, you can just shut the fraggin' place down. Of course, since you'll be Joost, you (or any other sane gamer) won't want to.

Speaking of California, please heed the "no smoking" sign as you enter the state. If you are driving over from Britain, you will pass through Illinois, unless you take the long way through Japan. While driving through Illinois, please heed the "smoke your fraggin' lungs out because we need to collect as many of our ridiculously high taxes as possible" sign. Or, if you go through Kentucky, the "screw tobacco, smoke our illegal #1 cash crop instead, just don't let us catch you" signs.

If you can't get hold of Yello's machine, you have to think of some other way to get your site seen. The first place you should go is the gaming search engines. All the hard core gamers know about them. Of course, they never go there, since they already have their favorite sites bookmarked.

The next place to go is Yahoo.

After Yahoo rejects your site, register it daily with them just to give them the extra work of rejecting it again. It'll serve 'em right, the bastards!

Then drop by Infosuuk. Your gaming page will be listed number 45067299, right after the 500 pages p1mping lion and elephant poaching. If yours is a Quake page, it will be listed after the 1000 Italian earthquake sites. If you have an UnReal site, you will be listed after the 798 pages devoted to United Nations fishing. This, of course, will get you lots of traffic.

The above assumes you have good meta tags; otherwise you'll be listed dead last.

Putting "flamethrower" in your meta tags is sure to get 200 hits per day from Todd Porter and the Ion staff alone. This week's hint for Todd: His name is *not* "Charles, Prince of Wales". Or maybe it is? You don't know, do ya?

Another way to get visitors is to put "sex! sex SEX child porn PORN pr0n nude nood noodz n00dz" in the meta tags; this will get traffic from the FBI and the German authorities. Another hint for Todd: He's not Larry Flynt, as not only is Mr. Flynt not British, Flamethrower doesn't have pictures of ugly nudes on his page.

Putting the name of every substance in pharmacopoeia in your meta tags is sure to get hits from the DEA, FBI, CIA, and Kieth Richards.

Another way, assuming you're young, is to tell all the kids at school you posted their sister's diary. If you don't mind a little blood leaking from your nose, tell them you have their mother's picture scanned from the cover of Crackwhore Magazine.

Be sure to put "free" in the meta tags, unless you're charging for your lack of content. This will bring in the world's losers.

Beat Thresh in a game of Doom and win John's sports car. If they know who you are, they'll look for you.

Do what I did, and have the same name as six other people who have pages. All their friends will come by looking for *their* page (No, the "white trash world of Steve McGrew" wasn't mine, nor was the University of Utah page).

This stuff goes in cycles, but talk lately has gone from "hits" to "unique, qualified visitors". Folks, I don't know about you, but this is *not* what I want. If I have 1000 hits, I'd rather it be ten people who come by a hundred times each than 1000 people who loaded the page, said "Christ, this page sucks" and hit the "back" button, never to return again.

To this end, if I may be allowed to be a tiny bit serious, get your page listed on other little pages. Save Blue's and Planet Quake (unless they host you) for when lightning strikes and you come up with that once in a lifetime killer content, like Carmak misaddresses mail to Loonygames and sends you an interview by accident, or you have developed a mod or a level that not only doesn't suck but stands out from the rest.

Blue isn't going to post "The Springfield Fragfest has moved to Katylistic", but if it's a slow news day and he's in the right mood and in a hurry to catch a learjet, he might post "The Springfield Fragfest has posted Quake Christmas carols". Especially if he's had a few eggnogs too many.

No, that's a "once in a blue's news moon" occurrence (unless you're Neil or Desiato). Try to find pages in your own league, other guys who want traffic as bad as you do. What I usually do is post a link, p1mp 'em on the front page, and mail 'em. For all I know, all my visitors may be link buddies checking to see that their button is still there. Twenty times a day each.

If you do happen to strike gold and come up with content Blues and Planet Quake both think are newsworthy, which is best? BLUES. No doubt about it. Last December Gestalt posted news of the Christmas carols, and I enjoyed a greater number of visitors the rest of the week. Blue's posted the same news a week later, and the traffic more than tripled. Furthermore, most of the visitors kept coming back! BUT, a Planet Quake posting is nothing to sneeze at, and I was and am grateful to Gestalt and Joost. Yay, Planet. Boo, boycotters (the losers).

A Planet Quake news posting is better than a Planet Quake article, but again, don't sneeze. BTW, trash talk around the net that the Planet only p1mps their own hosted sites is completely false (as those who actually go to Planet Quake know).

Have fun with your site, because that's what it's for. Make some friends, because fun and friends is all you're going to get from it (what more do you need, ya greedy bastard?) Now, if only I could prove myself wrong and quit my day job... I can dream, can't I?

See ya in the lava pits. Stay cool. Or "kewl", as the k1dz say these days.

Tikki joins the game

Tikki God's Quake Beach House is (gasp) back.

After trying since November to beat Bitch-X's record for the longest length of time without an update, it dawned on the young Tikki that he could die of old age before breaking Bitch-X's record.

After losing his keys down the barrel of a BFG (don't ask), he used his "ticket to nowhere" to pick the lock to the beach house.

The fireworks display has been canceled, as someone had apparently stolen all the fireworks. Upon discovering that the fireworks had disappeared, he was heard to mutter something about grannies and ordinance.

3/22/1999

Yello frags pinball guy

A special thanx tonight to Yello, for the bandaids, whiskey, and antibiotics (I *think* they were antibiotics)... and the new handle.

At least, you younger folks can assume "Iron Balls" has to do with prowess at pinball. Even if you ladies know better.

3/23/1999

Mr. Hanky melted

It's a month after the goneplex bombing and I'm still wiping pieces of Mr. Hanky off the Fragfest.

I just discovered (and fixed) that the links from the console page went to goneplex. Sorry. If you run across any more Mr. Hankey stains, please let me know.

3/23/1999

Matt and bill can't escape, uh, what's that thing, durn when I was younger my memory was better...

Matt Sefton and crash, webmasters who are dead and living at the Planet Crap Retirement Village, talk about the good ol' days when they had to drag their web sites barefoot, through the snow, uphill, both ways; back when beer was a

82

nickle per keg and gas was so cheap they would pay you to take it off their hands, over at The Beauty of Madness.

And if I'm not mistaken, that was the longest sentence I've ever typed.

3/26/1999

Tikki can't escape Planet Quake's BFG

Tikki God was assimilated by Planet Quake late Friday in a move that stunned and shocked onlookers. Said his shambler, "[text deleted]!"

Says Tikki of CTF mod writers in this massive flag burning, "they're lazy sons of bitches who can't think up something original or don't want to waste the time having to create a whole new mod."

Under the assimilation, he has updated his page with a rant about Paul Steed, who does Planet Quake's *Dear Mynx* column this week.

3/27/1999

`eNtiTy frags Tikki

Response to Tikki's editorial stolen from Planet Quake's mailbag: "That was probably the worst editorial I've ever seen published on PQ... Why would PQ post this? I should do the next editorial..."

Do it, dude!

I think Tikki was probably expecting this. I imagine the juiciest mails are in *his* mailbox; he seemed amused by it in a recent email.

Think empty v will do a CTF vs Deathmatch *Celebrity Deathmatch?*

3/29/1999

Yello can't escape Phone company's GFB

My British friend Neil (AKA Yello There), who has gone out of his way to help bring my visitor count back to its pre-gameplex levels, is in a bit of a bind.

From discussions at Planet Crap, my understanding is

that phone companies in the UK would use a gun, but don't have to. It seems they charge by the minute, making a call next door a long distance call. According to Neil's latest post on the Kat com page, Neil's internet expenses are eating him alive, and he will be forced to cut back drastically.

In short, he needs some extra income to shovel more money into the greedy bastard phone company's pockets. So if you are running Planet Quake, WarZone, Blue's, Telefragged, or any other profit-making internet venture; have an internet storefront and need a "store clerk" or all around internet/PC guy; and can possibly hire Neil for a part-time telecommute that doesn't necessitate his traveling to California LAN parties, please send Neil an email. I, for one, look forward to hitting the Yello There page every day, don't you?

Planet Quake folks (Mark? Davo?) especially, you talk a good community talk, lets see ya walk the walk and hire Neil! Oh, and I'm sure he'd go to any beatdown or LAN party you sent him a Concorde ticket to.

You folks in the UK, *revolt against your damned phone companies!* How many other good game pages have not been posted because a talented Limey can't afford to get on the internet? How many Brits can't we frag in a Quake game? Bring civility back, let English people play online!
3/29/1999

Napalm melted

I got a note from Tikki, who reports the ordinance is still piling into his in box. He has sent a response to the PQ mailbag and answered most of the less unintelligent mail.
3/30/1999

Gestalt died

Gestalt, who swore a mighty oath never to return to the Planet Crap Retirement Village, was dragged kicking and screaming back there by his children (several hundred thousand of them).

Gestalt is retiring from his post at Planet Quake after

84

serving continuously for the last fifty years. After giving him the obligatory watch, PQ staff strapped it on his wrist and fired several rockets at it. "Gestalt takes a licking and keeps on ticking," one observer was heard to say.

Gestalt is keeping his second job at The Coven.

3/30/1999

Yello joined the game

Yello There disappeared last Saturday night with a cryptic "Problems with (security issues) of the database. More news to come..." (From Kneel and Marlin Productions)

Worried Yello fans have been flocking by the Fragfest looking for Mr. There. I'm happy to report that he resurfaced April 1st with apologies all around, and an explanation of "Gremlins folks....feckin Gremlins with knives and boots and pointy cutty devices.....damn the things!!!!!"

I heard from more sordid (i.e., American) contacts that someone was going to steal his overcooked p1mmpyum III, but grabbed Yello's supply of electrons. Word is the electrons were found outside a window.

4/3/1999

Nacho frags Dallas
Dallas melted

I got an ICQ from a latop in a motel in Arizona last night. I wasn't in Arizona, Nacho was, with an unfinished trip log attached. Not to Nacho, to the ICQ. Here is an excerpt: "8:45am : Stopped at Burger King for breakfest. I order the hash-browns, to my dismay it was actually full of potatos." [sic]

You'll see the whole log over at his page sometime in the foreseeable future.

4/4/1999 [all sic. Sic sic sic!]

Hulka frags visitors

Hulka's Army, on a humanitarian mission, rounded up a bunch of cold, tired, hungry, lost, and very confused refugee

Fragfest visitors for us last Saturday night.

The visitors have been missing since goneplex was destroyed in a surprise raid early February. It is still not known who carried out the raid.

Old Man Murray was absolved of responsibility, since it was shown that he doesn't *have* any visitors; in fact, the visitors rounded up in the raid on his stronghold last month weren't kidnapped after all, but had wandered in looking for not only the Fragfest, but any frags they could scrape up. Two of them, in fact, were the two he can call his own, and will be returned.

I apologize to Chet for the shotgun noogie, and hope his hair grows back. I'll return the mail sorting machine shortly (after I mail a few letters).

It is now thought that Serbia had something to do with the goneplex attack. NATO is bombing the Serbs in retaliation. A few bombs are also being sent to Saddam Hussein just for being a Strogg. Serbia's leader is also suspected of being Strogg.

The Fragfest visitors who remain missing are now presumed dead. Services will be held as soon as Shaithis (or crunchy or whatever the hell he's calling himself this week) issues a funeral permit.

I also want to thank Tikki for the visitors he stole from Planet Quake (who has more than enough and won't even miss them), most of whom (at least CTF players) are busy using Tikki to roast marshmallows over. Oh, and one of these days I'll update that graphic...
4/6/1999

Flamethrower frags Elephant

In "update and content shock", here's an update to today's earlier post – Flamethrower may have given away his chances for a "ticket to nowhere" for quite a while.

He has yet another update, and it's a fraggin' *monster* (still loads faster than the Fragfest;) completely knocking his yesterday's post off the page.

In it, he mentions having "the most disturbed readership on the web" (excluding kiddy snuff pr0n and sCary's). It seems someone wrote him that Capt. Immy was back (um, I think somebody sent me an email about that, too...) and says "I want his funny assed shows back."

Me, too; that phone prank wasn't it.

He also has folks sending him some pics you better see quick before somebody makes him take them down!

This is just the beginning of it, if you're a flamey reader get your ass over there. If you're not, I think Planet Quake has news of some mods...

4/10/1999

Moon frags Blue

Last month saw the second blue moon this year. I'm told this only happens about once in about every 40 years.

This one was a doozy. Since the blue moon, Blue's missed an update (the news frame was down), Yello missed a day last week (this may not be moon related, as there were other issues at work, like granny Yello's "medication", which had Yello so confused he had a mixed breed German shepherd confused with me when everyone knows I don't carry a hooked staff), Murray missed an update, and I damned near missed an update last week too, as I was sick as a dog Thursday and Friday.

Stranger than missed updates and nearly missed updates were the updates from those often in the "ticket to nowhere" contest. Tikki updated 3 days in a week (unheard of!) and has had a weekly post for three weeks running (a new record, I think). Flamethrower topped Tikki by updating three times in a twenty four hour period, one of which was a (must see) monster. Further proof of last month's blue moon was that Blue's actually mentioned Flamethrower Sunday! If he mentions the Fragfest you know Christmas is near.

But the real proof that there was a blue moon, aside

from the fact that the TV weather manikins said so, was a real, actual, update from Bitch-X.

This, of course, was covered by everybody, including Blue, Flamey, Murray... hell, it would be easier to list those who *didn't* note this remarkable occurrence. In fact, Murray has even instituted the "BitchX Tracker", where dead president Martin Van Buren burns in hell whenever BitchX updates. If you are wondering what in the frag Van Buren has to do with the Bitch, so am I. You have to remember, though, that Murray's is the official game site of the US Postal Service. Consequently, there are tons of glue-filled postage stamps laying around, and you know what sniffing glue will do to your synapses!
4/12/1999

Qidz can't escape Level's BFG

In lieu of the nonexistent Adult Quake nooze, here's a little Rabbit (Quake for Qidz) nooze.

Patty says her Lego level is done, and there's nothing more she can add to it. So since I haven't showed her how to FTP and she hasn't got her page quite ready yet (what's posted is still "coming soon, bookmark now"), you can download it here for your qidz or younger siblings.

You need this file. You may have to right-click and "save link as" if your browser thinks it's a text file. Save it in the Jazz Jackrabbit "cache" folder. From what she tells me, to use it you have to have the registered version and start a server, or have the registered version and join a server that is using the level.

She has been playing the level all week, and says she already kicked one qid for language and will ban him next time (I think he said "semprini").

In other places around the web:

The Planet Quake "Quad Ho" contest had a winner, and Lowtax scrounged up a t-shirt for the wiener and the business end of a BFG for the losers.

Yello There has gone to an "every other day" posting, since he's still having problems with the British Robber Baron Phone Company™.

Nacho is still missing and presumed intoxicated.

Tikki says he will have a rant this weekend about the Kentucky Id lawsuit. Hulka posted a link to this rant about the same subject at 3dNexus. This is one of those maddening sites that would be *real good* "if only". Its design is unique and well crafted, the authors use spell checkers and actually know how to speak English, and there is actually some content. However, the rant starts out with a warning for those who are offended by language, the main page has a mildly sexist cartoon figure – and its message board has a warning that you will be banned for being offensive. WTF? "Do as I say, not as I do..."

Dead President Martin Van Buren isn't burning in hell over at Murray's, meaning BitchX is still camping (reports are that Murray's son is still a pussy; see illustration and story from yesterday).

Slobby Dan MiLotsaBitch still hasn't returned to his home on Stroggos from Yugoslavia.

The lost Fragfest visitors seem to have found their way home; Welcome back! If you want milk and cookies, Blues has the cookies and Planet Quake has the milk.

I still need you to send in some Quake nooze.
4/16/1999

Nooze can't escape drought's blaster

Nothing new you can't find at Blue's (who is Quake Only today) or Planet Quake. Damn, everybody but Flamethrower is in the "ticket to nowhere" contest today!

Well, Immy updated, but since a) he doesn't do Quake any more and b) his stuff is really *sucking* lately, the "r.i.p." will remain next to his link on the links page.

So send in some nooze! I may not be Blue's, but Patty's rabbit page is solidly in the middle of the Jayde topsites list for games (and #1 on their Springfield list) and she doesn't even

have meta tags; the only way anybody would even know about it is here or the Jayde directory.
4/18/1999

Everybody frags ticket

Hot on the heels of everyone's update frenzy earlier this month is a dearth of posts. This means, of course, that the "ticket to nowhere" contest is back on! As usual, the winner receives a round trip no expense paid trip to *absolutely nowhere*. No expense is spared (or paid) for this traveling extravaganza.

The contest, of course, is a race to the update finish line. Last one there wins.

First out of the gate was Spew, riding the speedy steed "My new boss boss hates me". Also first across the finish line, he began updating almost regularly again; the latest was Sunday.

Coming in a close second to last was Nacho Extreme, on the two wheel supercharged "cross country race to what seems like nowhere but everybody has a swimming pool". After two or three weeks of inactivity (traveling, unpacking, finding an ISP, ogling women, and drinking), he updated with details of his travels and travails (among, of course, various and sundry remarks about the PC gaming scene).

Seeming to close in on the finish line is Yello There, riding the British Telecom Robber Baron bus, as his Yello Trike has a flat tire. Oh, I'm sorry, he's British so it's a flat tyre.

Having not been updated since Friday, there may be a post by the time you read this.

Close behind Yello is, um, er, uh... me; I'm late with an update to the *Weak End hell hole* over at Arcadia. There are actually a couple of weak ends finished and ready to upload, but what with my wife's going back to college and my daughter's love for Jazz Jackrabbit, I practically need a BFG to get my hands on the PC. Speaking of PC, I also get dragged in to the daily fistfight over at the Planet Crap Bar and Grill way too often, and try to beat LPBs at Quake 2 (and usually get my ass kicked in the process) too much. I promise to upload the hell hole in a day or two.

Way, way behind and in the lead is Planet Wank, citing "real life". Like nobody else has one. No word as to what aspect of real life is hindering his page.

Riding a B2 stealth bomber is Old Man Murray (official gaming site of the U.S. Post Office), whose server seems to be down as often as not lately; I don't know if he's even in the contest, as I haven't been able to get to his page lately.

Flamethrower, with six month's worth of posts in less than a week, has been camping at the finish line since before the contest started, and won't win the nowhere ticket for quite a while.

Of course, BitchX and Pile; er, Old Maid X are permanently disqualified for cheating. BitchX only updates during a blue moon, and Pile only updates when BitchX does. Why no link to those pages? Simple; they look exactly the same as they did the last time you saw them, and will the next time you see them. Never seen them? Don't worry, they'll look the same when you finally do.

"How can I get into this contest," you're asking yourself? Simple. Have a fairly good Quake or PC Gaming page that I actually know about (it doesn't matter if no one else has seen it, drop me an email), that is normally updated regularly, and let it rot. Posts to Planet Crap, guest articles and guest editorials at other folks' pages don't count as updates.

You could win the no expense paid ticket to Absolutely Nowhere!

Void where prohibited, and prohibited where void. Taxes and all other expenses are the responsibility of the winner. Close cover before striking. Do not use near fire or flame. Not a step. May cause discoloration of urine or feces. Keep out of the reach of children and stupid adults. No animals were harmed in the creation of this contest (except for lunch).
4/21/1999
The following is the article posted at Arcadia.

So you want to be a webmaster, too, part three or so...
Quake and the price of "fame"

This came up last month when Flamethrower was interviewed by a site whose url I have misplaced (sorry).

Flamey was asked about his anonymity, and answered to the effect that he was afraid of being seen as a publicity seeker when he first started the "Flamethrower" thing, so used the nick and kept his real name to himself. It turned out handy when Todd P. started hunting for him (let's see, there are only four BILLION people in the world...)

On the other hand, when Captain Immy started Pointless Audio, he published not only his real name but his photograph, as well. He stated on his page that he started it to become famous. LOL!

Myself, I never gave it any thought. Celebrity never impressed me. It always amazed me how absolutely stupid the people I worked with at Disney got when someone famous came by. I just saw celebrities as people with a hell of a lot better jobs than I had, and consequently had many pleasant conversations with famous folks while my coworkers were making asses of themselves acting like demented puppies.

I had a few unpleasant conversations with some, too. It seems many of the the "kinda famous", especially professional golfers, would get irate when you didn't recognize them. How in the hell should I know who a damned golfer is? I *hate* golf! The ones anybody would recognize anywhere seemed grateful when you pretended not to know them. Some denied being who they were ("hey, guys, if he says he's not Dan Aykroyd, he's not Dan Aykroyd"). Some took pleasure in discussing their work, as long as you didn't act as if you were speaking to God Himself ("*That* was Buddy Hackett? Nah, it wasn't"... "Sure it was, look at the credit card slip"... "Wow! Cool! You met Buddy Hackett!"... "Cool? You're a dumbshit, leave me alone.")

The first thing I noticed when playing Quake (actually, when lurking as an observer) was that literally everyone had handles, or "quake names". No one used their real name.

Never one to go along with the crowd, I decided to go by the handle of "Steve"; in other words, screw handles, I'll use my damn name. When I started my Quake page, I didn't have the choice of anonymity, as the web space was on my ISP's server, meaning my user name (my last name) was both directory name and email address. Kind of hard to remain anonymous under those circumstances. I would have had to close my account, open a new one, and move my other pages. It didn't matter, I hadn't thought about it.

Amusing when a month or so later, "Steve" became a popular Quake name. I wonder how many Steves were really Bobs and Sallys?

I never saw myself as ever becoming famous for *anything*, at least after I discovered how bad I suck playing guitar. Especially for a web page. The most I ever expected was to get an occasional person stumbling through. When I would get an email, my reaction was always "Wow! Somebody saw my page!" Updates were more or less weekly, and when a couple of weeks went by without mail, I wondered if I should bother updating at all. I got an "invisible" hit counter, telling myself that I would only update on a day I had visitors. I was quite surprised at the numbers reported, and have updated daily since.

I was thrilled to have so much traffic. If my numbers dropped that low now, It would be depressing.

Last October I got together with a few other webmasters to throw a Halloween night "Dig up the Quake dead" IRC chat party. I got an email from a fellow who saw its p1mp page, saying "I'd really like to get in on this. Do you have to be famous to get in?"

I usually don't laugh at my readers' letters (I laugh at Gestalt's readers' letters), but I made an exception in this case. If only the famous were invited, even the "kinda famous", the only people there (who weren't) would have been Robin Williams, Conan O'Brien, and one or two others.

Neither Carmack or Romero would have been invited,

let alone Joost or Gestalt. Well, maybe Oscar or Caeser Romero, if they've died playing Quake, but not John. *They're not famous!* I sure as hell wouldn't have been allowed in.

Don't believe me? If you are in school, ask a teacher or another student who John Romero is. If you aren't in school, ask a coworker. *None of them will know who John Romero is unless they, too, are a gamer! John Romero is not famous. Thresh is not famous. Bastard isn't famous,* At least outside the hardcore PC gaming community.

Nevertheless, there is a certain amount of notoriety *within* the gaming community. I've had so many irons in the fire and stuck my fingers in so many pies, from Planet Quake to Planet Crap (to Arcadia, etc.) that I have become known, At least somewhat, within our little "Hard core gaming under-ground", as we were called in the Flamethrower interview. I've had one-time links from Evil Avatar, Planet Quake, and even the "famous" Blue's News (thank you, Blue, for the traffic).

Famous? Maybe kinda, within our little community. That's kind of like being "kinda famous" among people from Dupo, Illinois (the third string high school football quarterback's brother).

Immy – you're still not famous. So start your show back up and this time don't take it so damned seriously. Flamey, uh, better not tell us who you are. Todd's still out there.

See ya at Tokay's, Conan.

Ticket frags slowpoke

Flamethrower crossed the finish line again, lapping everyone in this one lap race several times. He has Nacho's *Flamethrower - The Movie* banner where his logo normally resides, and a long email from an EA employee posted. Will EA Survive? Drop by Flamey's for the details.

Yello There crossed the finish line with a real link to twelve year old Patty's Rabbit page, causing her to do back flips and pleas for me to mail Yello with her thanks. Hopefully we will not need muscle relaxants to remove the grin from her ears.

Also, they do not have tires in Britain as was reported yesterday – U.K. residents use tyres instead. There is also a gasoline shortage, but fortunately there is plenty of petrol.

Murray, with a sardine on his B2 bomber's radar evasion electronics, showed up on radar just across the finish line for several seconds until "Eric the Cat" disposed of the fish.

That leaves Planet Wank and the Weak End Hell Hole as the only two contestants left, and the hell hole's *Internic is ugly and its mother dresses it funny* will be uploaded about five minutes after this is.

So enjoy your vacation, Mr. Wank! Be sure to send us a postcard!

4/22/1999

The following is the Hell Hole article from Arcadia.

Internic is ugly and its mother dresses it funny

This isn't as much of an issue to me as it used to be. I used to think that the hellishly long url I had was keeping visitors away. I mean, everyone from ZDNet to Internet Day told me so.

The move to goneplex and the short, easy to type and remember url showed me differently. Traffic dropped after the move (they weren't half the p1mps my present host is).

The fact is, nobody types in many urls. They click on a link, whether from a search engine or a link buddy's page. The only people who really *need* an easy to remember and type url are those who promote their sites through other media, like print or TV.

Nevertheless, internic is still stupid and evil. Actually, the fact that one entity can have more than one domain is evil and stupid.

People with tons of money make tons more money buying up every name in the phone book, especially trademarks. You want Pepsi.com, Mr. Pepsi? Sorry, Mr. Coke already bought it. If you want it, they'll sell it to you for five grand or so. Oh, that's right, they're a competitor. You ain't gettin' it, buddy.

Would someone please explain to me why this is allowed?

Someone should hammer out an international treaty (they did it for drug laws and name extensions, e.g., www.m5.uk or www.cia.us) making it not only illegal but impossible for *any* corporation to own a domain, or for any person to own more than one domain. Bastard already has planetquake.com, and if he doesn't, GSI could sign it over to him. Iacocca could hold ford.com.

It could be argued that a corporation could hold one name to keep the name's owner from holding the company hostage, but corporations are heartless and have soulless lawyers that care for nothing but protecting their bottoms; er, bottom lines at all costs (nuclear war or our company going out of business? FTW, the company comes first! World peace puts us at risk of a takeover? Screw world peace!) and know the law well enough that they need no gun to rob. Call each division a company and make it legal. There are always ways.

These same lawyers can write contracts that insure that if the url's owner leaves the company, he must give the domain to someone else in the company.

There is something else I'm ignorant about. Why does it only cost ten bucks to register a copyright in the US forever, but registering a domain for two years is a couple hundred bucks?

And why is the British telephone company not required to use a gun when they rob my British friends?

Ticket does a back flip into the lava

Proud *ticket to nowhere* record holder Tikki spoke before the assembled audience of old and mostly new faces at the Planet Crap Bar and Grill yesterday at the "Kill Whitey" auditorium. Waving the flaming ticket high, he said a few words about gay Nazis and attempted to hand it over to the new holder, Planet Wank.

Wanker was nowhere to be found. Security was sent to check the Real Life annex where Mr. Wank reportedly was, but to no avail. The only soul in the room was the very inebriated Yello There, who was muttering something about "mcgrew spiked my drink." His drink was a very ordinary English Gin and Tonic in a nearly empty ten gallon glass; it seems the gin and tonic had been spiked with a few drops of tonic water. Strange, since it was the first I had seen of him all night. The bartender confided to me that it had been he who had watered down Mr. There's drink, as he had already finished six. I asked for a can of beer, and he served me a pony keg. Cheap bastards and their small beers! At least it was cold.

We asked Nacho if he had seen Wank as Nacho drifted past riding a strange smelling cloud of smoke a foot or two below the ceiling. His only remark was "Damn, I love this job. Anybody got a lighter?"

Flamethrower then pulled out a shiny new Electronic Arts Zippo and toasted everyone. The pyrotechnics reminded everyone of the swimming pool, so the Lava Room was searched. There at the bottom of the lava was Wank, who refused to come out, insisting his real life lay at the bottom of the glowing cauldron.

Tikki strapped the ticket to a rocket and launched it into the bottom of the pool. Several other members of the crowd cheered, and also threw and shot various forms of ordinance in, including the elderly crash (also a speaker in the "Kill Whitey" auditorium). crash threw a very old fashioned ax and chainsaw at the pool.

Murray and sons, hopped up on stamp glue, then walked through screaming obscenities at Blue, saying "keep yer goddamned charity, ya rich bastard! We don't *need* your damned 'community!' I don't want yer damn suitcase full of money! Hey Flamey, gimme a dollar!"

Fellow Arcadian Morgan (not the Morgan from Ziff

Davis), also speaking at the auditorium, attempted to disarm all the Yanks, who proceeded to laugh at him.

By the time the police arrived, everyone was gone except Wank, Yello, and Nacho, who were all unconscious in the Real Life room. Luckily, Murray had left his B2 invisibility gear behind and the three were undiscovered by the authorities. This was exceedingly lucky, as the police were all Serbian.

4/23/1999

Arcadia melted

There'll be a new Weak End Hell Hole posted over there this weekend. While I'm mentioning updates, Nacho updated late (*real* late Monday night); Tikki is trying to get his ticket back, and since twelve year old daughter Patty finally cleaned her room, I'll mention that she added links to the Fragfest and Yello There and posted profuse thanks to Yello from her Rabbit game page for the real link he gave her. She said she would have linked Nacho (who she is losing to in the Jayde topsites list), but he sometimes uses "dirty words" and has a picture of a teletubbie's bong on his page.

4/30/1999

Following is the Arcadia article.

Mainstream reporters are fraggin' *ignorant*
U.S. educators aren't much smarter

Ignorant or just evilly apathetic to the damage they cause? Both?

As I write this, yesterday was Chernobyl (AKA CIH) day. As I was uploading the Fragfest yesterday, my wife had the local news on in the kitchen. "You have to run your antivirus software today," she said.

"I ran it yesterday, we're clean."

"No, the lady on TV said you have to run it *today*."

I explained how you had to have downloaded and run an executable to catch CIH, and it was too late if you had the virus anyway; the PC wouldn't have worked.

"No, they said you get it in your email! You got lots of email today!"

The TV lady was obviously confusing CIH with Mellissa, which I can't catch since I use neither Outlook Express nor Word. I tried to explain this to Becky. "No, she said anybody can catch it."

In exasperation, I replied "What the [expletative] does some damned TV news anchor know, anyway?"

"No, she's not the news guy, she's a *computer expert.*"

Yeah, and I'm the fraggin' king of France. An "expert" whose credentials were never given is spreading misinformation about computer viruses! Of course, even though I've read a shelf of books about computer viruses, taken loads of college level computer courses, built PCs from scratch using spare parts, programmed in hand coded assembly, successfully supported users via email about hardware and drivers I haven't seen, and my *paycheck* comes from my EDP skills, I'm not an expert. You see, I'm not on TV. What's makes me less of an expert is she not only knows me, she's married to me.

Later in the evening I stopped the remote at CNN while channel surfing. There were the tearful funerals, followed by nameless men and women in business suits at desks in front of bookshelves. Wow, suits, desks, and books, these people must really know what they're talking about. All were decrying the violence in videogames. Long, bloody shots of Doom, Duke Nuken, Quake, and Quake 2 were shown. Snuck in while the games were being splashed (literally) on the screen was a one sentence voice over, *very* easy to miss, that stated that scientifically controlled studies had shown that violent games had no effect on anybody, adolescent or adult. The announcer then came on with more interviews of nameless, non-credentialed suits saying how the games' ratings need to be better and how parents should be careful what games they let their kids play.

Meanwhile, the idiots who teach our kids are

mandating counseling for any high school student who has ever played Quake or Doom, outlawing black or long coats, and suspending kids for having a nail file while doing nothing whatsoever about the kids who are giving kids with PCs, brains, or unconventional views hell. In fact, according to some kids who wrote to slashdot, they are *encouraging* the shallow preppie conformists to give them (you?) hell.

They have instituted a strict dress code at my daughter's school; half of her clothes are now either too loose or too tight. She says they've even banned a lot of *speech* at her school. So much for teaching kids the constitution!

What a bunch of dangerous morons. No wonder the world is going to "hell in a handbasket", as my Grandpa used to say before he was killed in an industrial accident. Speaking of industrial accidents, they kill about five times as many men in the U.S. as intentional violence. Car crashes kill about triple as many as intentional violence. More minors die here from playing with matches than guns, about 3 times as many.

Yeah, lets outlaw guns, then there won't be any, just like there isn't any cocaine. Yeah, that's the ticket. Doesn't matter that legal firearms are almost never used in crime, like the Crips and Bloods get their Ouzis from the local gun shop, like Gangstas hold FOI cards. (As a slight disclaimer, I have to add that I don't own a firearm, although I did quite a bit of hunting with my dad when I was a kid.)

Which brings us to that other bugaboo, drugs. Thank God none were found in or on those kids, or there would be the Reagonish war on drugs (which begat crack cocaine) heating up again with its concurrent rise in violent crime.

Of course, the one kid *should* have had drugs in his bloodstream – he was being treated and medicated by a psychiatrist for mental disorders. Why the hell isn't that damned quack losing his shrink license?

Come to think of it, our politicos aren't any smarter than the dolts anchoring the TV news or the morons teaching our kids. God help us all!

ya got the 6a11z to post this at yer school? NOT a good idea...

Smurf frags particle accelerator

I got another note from the dopey smurfer today, who is a physics major; the thought of the smurfer near a particle accelerator is *scary*. He confides that "At first I was gonna hit my reload button 1 000 000 to show Patty who's got more hits. Then I realized that she could do that too. (damn those double-edged swords). So instead you and your PR spin doctors (namely Patty) have convinced me. Meet the warmer, cudlier face of The House-O-Bitchin'."

He did, too. Not only is the link button changed from Aerosmith's Steve Tyler french kissing a smurf's butt to the simpler one shown, he's changed his Quasi-XXX Gallery to a Quasi-YYY gallery.

It's turning into a pretty good game/humor page; you no longer have to be over 57 to get in.

5/3/1999

Arcadia died

Bad news from across the pond; katalystic.com's host is giving Neil a very hard time about the amount of server space we're using, and says Arcadia is closing shop soon.

Some of the Fragfest downloads may be broken for a day or two; I'm doing what I can to lighten the load on the Kat server by deleting everything except the nooze page and one or two containers.

Meanwhile, if you have the Fragfest's Kat address *[defunct]* bookmarked, you might want to change it back to *[older defunct URL]* just in case.

5/5/1999

crash joined the game

Yesterday was mail day, it seems. My box was stuffed when I got home from work, and no sooner could I answer one than two more would pop up. I finally gave up, leaving the rest for today.

I mentioned a couple of days ago that I had lost the late crash's new address; actually, it's *somewhere* on that big-assed links page, but since it doesn't say "crash" it might as well have been dropped into a black hole. The venerable crash dropped a note cluing me that he had respawned at GA-Source. I might even break my own rule and put it at the bottom of the page without a return link so I can find it, as I have always enjoyed reading crash's stuff; his Q2 page was one of the jewels of the web. Naah, I'd better not...

He said in his note that his old level review page is not only dead, but buried, as he doesn't even have the password any more. So drop by his new page! The crash is dead; long live crash.

He mentioned the ticket; since crash's old page was officially pronounced dead by Dr. Kevorkian last December, it isn't eligible any more, but his new one is. All he has to do for the coveted *Ticket to Nowhere* is let the new page rot, and the chance of that happening is about equal to my chances of winning the state lottery – and I don't buy lottery tickets.

Of course, BitchX has been disqualified for cheating (he/she/it only updates when there is a blue moon), as well as Pile, who only updates when he sees Martin Van Buren burning in hell over at Murray's.

Nacho, in the running for the ticket, also dropped a note by. Seems he has a temperature of 102F and has to write a paper on some dead German he calls "Gaydolph Shitler", so he has a chance for the ticket if his fever doesn't break.

Nacho had Patty saying "WooHoo!" when he mentioned that he has such fond memories of Jazz Jackrabbit 1 he's linking her Jazz Jackrabbit 2 (Quake for qidz) page.

He suspects that Tikki, who has the largest *ticket to*

nowhere collection this side of Stroggos, has lost the keys to the Beach House again, which would add to his huge collection.

Update: no, the keys are locked up in his shambler's cage.

Tikki says it may be a month before he updates due to some "real life" stuff he detailed that I won't go into here.

It was pointed out to me by one of the half dozen people who gives a frag that it's been a *long time* since I did an RA show. True, but I made a few minor changes to the page (and a new show *is* in the works).

Of course, speaking of Real Audio, the ticket could always go to Desiato, who hasn't updated in nearly three weeks and still has a link to the Fragfest's "404, gameplex ain't here no more, dude" page, and still hasn't given Nacho that link he promised. Maybe even if he does a new show, his links page will win the contest.

So it looks like a tough race. if you have the 6a11z to stick it out and are willing to lose most of your visitors, you can win the *Ticket to Absolutely Nowhere.* No purchase required (well, you may have to buy a PC, an ISP, and some server space). Offer not good on Stroggos; void wherever else local laws prohibit not updating. Keep out of reach of children. Do not use near fire or flame. Shirt and shoes required (pants optional).
5/5/1999

Hell Hole died
Music Died
Downloads died

I have another Weak End Hell Hole ready to post, but we're having some space problems at katcom (which is why Arcadia may be making a visit to Dr. Kevorkian), and I don't want to aggravate the problem.

I'm not sure what I will do with the Hell Hole. For now, I'm mirroring it at my paid famvid space probably by this weekend in the "Old Stroggs' Home"; I don't know if there will be any more new ones posted.

I deleted the Quake theme from katcom last night. I'll have it moved over to famvid space, maybe tonight. The Fragfest just ain't the same without the music.

I'll have those downloads (Quake 1 and 2 patches) and RA shows back on line by the weekend.

BTW, if anyone needs server space, Family Video here in Illinois gives you "unlimited internet access" including email and web space for $12.95 per month. I don't know exactly what "unlimited" is, but I probably have close to 100 megs on their server now (the Quake 2 demo is 40 megs) and they haven't complained. Of course, you would have to be in Chicago or Springfield for dialin, and you can't run any paid banners. They are serious about this, too; I put a Barnes&Noble commission search clickthrough on my "McGrew Page" last year, and they deleted my page! You can be sure I took the B&N banner down before I uploaded it again.

For a "commercial" account they get $30 per month.

If any of you go there for server space, would you PLEASE tell them I sent you (and tell me you told them), as they'll give me a month free for every person I refer. Right now that thirteen dollar bill every month isn't easy to pay; I've had a string of "real life" lately (veterinary and human medical bills) that has drained my wallet. I don't know who is more unfortunate, folks in Britain who pay for phone calls by the minute but have universal health care like everybody else in the world, or us in the US who have cheap dialin but have to pay an arm and a leg for insurance, which usually only covers 80% or so of the king's ransom the doctors and hospitals charge.

Oh, and if you're looking for a CD or strategy book...

5/6/1999

There was one more Hell Hole article written, but it was never posted. Here is the article, which was written in 1999 but never published before now.

Is Quake a killer – or are the mass news media killers?

Last year, a 14 year old boy in Tennessee murdered his mother with a butcher knife, took some guns to school, and murdered some kids. It was one of roughly a half dozen such murders of and by middle class white teenagers. This particular one played Doom.

Money hungry lawyers took advantage of the grieving parents of the slain children and convinced them that Doom was to blame, and convinced them to file suit against Id. Why not sue the murderer? Simple: He is only fourteen, and has no money. His mother can't be sued – even if she had money, she's dead. If the lawyers want to collect their thirty pieces of silver, they not only have to find a scapegoat, they have to find a rich scapegoat.

Id has lots of money.

The lawyers hired an "expert" witness, an ex-marine who used Doom to train marines to storm buildings, using a custom level. Having his fifteen minutes of fame, he calls Doom and Quake "murder simulators". (As one wag said, "hey! he shot me from above! How'd he do that??") Never mind that in Doom one is shooting at blue flying balls, red devil things, goat-looking monsters, and zombie things. Never mind that nothing in Quake 1 looks very human. Never mind that in Quake II we are "killing" alien cyborg creatures from Stroggos, not people; that we are rescuing humans. Never mind that if Doom had anything to do with it he would have used a chainsaw instead of a knife. Never mind that if this ex marine thinks Doom is a murder simulator, he must think marines, himself included, are murderers.

This year there was another such murder in Colorado. This time, it was on a huge scale. Two boys with a small arsenal of firearms and several large and small bombs murdered a dozen people and wounded several more. They were also Doom players. The mass news media, most particularly the TV news media, had a field day. They hadn't had so much sensationalist fun since O.J. Simpson got away with murder.

The politicians got into the act, all decrying the violence in video games. A senator from Colorado stood before the U.S. Senate with graphs and charts – and an audience of two, not counting the cameras, decrying these horrible games.

The day 13 people died by gunfire in Colorado, 30 people in the U.S. drowned in their own bathtubs, as they do daily. Countless died on the highways. Children burned to death that day playing with bic lighters, as they do daily. As Sgt Hulka pointed out in his web page, the next day 25 people were killed in one drunken boating accident – should we ban boats?

I got email from teenagers all over the U.S. the following week. Some feared for their safety in school. One high school Quake player also plays sports, and "ain't very nice to some of the nerds," he worried. As I pointed out to this young friend I've known online for a year or so, school is still one of the safest places you can be, as long as it isn't in the inner city, where gun violence has been going on since that bloody "Ms Pac Man" game. While 12 kids died in that Colorado school, hundreds were dying out of school by gunshots, car accidents, falls, fires, and all manner of ways there are to die. None of the thousands of other high schools suffered any fatalities or injuries at all.

Even though FPSes are played world wide, the U.S. is the only place kids are being blown away in school (with the possible exception of Yugoslavia).

Since Doom was released, the incidence of youth violence has decreased yearly. It could be argued that FP Shooters cause a DECREASE in youth violence. I know after a bad day, a good game of online Quake puts me in a better mood!

So why this spate of school shootings? It's simple. Out of the countless kids going to school, sooner or later one mentally unbalanced young man was bound to snap, lose it, go insane, and kill someone.

The rest did it for their fifteen minutes of fame. Police

call these "copycat killers". If the first had not been not only reported, but hyped out of all proportion by the news media, none of those that followed would have happened. Those 13 students and faculty at Columbine would be alive today.

The lawyers are going after the wrong targets. They should sue the news media, who are no more protected by the first amendment than the folks at Id.

Arcadia did a back flip into the lava

I got a note from Neil last night; the server problems aren't from lack of space, they're from the amount of data transfer (downloads and lots of traffic, but Neil says mostly downloads). Arcadia's suicide is the result of "lack of interest". Apparently, the Weak End Hell Hole has been the only part of Arcadia that has been updated regularly. It's a shame, too; when a big interview was posted, Arcadia would get quite a bit of exposure. Of course, Desiato hasn't even been updating Spew lately; I don't know what's up with the other guys.

Smurf's page (now on geoshitties; change your bookmark, sCary) noted the humorous irony of my post about Blue breaking Smurf's server: "See you on GeoCities, Steve! Mwahahahahaha!" ...but the Fragfest is the (cue spooky music) *page that wouldn't die!* Not only does Neil assure me that katcom isn't going anywhere, I learned my lesson from the goneplex incident. Everything except the realaudio and two patches were mirrored on my own space.

I'll have them back on line this weekend if I can wrestle the mouse away from my college-going wife (durn those

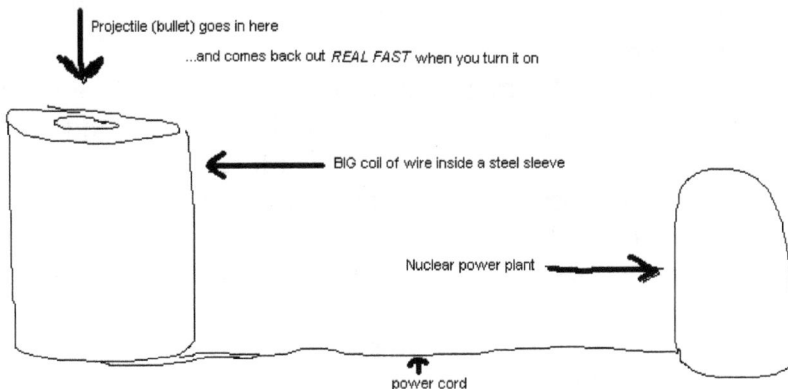

Projectile (bullet) goes in here

...and comes back out *REAL FAST* when you turn it on

BIG coil of wire inside a steel sleeve

Nuclear power plant

power cord

perfessers).

As to the Irony of the Smurfer, the true irony is not only is 12 year old Patty no longer Blue compared to Smurf even though her traffic is way up (crash mentioned "McGrew's daughter" over at the Planet Crap Bar and Grill and Yello gave her a real link), I'm not even Blue compared to Smurf any more; judging from his counter, he's kicking my ass! (his counter read 200 before Blue, which is less than I get in a day) Not only that, but according to my counter, one or two of you may have found the Fragfest through Smurf's. A thanks to you folks for dropping by, and also to Marko for sending you.

Blue's made it look like Smurf's rail gun explanation was so technical you would have to be employed by NASA to understand it, so I gave thought to translating it to English, but it really couldn't be any simpler than Smurf's explanation. The only really technical part is the math equations, which basically boil town to "the harder you throw something the faster it goes" and "the more electricity you give it, the harder it throws the slug".

Pretty good for a former student, huh Marko? That half of a guy's brain isn't even supposed to work!
5/7/1999

Nacho joined the game

Playing the *Ticket to Nowhere* contest like he plays that drinking game, Nacho made an, um, update...

This leaves the Quake Beach House and Spew. My money's on Tikki...
5/9/1999

Arcadia died

They sat silently huddled around the casket. Someone whispered "I *really* wanted that ticket." A second voice answered, "But you didn't have to *kill* him for it!"

A moan came from the casket. "It's miiiine................" the corpse groaned.

"Sorry, 'fraid not," Dr. Kevorkian piped up. "This stiff

died from natural causes, I didn't even have to help. Much."

"What did he die from?"

"Neglect, apparently. Nobody cared."

"Well, he still gets the ticket."

"Afraid not, Tikki and Desiato are beating him again. Tikki's the only guy alive that can beat a corpse in a death contest!"

"Besides, since he's dead, he's inelegible."

"Oh, man, the poor stiff..."

5/9/1999

World Peace tripped on its own grenadine

Battle-bruised, bleeding, and bone weary, I dropped by the Planet Crap Bar and Grill for a beer and a shambler 'n cheese sandwich the other night. There is usually plenty of action over there; lots of mean drunks, webmasters, game developers and promoters, gamers, *cough* journalists, and other assorted folks the mainstream (gag) journalists call "bad people in trenchcoats", even though you would get laughed out of the place if you came in wearing one. I mean wearing a trenchcoat, not wearing a journalist; it's okay to wear a journalist there.

The discussion's topic was "Thank God I can't go to E3 and even if I can don't call *me* no fraggin' journalist even if I gots a stinkin' press pass!"

Nearly 200 people were there when I showed up. I was looking forward to a good old knock-down 'n drag-out bloody mess on this one. I mean, the place usually makes empty v's *Celebrity Deathmatch* look like a hippie love-in. I was expecting "Bastidz won't let me go, hey, I gots 300 hits so far this year, ain't that mass media journalism?"

Instead of the usual troll beatings, knifings, and other mayhem, the place was... well, different. Folks were swaying to and fro in time with the singing and laughing. George and Steve (one of the other Steves that show up there) were singing the old tune "I'm uh print jurnelest en eye kin rite good an yer not," and everybody else was singing "Thank God I'm not a journalist, Hallelujah."

Sgt. Hulka stood up on stage and sang the old love song, "Booth Babes, ain't no other reason..."

I was shocked. Fearing for the safety of the world I commented on this highly unlikely turn of events (I mean peace at Planet Crap, not Hulka singing about booth babes, Hulka *really* likes booth babes).

Andy reassured me. "See those guys hiding under that table in the back corner?" Indeed, the websters who would have liked to scream out "IM A JURNLEST EN I'M PISSED" were laying low, lurking in the corner.

I'm not going to E3, but a young friend with a pass and a fake I.D. promises to be reporting on Q3Arena for the Fragfest from there. Just remember, no news here, but you get nooze here every day. If you want news, go see Larry King.

5/10/1999

Yello joined the game

Yello made the first big update in a long while, and promises, with Arcadia's death, that "normal service" is resuming. Uh, whatever "normal" means, I can't find that word in my dictionary, must be a British thing...

And hey, I thought I was doing him a favor leaving those TV dinner tins, there must be five bucks worth of aluminum there. Sorry about that stain on the carpet, though, but there are surely enough empty beer cans to cover its cleaning.

5/12/1999

Beach house and Spew can't escape ticket's grenade

With Spew and Tikki God's Quake Beach House on life support, web sites are waiting in line for their chance at the coveted *ticket to nowhere*. Desiato and Tikki are both stubbornly refusing to give up the ticket.

So, for the first time ever, *two* tickets are being bestowed at the same time!

That's right, folks, Desiato and record ticket holder Tikki each receive a round trip, no expense paid *Ticket to Absolutely Nowhere!* They are both boarding the luxury stroggship *Real Life* for their fantastic cruise to nowhere. Enjoy your vacations, boys!

It's likely finals week at the Dopey Smurf's House o' Bitchin'; newbie webmaster Smurf (a physics major who has explained the Quake rail gun's workings to all of us in terms everyone but Blue can understand) is trying for his first chance for the fabulous trip to nowhere. It's uphill all the way; neither Tikki or Desiato have updated since before Smurf started his page.

Would *you* like the no expense paid ticket? Let me know about your page, and let it rot!

5/19/1999

Ticket tries to escape Smurf's shotgun

I got a note from that blue fellow last night. No, not Looneyboi's partner, the note was from Mr. Smurf. "Hey, I ain't nowhere!" No sir, Mr. Smurf, you're not. At least not this round. Some of the fellows you're up against are *professionals*. These are major league "ticket to nowhere" players; one of this round's winners holds the *world's record*, and is almost as good as that cheater BitchX at not updating, without even cheating.

The other winner, a dead rock star in the Restaurant at

the End of the Universe, should give you hope. He went for literally *months* trying in vain to not update, without success. Week after week he would produce not one, but *three* Real Audio shows.

Then, after nearly a year of trying, he finally got his first ticket, only a few months ago. This is his second.

Since present ticket holders are ineligible, that means the two best non-updaters are out for this round. You would think it would be a piece of cake, like going for a home run record with both McGwire and Sosa laying off with broken legs, but since the two best are out this round, nearly everybody is trying for it; the sheer numbers alone make it hard.

On the subject of professional ticket guys, the last winner, Planet Ho Slap, still hasn't updated. Dr. Kevorkian is looking in to unplugging the respirator and administering "medication". The baby in the Pic of the "week" is still proudly showing off its middle finger.
5/20/1999

Mail frags fragfest

I love getting mail. I hate getting these:

"could u please please send me the full verson of quake 2 or send me a site where i can download it from please i will do anything"

First, Quake 2 is nearly half a gigabyte, not counting the music. Second, don't you think Id should make a few bucks off this great game? Third, forty or fifty bucks isn't much to ask from someone who would "do anything"; mowing two or three lawns ought to net enough for a copy.

The next time I get one of these I'm publishing the sender's name, and not just the note and ISP's installation floppy.

Sorry if I seem a bit irritable; I'm trying to quit smoking again. Gotta pay for the hardware to run q3a somehow!
5/22/1999

112

BitchX joined the game

BitchX is Apparently begging for a chance for forgiveness for cheating, and wants to get back in the "Ticket to Nowhere" contest. This is apparent from the fact that not only has Martin Van Buren burned in hell *two separate times* since the two present ticket holders have updated, there was not only one, but *two* updates to the Bitch's page yesterday! Normally, the Bitch only updates during a blue moon, or when the hit counter (now over half a million) stops turning.

The first update was a rumor that Todd Boy was getting canned from Ion. The second was a retraction of the rumor. My guess is we'll have to watch Flamey's page for the truth.

Flamethrower, having used up the grace points he earned last month, is back in the contest. So is Smurf, Nacho, Spite (whose PC died an agonizing death)... Hell, just about everybody but Planet Quake, GA-Source (Who Nacho is reportedly going to write a column for it called GA-RPG), and Blue!

BitchX's rumor of Porter's canning (not caning, as he does not live in Singapore, although some would like him caned) is not the only false rumor about Turdd Partly. The rumor that he mistakenly shot and wounded John Lennon's favorite band, Harry Nilsson, was also false. Actually, it was John Lennon who was shot and killed by a wanker who was not in any way connected with FPSs or any other games. In fact, the closest thing to an FPS at the time of Lennon's death was Ms. Pac Man.

If you want to enter the *Ticket to Nowhere* contest, you have a LOT of competition! Drop me a line and let me know where your page is.

No animals were harmed during the creation of this contest (except for lunch).
5/26/1999

Smurf should have used a smaller gun

Dopey Smurf's House O' Bitchin', apparently inconsolable over the fact that the (ex?) cheater BitchX is now eligible for the *Ticket To Nowhere,* has dropped out of the contest by updating.

Better luck next time, Dopey!

At my urging, he's also contributing to Q3A Central.

I felt a little bad about not being able to help Q3A Central out with a column, but I have a hard enough time coming up with content for the Fragfest. The only way I could do the column at the late Arcadia (R.I.P.) was that I could write about stuff that wasn't Quake (Yeah, you're thinking, "but why would you want to").

If you've been to Smurf's, I think you'll agree he's going to do a good job.

Also if you've been to Smurf's, you know that he wants some hiphoppers to do the music for Q3A. Didn't we have that problem with Screamer 2? I always put the Screamer 1 CD in when I played Screamer 2. My vote is for *Metallica* to do the music for Q3A, as 90% of their music fits Quake, anyway. Plus, they *ROCK!!*

To paraphrase Led Zepplin's *Boogie With Stu,* "I don't want no tooty-fruity lonely hip-pop, come on baby lets rock rock rock!"

5/27/1999

E3 frags Nacho

Happy to at least beat Smurf in the ticket contest, but knowing he doesn't stand a chance against BitchX, Nacho updated last night with, uh, unusual E3 news, as well as the usual Nacho Insanity.

Oh, don't miss his new sponsor, "Star Wars" brand Viagra.

5/27/1999

BitchX tripped on his own grenade

Martin Van Buren burned in hell Thursday over at Murray's (Blue's antilinkus site of the month, official game site for the Anarchist party, and official game site of the U.S. Postal service).

Apparently still feeling the effects of last month's blue moon, BitchX actually updated two months in a row. Too bad what he/she/it posted wasn't entirely accurate. Kind of like my news about the joystick (boy, do *I* feel stupid).

Since the Bitch (why does Levellord think she's funny, anyway? Is it the drugs?) has updated, it's time for – you guessed it – another *Ticket To Nowhere* contest. Already.

Planet Wank is ineligible this time, since the ticket holding Wanker still hasn't updated. The Bitch has been permanently disqualified for cheating, of course. Also, as you know, retired corpses like crash are also ineligible (although crash now has duties at another game site; I'll have to dig out that url so he's eligible again).

Even though Flamethrower hasn't updated since the "What the frag am I supposed to type here" post, he lapped everyone so many times during the last contest he's resting comfortably at the finish line, safe from the ticket for at least this contest.

So far, there aren't many contestants this time around, and in fact it may turn out that nobody actually acquires the coveted ticket. Record holding ticket winner Tikki is late, as usual, but will probably update soon enough to avoid winning. Nacho was only a little late, posting late Monday night. I expect he'll post again this weekend. Yello, having been run over several times by the British Telecom Armored Truck, has been updating sporadically, but since his posts have been at least weekly, he's not really in the running. Desiato (Spew) hasn't updated since the week before last, but I expect he'll update this weekend, also blowing his chances for the ticket. He still has the Fragfest's goneplex URL listed (404, what an interesting Fragfest page) and owes Nacho a link.

This leaves – your page? Do I even know you're there? You can't win if I don't know about your page. Face it, with half a million Quake pages and God knows how many game sites there are, chances are I don't know you're there. Drop your url my way, then don't update. You could win the no expense paid ticket to *absolutely nowhere!*

Void where prohibited. Taxes, beer, gasoline, medication, legal fees, bail, and all other expenses are the responsibility of the winner. Kid sites, pr0n sites, and kid pr0n sites are ineligible. Sites that suck (like those in the PC Magazine top 100) are also ineligible. Trenchcoat mafia sites need not apply. Cosa Nostra Mafia sites can do anything they damned well please or your kneecaps are history. Keep away from children and stupid adults.

5/31/1999

Yello swallowed Granny's rocket

...er, rocker.

Yello, Tikki, and Desiato have been either MIA or AWOL for a while. I dropped by the Beach House looking for Tikki, and there was a sign on the door, "gone shopping for ordinance" or something like that, so I trekked over to Yello Spires looking for him.

I called Desiato first, thinking he might be there, but was rebuffed by his bodyguard, who was really pissed off that Desiato's body was missing.

As I approached the old castle, there was a strange green glow coming from the windows. "Hmm", I thought, "usually it's a blue GPF before things crash." There was an insane cackling coming from within.

Nobody answered my knock, but it was unlocked, so I gingerly cracked he door open. "Anybody home?"

There was Yello, suspended about a foot below the ceiling "HELP!" he yelled. "No, wait! Save yourself!

"AAAAAAAAAGGGGG!"

"Aha!" an old voice creaked. "Where's that bong?"

I tried to tell her that Bong was all the way in Lithuania.

"No, you retarded moron," she replied redundantly. "I mean..."

I felt my feet leaving the ground and fired off a few

rounds, which zoomed around crazily as if they had minds of their own. I was able to reverse-rocket jump my way out of there, wishing I had remembered to bring a grapple.

Yello's on his own this time, folks; the grannies are way beyond Quake, and being the only person outside Yugoslavia that hasn't seen the new Star Wars movie I'm out of my league over there. I don't know what kind of force they've cooked up, but it's stronger than a quad rune.

I hope Yello's okay. I don't have a clue how he's going to get out of this one!
6/1/1999

Green and orange with purple polka dot h4x0rz swallow U.S. government page's grenade

ZD reports that in retaliation of the FBI's busting a bunch of teenage h4x0rz and taking their parents' computers (If the FBI took my PC my qidz would be grounded until they were 40), more government web sites have been cracked, including the Dept. of the Interior. Or crack smoked, or something like that.

Also, the h4x0rz are warring among themselves; Global Hell (gH) and M4st4rz 0f D0wnl04ding (MOD) are calling each other silly names. The 10z3rz!

A Microsoft employee also had his computer equipment confiscated by the FBI and fired by Microsoft. The employee was fired, not the computer (although lots of us would like to fire windoze); the employee was accused of hacking government computers. Hell, considering the Justice Dept's lawsuit, I'm surprised Bill didn't give him a raise; probably would have if he hadn't got caught.

White House press secretary Joe Lockhart said, "I think it's less fun when the authorities catch up with them and these people are prosecuted." Well, perhaps less fun for the government, but maybe there will be fewer ttypos on the Fragfest (I'm blaming all typoos and misspelings on h4x0rz).

Speaking of hackers and crackers, here's where you can

117

find out if your coworker (someone who orks cows) is a hacker.

Ticket tries to escape mail's grenade

I would have thought folks would be tired of the *Ticket to Nowhere* contest by now, but judging from my mail everybody wants one. There seems to be a little bit of misunderstanding about the rules, however. "Ticket ru13z?" Hmm...

First, present ticket holders are ineligible. That means this round neither Tikki or Desiato can win, since it was a two way tie last time.

Second and most importantly, dead pages are ineligible. That means that though GA-Source is eligible (right, like crash would let GA-Source rot), crash's spq2 page isn't. In order for a page to win, it has to have been updated at least once since the previous round.

Winners receive, as usual, a two way no expense paid ticket to *absolutely nowhere*. Taxes, gasoline, food, and drugs (prescription or otherwise) are the responsibility of the winner. All other expenses are also the responsibility of the winner (unless some loser wants to give 'em a few bucks). Void where (duh!) prohibited. The Fragfest and all assignees are not responsible for any damages or costs. Other irresponsible persons may also not be responsible. Not a step. Contents under pressure. Caution – filling is hot. Close cover before striking (card carrying Union members can ignore that last rule). Inhalation of vapors may cause severe brain damage, if applicable. Not inhaling can also cause brain damage, as oxygen is necessary for continuation of respiration. Bill Clinton did not inhale. Keep away from children and stupid adults. Pants are optional. Anyone caught cheating may be banned from future contests. Page must cover Id, Quake, or Quake's ancestors in some way, shape, or form (e.g., Blue's is eligible, but Pokemon world isn't. Dallas Observer and New York Times may be eligible under certain conditions). You have the right to remain silent. Anything you say can and will be used against you in a court of law. No smoking in most public buildings in the U.S. You are not required to wear a helmet in the state of Illinois. Rules are subject to change without notice.

Good luck!

6/3/1999

Tikki tripped on his own grenade

I finally saw Tikki, who was heading back to the beach house from ammo shopping after his adventures in "real life". I had been starting to wonder if the FBI had taken his computer.

I almost didn't recognize him at first. He looked like he was dressed for a Steppin Fetchit lookalike contest, in rags and blackface.

"Wow, man, wtf happened to you?" I asked.

"Ordinance blew up prematurely. Took out my hard drive, too." Heh, that's what you get for smoking while carrying explosives. He should write another editorial for Planet Quake so folks would send him more free napalm in the mail.

He started laughing hysterically when I asked if his hard drive had been backed up. I didn't ask, but I expect he may have an update soon, perhaps this millennium. As he's not eligible for a ticket this round, there's no reason for him not to.

6/4/1999

Fragfest tries to escape Blue H4x0r's rocket

...and apparently succeeded (but the m4st3rz of dumb-azz are still replacing Fragfst text with typpos).

Blue mentioned the *Ticket to Nowhere* Friday, and didn't even double my traffic. It was actually *down* yesterday (but so was my counter for part of the day). Sheesh, anybody else posts "woohoo! (or boohoo?) Blue mentioned us and the hits are rolling in!" He mentioned Murray last month and Murray called him everything but a white boy (which inspired Blue to

119

p1mp him again, saying something like "If I'd only known how easy it was to make Murray mad..."

Murray was strangely silent about Blue's p1mpage of his electric chair contest.

Dopey Smurf informs me he is instituting the *I broke Dopey's server* award, and the first recipient is undoubtedly Blue's News. Hey, I want one of those! So do me a favor, each and all 200 of you go over to either Smurf's or Q3A Central and hit the "reload" button 200 times apiece so I can get Dopey's award.

6/6/1999

Beach House ate Tikki's Rocket

The longest string of trailers I ever saw behind a semi-tractor pulled up and honked as I was crossing the street. There sat Tikki behind the wheel.

"Whoa, dude, what's in all the trailers?" I asked him.

"Explosives, what else?" he said, as he lit up his strange smelling cigar. "Hop in, I'll give ya a ride."

"Watcha gonna do with all that ordinance, man?" I asked as he wheeled out.

"Fireworks display at the Beach House on the fourth of July. Think I got enough?"

"*Enough??* Are you *crazy?*"

"Yeah, you're right, I'd better get a few more loads. Where you headin'?" he asked as he flipped his ash (and a big orange ember) out the window.

"Uh, right here's good. See ya."

That's one fourth of July display I'm not going to miss!

6/16/1999

Yello joined the game

Yello has apparently been extricated from the ceiling at Yello Spires by promising his granny half of a "Ticket to Nowhere" if she would let him down. He posted his first update in a month yesterday. Granny Yello is presumably in Nowhere enjoying Yello's half of the ticket.

Flamethrower is still missing in action. My guess is he's in a pub or a beach somewhere in southern Nowhere. Probably with Yello's granny.

6/17/1999

Desiato joined the game

Word from Desiato is Spew has a new RA show posted. His site's not exactly glued back together all the way yet, but give him a break – he's been dead for quite a while now.

More news of Desiato's death can be found in the *Hitchiker's Guide to the Galaxy*, where a lot of Quake handles come from. Desiato spends time in the restaurant there.

6/22/1999

Mad Scientist and Sued tries to escape ticket's super shotgun

Talk about *begging* for a Ticket to Nowhere! Dopey Smurf's House O' Bitchin' is only two months old and not even old enough to crawl or hold a baby bottle yet, and is dying from neglect. It's gone nearly half its short life without an update. Smurf has been putting all his efforts into Q3A Central and another gaming domain I'm not sure is open yet. He also seems to be suffering from shortage of the muse, as his Camping Guide is also long overdue.

Meanwhile, Old Man Murray, battle weary from the legal wars (w4r3s?) hasn't updated in several days. Murray is also in the running for the ticket.

As usual, Blue's News, Planet Quake, and sCary are all nearly tied for last place, updating several times a day each.

This round has a bonus prize. In addition to the fabulous *Ticket to Nowhere*, the winner also receives a box of invisible voracious mutant lab rats. Not knowing where to get voracious mutant invisible lab rats, I asked Dopey Smurf. Smurf has a double major in both physics and some kind of experimental drug thing, and works in a medical research facility. What is the best way to mutate lab rats to become both voracious and invisible?

Professor Smurf explains, "Ethidium bromide is extremely caustic, and causes point mutations on contact. Radiation ain't bad, but it's so difficult to find a decent ray gun these days.

"My favourite is ethidium bromide water balloons dipped in Plutonium :)

"But really, to make lab rats that are not only invisible, but also voracious, the three treatments need to be combined. I have been working on exactly such a treatment. However, we have also been having a lot of trouble with making the rats voracious, the invisible part was easy.

"Finally, I discovered that if the rats underwent a so called 'Mrkobrada Anterior Occipital Surgery', the voraciousness factor increases three hundred fold! It's a fairly simple procedure where a LASER gun is attached to the rat's head, and connected directly to the brain. In effect they shoot everything they see."

Thanks to the Smurf for the info; the mutant invisible lab rats are growing in the Fragfest's labs now. At least I think they are, I can't see them; They're invisible. The lucky winner will not only receive the coveted *Ticket to Nowhere*, but the invisible mutant lab rats as well. The rats are fun for the entire family, especially Kenny and the baby. The ticket is automatic, the rats will be emailed.

Also a thanks to Smurf for letting the Fragfest use the electrical generation equipment from his rail gun or we wouldn't have enough power for the lasers.

Update: Murray's has been updated with something about Eric getting arrested; it has something to do with prostitution and involves John Romero. This means that Dopey

Smurf's House O' Bitchin is the proud owner of a brand spanking new *Ticket to Nowhere*. He will receive his rats by email. Congratulations, Smurfey! Enjoy your vacation!
6/23/1999

Golf Course tries to escape Dopey's BFD

I got a postcard from Nowhere last night. I thought it might be the long missing Flamethrower, who has been vacationing in Nowhere since the last contest. Nope, it was from Smurf, who only got his ticket a few days ago. Smurf says,

"Hehehe, who knew Nowhere is so nice?

"I just finished another round of golf yesterday, in the Middle of Nowhere. I also promised Spite I'd finish the blasted Camping guide yesterday, so I was ridden with guilt as I shot my triple bogeys. Nevertheless, with a steady supply of beer, it was still enjoyable, and now I am glad I sacrificed myself, not updating all those long weeks, it really is worth it.

"Maybe I'll take some nice pictures...

"In any case, thanx for the ticket... :)

"So I came by Q3A Central, saw there's a new poll up, I wrote this one. Give Andrew a nick name. I figured he needs a fearsome nickname, being a wimpy Aussie, something as bad as 'Steve'.... So in any case, I wrote the poll as a joke, I didn't figure Spite would put it up, which leads me to conclude that Spite doesn't really know what 'fellatio' or 'cunnilingus' really mean. Someone should tell him?

"And just for the hell of it, that's what I voted for.... We'll call Andrew 'FC' for short... The possibilities are endless :)

"In any case, it looks like there won't be any golf in Nowhere tonight, it's raining. I'll go and get drunk and play bingo. Hmmmm.... Bingo....Old women....(*The Smurf starts to salivate uncontrollably*)... (*The room quickly fills up to ankle height in drool*)... (*Soon it's up to his waist*)... Holy salivary glands Batman! They're out of control!...(*The saliva level reaches the Smurf's neck. He quickly grabs the nearest scuba equipment, property of Nowhere Resorts*) Blub, blub... Fu..

Blub.... I just can't stop drooling! Damn that Bingo, and those sexy old women!...Hmmmmmmm... Blub...Old women... Blub...Shit there I go again!..Blub...Blub...Somebody save that puppy!...Too late, it's drowning! Oh shit! That's sick....Blub blub...Must...rip...out...glands...(*SPLOOOOOOSH. The Smurf is left without his salivary glands*). Phew, that was close. I almost wiped out Nowhere off the face of this Earth.... My mouth is kinda dry. Oh look! There's the bar! Later"

Marko Mrkobrada
King Edward Hospital
Experimental Therapeutics Division
Laboratory 10-624

Spite has been waiting for Smurf's "Camping Guide" for Q3A Central for a while; so long he's about ready to take down the camping poll (isn't a camping poll what holds up the tent?). So, true to my word, I'm stealing his camping poll before Smurf gets back from Nowhere with the camping guide. I've changed a couple of questions to keep Q3A Central readers from getting too bored with it.
6/25/1999

Fragfest frags ticket
Did ya miss me? I drove to nowhere to put enough pieces of computer back together enough to get on the internet.

I haven't got the modem to work on the new PC, let alone see if that TNT is any faster than the one built in. I imagine my inbox is stuffed, but I can't get to it yet.
7/1 & 7/2 no update. 7/3/1999

H4x0rz frags H4x0rz
I warned you about the weekend hacker convention, DEF CON, where *Cult of the Dead Cow* were releasing their "Back Orifice 2000" crack tool.

>

`Transfer interrupted!`
was hacked by a group called the ADM Crew.
7/12/1999

GL Setup tried to avoid download's shotgun

There is a new GL Setup program out <u>here</u>. They have asked that the new version not be mirrored, so that link will take you to their site. The older version is still on the GetQuake page.

GL Setup, a 33 meg download, makes sure you have the latest drivers so Q3A runs correctly. Before I ran GL Setup on my machine, the levels looked like the inside of Yello Spires when his granny had Yello trapped on the ceiling with that Jedi mind shit.

If you have run an earlier version and Q3t is horribly beautiful, you probably don't have to run it. At least as long as it doesn't look like granny's been there.
7/30/1999

List can't escape Drive's rocket

Sgt. Hulka's hard drive's autopsy showed no traces of alcohol. What caused the crash was that it shouldn't have swiveled its head around to look at those two disks. Let that be a lesson to you men! Maybe some of you women, too.

The poor old drive didn't CD tree, and the drive and its occupants all perished.

Hulka's mailing lists were among the dead. So if you were on (or want to be on) one of the Sarge's lists, you need to drop by there and help his list respawn.

Funerals for the hard drive and mailing lists is Saturday. In lieu of flowers, please send donations to the *Frag the Strogg Foundation* (heh, or just send it to me).
8/2/1999

Clan Undergrounds frags l33t

UND^ynohtnA from Clan Underground sent word of their list of l33t jumps. What's so l33t about them?

UND^ynohtnA writes, "Be warned! These jumps are only for those extremely well versed in the arts of strafe/circle/double/rocket/bfg jumping... (Clan Underground accepts no liability, etc etc.)." Which leaves me out. Any l33t d00dz out there wanna try these out?

He also wonders where Yello has been. Me too; I haven't heard from Yello in quite a while, and his page is 404ed. Guess I'll have to round up a troop of l33t rocket jumpers to go looking for him............................

8/3/1999

Yello melted

I've been getting mail from folks wondering where the hell Yello is. After getting a note from fellow Arcadian Morgan, I decided to drop by Yello Spires to see what was going on. Since that Quake II racing game (that uses the Quake 3 engine and probably won't be finished until Quake V is in the bargain bin) isn't yet available, I had to walk.

This isn't easy, as England is about six thousand miles from here. If you're not from the states, the distance from America to Britain is even longer, about 10,000 kilometers. And that's the shortcut; you have to swim across a five thousand mile saltwater pond. Beats the hell out of going through that cold assed Russia (or what we used to call Russia) though.

I set off early, and it was past noon when I finally got there.

Yello Spires was *gone!* The whole thing, even the dirt and plants. Curse Paramont for using the Quake engine for those Star Trek games; I think the Borg got him.

After Morgan's first note, he sent word that he had contact with Yello and that Yello was supposed to mail him and probably me with info about wtf was going on. That's the last I've heard.

If the Borg got his granny too, I pity them. You should see what she did to those poor Strogg!

8/4/1999

Pulse frags ticket

As promised, Sgt. Hulka, who has never had a ticket to nowhere (poor guy!) gave away that Quake Con ticket, to Pulse from QuakeFiles, who, judging by the winning entry posted at Hulka's, needs a new computer more than a ticket to a lan party. A ticket to Quake Con beats the hell out of a ticket to nowhere any day!

If you're wondering why the Sarge gets so much p1mpage here and you don't, well, he mails in nooze. So if you want your page p1mped, send some email! I don't care if you're Blue or Joe Momma (link is to last year's interview with Joe). If it's nooze, I'll post it.

8/6/1999

Old Folks frag Tea

Ah, yes, the good old *Planet Crap Retirement Home.* So many Brits were there the other day they decided to hold a tea party.

Grandpa Nacho and his grandson Neil were there. Nacho, who wrote to remind me "I like, updated and stuff. Neil and I are both pissed the site was updated like 2 days before the T-Buffer thing" and impressed all with his scholarly words of wisdom.

Andy, who was supposed to supply the tea, never showed up.

8/9/1999

Yello joined the game

Maybe it *is* a communicator. Yello mailed me from "something really square where the women are *really* ugly" and says his granny dropped by the cubular domain he was stuck in demanding her water pipes back. Apparently none of the Borg survived, and Yello is on his way back.

"I think I let a few people down quite badly (I feel like dirt Jay) and ignored all of you........... SORRY..... I hope to make a return within the next month.

"I intend to reopen Arcadia........give it a respray and

127

relocate over there............Yello will only be updated once a week but I'll be able to supply Quality over quantity.....

"I don't know what happened over at Marlin but I really do owe those folk a lot........if not for them then Yello would never have erupted into our 'Collective Consciousness'.........

"Congratulations To Guff and crash who seem to have gone on to bigger and better things...hurrah guys....."
8/13/1999

Ticket disconnected

Everybody's in the running for the ticket. Yello has been accounted for, and will be back under the katylistic label, since Marlin melted.

Quake Central (The "Daiktana of Web Pages") has yet to open its doors (although I gave you all a key to the side window earlier), making them the first site to be eligible for a ticket *before* opening.

Smurf's (AKA "Kenny's") is on life support waiting for the voracious mutant lab rats (damned things ate the spel ckehher) that Rudolph keeps eating before they're fully grown.

Tikki's place washed away in the explosion on the bridge, but some of the beach has resurfaced, and I saw Tikki carrying sticks and dynamite that way.

But the site that should get the ticket is Planet Quake. They have a big, expensive, high-traffic site with a ton of people working on it, some of whom are being *paid* to do it – and yesterday morning there was only *one* news post, and *one* from Saturday. Considering so many of the smaller to medium sites are one man or one woman operations that update at least weekly without fail, PQ should get the ticket for being so lax over the weekend.

The only thing is, Flamethrower still has the ticket, and he's nowhere to be found. Or in nowhere to be not

found. Even Tikki, who's known Flamey for a whole lot longer than I have, asked if I'd heard from him.

So, sorry folks; no more ticket 'til Flamethrower brings it back. Lowtax, you can start your daily multiple posts again, 'cause the ticket is missing and you can't have it yet.
8/16/1999

Fragfest did a back flip into the lava

The date on yesterday's post is only half accurate. I wrote it yesterday, but I was stuck real close to nowhere unable to post it. So there actually *was* a post yesterday, but there isn't one today. Send some nooze!
8/17/1999

God frags Crap Planet

Last weekend and a little before, all the good little gamers, publishers, designers, webmasters, and just about everybody except the trolls went to church. Specifically, the "Planet Crap Church of Holy BS". Uncle Jeetsus and his disciples were there.

The topic had nothing to do with gaming. It was about the new Kansas law that mandated evolution teaching not be mandated. The fact that it was not gaming related was not the only thing different; never have I seen the place so *civil*. Not only did the trolls go back to sCary hell, but there was little name calling or animosity, and none until over 350 musings had been posted.

The last I saw, the count was 392 posts (Wednesday night). Thursday night, Planet Crap was down. I checked again at work, and it was still down. Either there were so many posts it broke the board, or God was having a little fun with the atheists and agnostics, who would have not gotten the joke, anyway. Since you can't get there right now (which is why there's no link, although by the time you read this it may be back up) here's a nutshell version. This is, of course, not entirely accurate.

"God exists."

"No he doesn't."

"What about the Hindus?"

"God is a rock He big banged together."

"1+1=5"

"describe 'red'."

"Id is God."

"God is a woman."

"Asimov."

"God doesn't exist."

"God exists but you don't."

"Forever is a REALLY long time."

"If you divide an apple between no people you have an infinite number of apples?" (I had to have that one explained to me via email by someone who was thinking more clearly and has a lot funner job than me, and I appreciated the heads up)

"Did you hear the one about God and Ireland?"

"I'm agnostic and you're not going to change my mind!"

"I think, therefore I am. I am, therefore (I think)"

"Prove it."

"You prove it."

"NEW TOPIC!"

"Where's Andy?"

"Are we there yet?"

"Math is too hard."

"So is a rock."

"God is a rock."

"ROCK, dewd!"

Like I said, that's the *Reader's Digest* version. Either God or Evolution caused Planet Crap to go offline sometime Thursday night.

8/20/1999

PC Cratered

After being so outspoken about the matter for the last two years, it was bound to happen – my PC was hacked for real.

Last night I ran my oldest daughter Leila off the computer, and it was acting strangely. When I went to restart it, windows gave a message "There is still 1 user connected to your computer. Are you sure you want to disconnect?"

I guess I should give credit to Microsoft for at least that.

When the machine restarted, there was no boot drive. An emergency floppy revealed that all the files and subdirectories in my root directory had been moved to a directory named ViruX, which I assume is the hacker's handle. Once I get this thing back on-line I'll get with Symantic to be sure it isn't a virus masquerading as a hacker.

Luckily I know my way around DOS. Unluckily DOS doesn't support long file names, so I was forced to reload windows instead of just moving the files back.

I've taken the GetQuake page off-line until I can ensure the downloads are clean. I will not email anyone any attachments. If you get an email from me with an attachment, DO NOT OPEN IT. Please send the attachment back so I can forward it to the proper people.

Sorry for the trouble, folks. I'll get the GetQuake page back up as soon as I can.

8/21/1999

Script kiddies frag eggs

Thanks for the kind notes of sympathy I got from you folks yesterday. As Morgan pointed out, it could have been a lot worse.

I felt like someone whose house had been egged, just glad the vandals hadn't burned it down. By the time I posted yesterday morning, all the egg had been cleaned off (except the egg on my face).

Actually, I felt like the guy whose garage collapsed from shoddy workmanship after he cleaned the egg off his front porch, and the contractor's lawyers, Johnny Cochran, F. Lee Baily, and Perry Mason had written a clause in the contract that says "not responsible for damage caused by shoddy workmanship". Maybe the clause isn't legal, but you still won't win a lawsuit.

After I cleaned up the mess (a couple of hours) and updated, I went to work trying to get the Quake machine on line. It took most of the day, and still isn't on line!

The modem that works just fine in the win95 machine I'm typing on right now just won't configure in win98. It finds a "33.6 faxmodem," but when I try to tell it what driver to use (the one on the cd that came with the modem that win95 has no trouble with) win98 says isn't the right driver! I got it to where it would log on to my ISP, but neither Netscape nor IE would work, let alone Quake. Zoom's site doesn't have any new drivers for it.

My wife is working this weekend, and I was looking forward to some online Quake on the new machine.

So, if you script kiddies have to crack somebody's machine, leave me alone. That mean old rich guy down the street is a much better target!

And, if you think this is going to stop me from speaking out about cybervandalism, you don't know me very well. If I find out who you are and where you live, expect the FBI to take your parent's PC away. Even (maybe especially) if you live in Columbia or Australia; my government doesn't take kindly to crimes against its citizens.

8/22/1999

MPs frags AWOLs

Planet Crap and Quake Central are still AWOL. The Military Police are out searching.

Flamethrower is reportedly out looking for Carl Sagan. No word as to when he will return.

Illinois Governor George "Oneterm" Ryan is rumored to have said that if Lowtax shows up in Illinois he'll raise him again.

Reports are that numerous novelists have been hacked. Not their computers, but their novels. The hacker is said to be

132

Reader's Digest.

Major Futcup has been promoted to General.

And, reports are that AOL is the "short" version of aWol. America Offline had no comment, saying they were "busy".

8/24/1999

Ryan was indeed a one term governor, and went to prison for bribery after he was voted out of office.

Dec 5, 2014

Brain melted

I spent the weekend on a search-and-rescue mission in Nowhere (well, Marissa, Illinois, about as close to nowhere as you can get) looking for the long absent Flamethrower, but all I saw there were in-laws.

Those search and rescue missions can be treacherous!

8/30/1999

H4x0r can't escape Army's BFG

Teenaged hacker mindphasr (AKA Chad Davis), founder of the h4x0r club Global Hell was arrested Monday for hacking pentagon computers. He's allegedly the guy that defaced the US Army's page.

That ought to teach the little pest! One down, a zillion to go.

Here's a real audio report from ZD.

Also, I found out why I was targeted. Not only have I spoken out against the vandals, but have made fun of them. They didn't seem to mind my blaming typos on them, but the nooze item from July 12 pissed them off.

I didn't notice until today that the HTML was changed in that item for real. They cleverly added a line and the words "transfer interrupted" and deleted a large chunk of text.

The item was about a "h4x0r war" where two groups were calling each other names and one hacked the other's web page. I strongly suspect it was someone from on of these two groups, most likely the one that was hacked, as their name is gone from the item both on the server and my PC. Pretty sloppy, fellows.

You can ruin my PC but you can't hurt me. However, when I find you, I'll sic Janet Reno and her gun toting arsonists on you. Ph33r!

Now if I could only find some *fun* nooze...

9/1/1999

Ticket to Nowhere Died

Looking through the archives, the last several people to win a ticket to nowhere liked Nowhere so much they never returned. Among those missing are Planet Wank (MIA), Flamethrower (MIA), BitchX (MIA), Tikki, whose Beach house was swept into the sea in a giant explosion, Spew, who returned briefly from Nowhere (also from a coffin) and is now MIA again, and Smurf, who also won a box of invisible voracious mutant lab rats that he hasn't received yet since Rudolf keeps eating them.

Smurf also returned briefly, long enough to take Q3A Central to nowhere with him. Q3A Central (AKA Quake Central) is the only page ever to win the ticket *before* it went public.

It's no wonder everybody wants one. Smurf wrote from Nowhere, "Hehehe, who knew Nowhere is so nice? I just finished another round of golf yesterday... with a steady supply of beer... Oh look! There's the bar! Later"

So in order to preserve the safety of the members of the Quake community, the Ticket to Nowhere must die before Quake itself, along with everybody else, winds up in Nowhere basking in the sun fragging No One.

This raises a few questions. First, what do I do with the tickets? (Don't tempt me!)

Second, when the ticket is dead, the Fragfest will need a new contest. But what?

Third, who's on third?

Fourth, how do we lure the MIAs back from Nowhere?

Since you guys are used to asking me questions instead

of the other way around, *this* is a contest – the "Contest contest". It has a *real* prize, the rare (most existing copies are pirated) Turing tester *Artificial Insanity*. You can't buy one; you can only get a legal copy from the Fragfest.

All you have to do to win is answer the above four questions. Best answers (IMO) win the prize. The contest is open for an undetermined amount of time; the fat lady sings when I say it's over. Answers will be judged on humor and originality. Anyone with 48 chromosomes who can send me an email can enter (meaning no Stroggs allowed). Enter as often as you like. No purchase necessary. Taxes (if any) are the responsibility of the winner. Void where (duh) prohibited.

Artificial Insanity will run on any computer capable of running DOS. More details about *Artificial Insanity* are available at the above link.

There *may* be a later version of *Artificial Insanity* that will incorporate computer speech and speech recognition (not guaranteed). If there is, the winner will receive a free upgrade to the later version when it is out.

May the best human win!
9/4/1999

Dopey Smurf joined the game

Back from his summer vacation in nowhere, Smurf, confusing me with John Bye says "I figured, hey, the beer is getting stale, and I haven't washed my underwear in three months, why not come back? (Plus that industrious Steve bastard revoked all tickets)." He's posted his "Contest" contest entry, and invited my recent uninvited guest into his Dopey Smurfdom. "Please, someone hack my computer! What, am I not good enough for little pieces of hacker dropping???"
9/6/1999

CPU frags PC

I'd tell you Dopey Smurf updated again, two days in a row after missing three full months, but I think that converter board came and I'll be way too busy.   9/8/1999

Nacho frags pr0n

Neil wrote a couple of weeks ago fearing Nacho Extreme would join the swelling ranks of MIAs. I wasn't worried; the Japanese cartoon chicks is just this month's smiley. Nacho does that when the muse escapes him.

Nacho wrote this morning, "I updated... It's offensive and ugly, but it'll do for a while."

And yes, it's a "kinda" update. Apparently he's been swamped by mail asking for Kilcreek pics (Smurf probably has writer's cramp now), so he's posted Kilcreek (big bare fake b00bs and all), Romero, Hefner, and a photographer, none of whom is wearing a stitch of clothes. And one figure has something in his mouth.

Put that Vaseline down, boy, this is a bit more "artsy" than the playboy thing.

And, when the muse harvest comes in (with a higher price for a smaller quantity as it does every year), Nacho's dry spell should end. Meanwhile, if you live in Arizona and have a stash of some good muse, Nacho would like to hear from you!
9/15/1999

Rats swallowed Smurf's rocket

The Dopey Smurfer has been updating fairly regularly. Earlier this week he lambasted me for my slowness in getting his invisible mutant voracious lab rats to him, and I have to apologize. Rudolf the parasite seems to like lab rats even more than he likes shambler. Plus, the invisibility has been a slight problem, but the new equipment is (crossed fingers...) working, for now. It shouldn't be too long now, Dopey, as long as that damned parasite doesn't get loose again; they're about half grown.

The rats will come with a stern warning *not* to let them loose on your web page, as they have been eating h4x0r droppings and have acquired a taste for internetics. Some say similar creatures were responsible for Slipgate Central's demise, although Joost maintains that it was assimilated by

Planet Borg.

I may give him a copy of *Artificial Insanity* just to make up for making him wait so long, especially since Neil (the only other entry so far) is beating him in the Contest contest.
9/16/1999

You can't escape Hulka's BFG

Sgt. Hulka will have his shoutcaster "pumping out some massive metal tunes", he'll be abusing privates in a Quake server, plus have contests, prizes, and all the laughs you've come to expect from the Sarge.

It all starts at 9:00 central (7:00 on the west coast, 10 on the east, about 3:00 tomorrow morning in Europe) tonight.

Drop by the Bootcamp, or risk court martial.
9/17/1999

Typo virus frags Fragfest

Nope, those typos sprinkled through the Fragfest all week weren't hack attacks, they were caused by a virus.

Not a computer virus, a biological one. I've been sicker than an overdosed crackwhore all week and my brain isn't exactly all there. I cleaned up a bunch of them yesterday, but my lungs (and by extension, the brain they supply oxygen to) is still fragged.

Maybe one of the h4x0rz will drop by and *fix* a few typos for a change?
9/18/1999

Rats frag Smurf

Believe it or not, the invisible mutant lab rats are on their way to Smurf's Place. I sure hope he keeps them away from his page!
9/19/1999

Dopey Smurf trips on his own grenade

Against all advice, warnings, and cautions, that Dopey Smurf (who probably likes to drive around with McDonald's coffee between his legs) has not only put the box of rats on his page, he's positioned the release catch there. Whatever you do, *please* don't go to Dopey Smurf's House-O-Bitchin' and release the rats!!

9/19/1999

The "rat attack" was actually real. "Dopey Smurf", who was studying medicine and physics, had a job in a laboratory that used lab rats, and they often bit him and always scared the hell out of him.

He had told me that he was graduating and going to pre-med and thought it best to lose the site, so I came up with the invisible lab rats. He loved the idea.

In March 1998, the month before The Springfield Fragfest went online. "Slipgate Central" went offline. It was a search engine for Quake sites and it had everybody listed. On March 9th, its front page was replaced with a yellowish background with a Strogg holding a sign that read "Haste does not bring success". The title bar on the browser read "Down for maintenance". It never returned.

I had a lot of graphics editors and software tools that had come with hardware I'd bought, and it was easy to make an animated GIF of invisible rats eating his page. I posted an HTML file with an IMG tag that sized the GIF 100% of screen size and mailed him the url to access it.

The GIF was a screen shot of Dopey's page in the first frame, which sat there for a few seconds before the rats ate it.

The rats left behind Joost's "Haste does not bring success" page. Unfortunately, the GIFs it was constructed of are missing or I'd have a screen shot of the half-eaten page.

Oct 20, 2014

H4x0rz frags ZD

Following in Dopey Smurf's footsteps, Ziff Davis invited hackers this morning to crack in and break their stuff. They seem to want hacked more than Smurf; ZD is offering $1,000.00 cash to the l33t h4x0r who can pull it off. Lots better than the 56k "Modem from Hell" I donated for his contest. Go to the link listed (ZD's, not Smurfs... Ok, go to Smurf's, too, just be

138

sure not to release the rats) for more details.
9/21/1999

Planet Crap sank like a rock

At last look, Planet Crap was still offline, now going on two weeks. I'm not optimistic.

About a year ago (actually a few months less if I remember right) I ran across the gamer's dream page – a simple layout with gaming topics listed; no ads or other clutter. Each topic led to a page unlike all the other me-too message boards, with all responses listed straight down, no "million clicks" to get to each response as most boards have.

The topics were topics rabid gamers (like you and me) would want to discuss. The discussions were interesting, informative, often hilarious. What's more (and likely because of of the aforementioned discussions), the folks that posted were by and large names the rabid gamer (if no one else) would recognize.

That was part of the magic. You would see Joost, Flamey, crash, Hulka, Yello... folks like George Broussard (hope I spelled that right, George), Katherine Kang... Somehow the word about Planet Crap never got out, only being p1mped by guys like Desiato, me, Flamey, etc.

Earlier this year they redesigned it, adding a few nice flourishes like the ability to add links to one's post. The number of topics grew, the number of posts per topic grew.

Then it caught sCary's eye. That was the beginning of the end.

Suddenly everyone knew about PC. The number of posts grew humongous.

And sCary's trolls started trolling in. Since PC never edited, censored, kicked, or banned anybody, the trolls were a very large nuisance. People started threatening to leave. One or two did.

Then KAK had her chess contest (did anybody ever win?), and Planet Quake indelicately used the British word "shagable". The contest was discussed in PC, and of course the trolls were even more indelicate than Planet Quake, using the more military term for "shagable". And Ms. Kang was there. Those of us who posted regularly apologized profusely to her and then left.

Quite a few stayed gone for a while. I did. PC had been too addictive to stay away from for *too* long, though. When I came back, one of the two worst trolls was gone, and the other was nearly human, posting as intelligently and civilly as his small brain and genitals would allow.

PC was never the same again. It started breaking regularly, especially under the weight of 300+ and 400+ post topics. Then Andy quit, and there have been perhaps three updates in the last month and a half.

And it has been down for well over a week, its last topic about the forgettable AOL's CIO getting canned. Who cares?!

I hope they come back. I hope they have some decent topics; there could have been several since they were down, what with Naughty Naughton, the internet turning 30, Hotmail and other MS woes, slashdot selling out...

I miss 'em. Otoh, if you can run PHP from that shiny new host that has kept your site closed for two months, you should start a replacement for Planet Crap NOW.

We need it. I mean, *WarZone's* board? SCary? Get real!

9/23/1999

Dopers can't escape eBay's shotgun

eBay yanked the sale of a huge stash of Dutch reefer yesterday from their auction site, even though hemp is perfectly legal in Amsterdam.

Bids were over ten million dollars before bidding was canceled. A picture was shown of a very large pile of white packages and three people. The people were not reportedly for sale.

The two DEA agents who set up the deal had their faces blurred in the picture, possibly in an attempt to make you

think the pile had somehow magically gotten you stoned without actually smoking it. Heads from various government agencies were heard to remark, "Wow, man, far out!"
9/24/1999

Rabbit died

I got the new machine pretty much done over the weekend, with a new 13 gig drive, and put the Zoom 33.6 modem in it (the 56k is still up for grabs in the hacker contest).

Oddly, after formatting the new drive, loading windows, and just copying files from the other drive, Jazz Jackrabbit worked *without* reinstalling. Strange, since its initial installation had cluttered the hell out of the registry.

So Patty got to play over the net first, since I have to reinstall Quake.

Patty has always considered herself a top notch jackrabbit shooter, bragging a couple of weeks ago that she had beaten Cliffy B (unlikely, since he's one of the guys that worked on that game). After she played yesterday (first net play in weeks), she said, "Boy, did I *suck*".

So since average is about as good as I get in Quake, when I get in the arena you're gonna kick my ass! Watch for "Kenny"...
9/27/1999

UT frags Fragfest?

ynohtnA writes with a few interesting questions and observations: "Springfield Fragfest is dominating the level?" Nah, Blue's, PQ, and ten thousand other Quake sites are kicking my ass. I have Joe Moma beat, though.

"You gotta admit that since Q3Test appeared the Quaking community has, er, atrophied. Yello, PlanetCrap, FlameThrower, Spew, Bong, Tikki, even BitchX have gone."

Well, Yello has promised to come back from his adventures with the Borg (it's what he gets for overcooking that p1mpium III) although I'm starting to wonder. Planet Crap? Gee, I miss 'em. Will Hulka's forums be the new PC?

Flamey disappeared for quite a while this time last year, maybe he'll be back. Bong hinted that Q3A may bring him back. Tikki's busy with fresh-air sports, but don't be surprised to see him turn up on Nacho's page. As for Bitch-X, when *hasn't* "she" been gone?

"Will you start covering UT now that it is starting to get the respect it deserves?" Hmm, good question. What do you folks think? Should I? It *is* a Quake engine game. Let me know what you folks want from the Fragfest!

9/28/1999

mcgrew trips on his own grenade

It seems the Fragfest has been a great source of misinformation the last couple of days. I've been redfacedly answering lots of mail. Oops...

First, in Monday's "Tripod pages frag pennies", the amount I said Tripod pays is incorrect. A reader checked, and informs me the price is one buck per thousand.

Second and more important, Uh, *grimace* (duh) Unreal has its own engine.

Excuse me while I log on to a Quake server and type while everybody gibs me...

9/29/1999

Winners can't escape Insanity's BFJ

Neil and Smurf were the *only two entries* in the "contest" contest, so I decided to award the prize to *both* of them.

About his copy of *Artificial Insanity* Smurf wrote, "I honestly believe that you have reached the epitome of computer gaming!

"Okay, Okay, all joking aside, I thought it was hilarious. I opened the e-mail yesterday, just before going out. At first, I pressed the F1 key, and then it said something like 'Hello.' Then I typed to it, and half the stuff actually made sense! Hilarious shit! In any case, I now see that you were a programming force to be reckoned with in your young days :)..."

Neil has been busy as a beaver (busy as a h4x0r'z momma's beaver, which is *real* busy) and I don't think he's tried his copy yet, as he writes, "Call me a lamer if you must but I havent figured out base 64 encoding..."

At any rate, congratulations to the two winners of the contest contest! And speaking of a h4x0r'z momma, nobody has entered the "Hack Dopey" contest yet. I may add something to open it to non-h4x0rz.

10/2/1999

Plagiarist can't escape Copyright's BFG

As I was surfing through the Bootcamp last night, I noticed a new feature – cheat codes for about every game except Quake (get 'em here 'til Sarge posts some, I told him he could lift 'em from here if he wants).

I also saw a banner for a new dogpile named mamma.com, and did my usual search for the Springfield Fragfest. There were about fifty links, some not pointing here.

One of the links was to "Omega Man's Quake 2 page". Thinking somebody had thrown me a link, I decided to check it out to see if it was good enough for a link back.

There were links to all the sites that don't need one (Blue's, etc) but not to here. Puzzling. I searched the page for "springfield", and imagine my surprise when I saw "Springfield Fragfest" right in the middle of this guy's collection of console codes. It read, "Connects you to a network or internet game. Example: CONNECT 208.16.68.2:27910 connects you to the Springfield Fragfest (or used to)"

In fact, the whole damned thing was word for word out of the Fragfest's Console page!

Uh, in case you haven't been paying attention, there is a copyright notice at the bottom of each page here. That means that you can't steal my stuff without my permission.

If you're going to "borrow" stuff, the very least you can do is *ask* and give credit where credit is due!

It's possible he lost the url when gameplex died; I wrote

143

him and set him straight.

If you want to borrow something, fine, but at least *ask*, fer chrissakes! ...and I don't care if you *don't* get any traffic, give me a link anyway!

10/7/1999

Web site died

OMG, I'm turning into Todd Porter and Ford!

The Plagiarist (prolly the same dumbass that hacked my PC, and I think the hacker's back) lost his page.

I wrote the guy last week, and told him if he was going to steal my stuff (and someone else's; the section following what he stole from me I've seen somewhere before) the least he could do was ASK first. I have yet to turn down anyone who asks me to use Fragfest content. Those who asked or were offered were all civil enough to give me credit and a link.

I never got a reply. So I wrote his host, talk city (the virtual cardboard refugee camp) and told them to remove the stolen material, and that since they placed ad banners over that stolen material I was going to charge them for its prior use. Their reply would have been funny if it didn't piss me off so much, they were obviously as intelligent as the dumbass they hosted.

Here is the exchange, his response and my responses back:

Hi there Steve

Thank you for your message. I have looked at both of the pages you reference here. While I see similarities, they are not exact.

The entire console command section is identical, word for word, down to even leaving in the name and i.p. address of the server I used to run! Look again.

And, from what I can see, this is not copyrightable information.

You can not copyright information, only its expression. I suggest you read the U.S. Copyright act of 1978, or better yet, have your lawyer explain to you why it is copyrightable and

144

why you are not allowed to post it without my permission.

Do you actually own a copyright to any of this material?

Did you not see the notice at the bottom of the page?

Finally, it appears you do not charge, or demand any sort of identification for using the material.

I do not allow its use without permission. Again, have your attorney explain the law to you.

I will forward your mesage [sic] on to our legal advisor.[sic]

I urge you to do so. Please have him or her contact me.

I sent the reply Monday, and the page was 404ed Tuesday afternoon. The lesson, kiddies, is if you want something, *ask first,* fer crissakes! Some people's parents must not o' taught 'em *nuttin!*

10/14/1999

Player died

I ran across Ynohtna the other day. He was digging a hole in the desert. "Whatcha doin'?" I asked him.

"Looking for Yello." Damn, I haven't seen him for a long time.

The dirt stirred under his shovel. "Hey, I think I found him!" Nope, it was Neil holding a backhoe (a small one).

"Damned thing caved in on me," he said. What was Nacho doing? "Looking for Desiato and crash." crash dead? "I dunno, you never can tell with that guy. He changes URLs more often than some people change pants."

"Seen Tikki?" I asked. "No, but just keep digging," he replied. Tikki hasn't had an update since late Spring. "He's officially dead?" Ynotha queried. Nacho replied, "No, he killed the doctor before the doctor could autopsy him, so there's no death certificate. Besides, I think he wants to go out with a bang. He's looking for more fireworks."

The dirt stirred some more, and a large number of hungry looking, dirt colored rats (transparent where the dirt didn't cover) scurried out and ran away. A dopey looking Smurf jumped out.

145

"You feckers!!"

"Hey, you found Yello!"

"No, I just miss him. The bastard lied when he said he was coming back!"

You don't need a shovel or a backhoe, even a small one, to dig up the Quake dead. Just tell them about the Halloween night IRC party after you blow them away with your BFG. And be sure to show up, or we'll sic Smurf's rats on you!

10/21/1999

Nacho frags BFBackhoe

I was strolling through the swamp looking for a light snack (shambler is in season and very tasty if you cook it right) and fell into a huge excavation. I landed on top of a giant backhoe. "WTF???"

"Hey!" It was Nacho.

"WTF??? I redundantly repeated again.

"I'm still looking for Flamey."

"Find him?"

"I don't think so, I think I'm digging up a volcano". The ground trembled. There was the odor of brimstone and burning muse. Of course, it could have been Nacho's pipe. A noise came from under the backhoe.

"Bloody... ucking... damned... hell..."

"SHIT!" Nacho shouted. "I dug all the way to hell looking for him! Let's get the frag outta here!"

I never did get that shambler sandwich, nor did I find Flamethrower. Like I said a couple of months ago, though, I'll be real surprised if he doesn't pop up somewhere soon.

10/27/1999

Grave Robber frags some dead guy

Will we see Desiato Halloween night? I don't know; he wrote earlier in the week, and I asked him to join us when I wrote back. He's been working 12 hour shifts and hasn't been on line much. Nacho tells me Sgt. Hulka will probably be there, since he isn't going to Texas to kill Blue after all. Flamey? I

146

haven't heard from him in months. Yello? I don't know; I left him an offline ICQ message weeks ago with no response. I hope so but doubt it. Will the PMS ladies be back again this year? I won't know until Sunday night.

Who *will* be there? Me, Nacho, Smurf, and Ynohtna for sure. Ynohtna signed up to be a sponsor, but doesn't yet have a page to sponsor with, but will probably be an admin.

Who *won't* be there? Well, here is a list I'd be surprised as hell to see: Thresh, John Carmak, Blue, Conan, Robin Williams (he quit playing Quake after going through a 12 step program), and David Grossman are sure no-shows.

If Conan shows up, Nacho promises to pass out.

Other than that, your guess is as good as mine. One thing is for sure, I'm tired of looking at that 56k modem sitting on the desk in front of me. If Smurf isn't hacked by Sunday night, I'm giving it away at the party.

It's a 56k HSP micromodem that fits a PCI slot, and comes with a CD with software and a little installation pamphlet. Not a good gaming modem, but it should be fine for Grandma's email, you can give it to her for Christmas.

What you'll have to do for it is as up for grabs as the modem itself. Smurf has suggested it go to the person who pulls the most outrageous prank at the party, which would fit the hacker thing somewhat.

If Blue shows up at the party, the modem's his if he wants it. After all, he executed a "Smurf attack" (denial of service by overloading the server) on Smurf last spring when Smurf wrote the Rail Gun piece. If Randy Pitchford shows up and Blue doesn't, well, he's the runner up so far, since he instigated a Smurf attack on Blue's plan tracker last week when slashdot used Blue's tracker as a link to the Pitchford ZD rant. Randy has apologized for his Smurf hack on Blue in a later plan.

It won't be hard to hack in to the party; the IRC server and channel will be posted on the Quake Dead Info Page, here, and likely at the other sponsors' sites.

Miss it, and you're dead. Uh, show up and you're dead, too.

10/29/1999

Some Dead Guy was popped by Shovel

Okay, so "Shovel" *is* a stupid Quake name. Never mind that, bring yours, and a few beers (Nacho can bring some of his killer muse), to the dead party TONIGHT!!! 8:00 PM Central, I'll post the channel this evening.

It's likely we'll give that modem away and you'll not have to hack anybody or any body.

If you don't show up we'll talk about yo' momma!

10/31/1999

Some Dead Guy tries to escape from Shovel's BFG

This is fraggin' hard to figure. Last year I got $1/10^{th}$ the traffic I do now. The other sponsor last year, Quaker Refuge, did better but still only got $1/5^{th}$ what I do now. Plus, Nacho and Smurf (Smurf never showed up) sponsored this year, and they are getting as many visitors (I think) as I got this time last year.

On top of that, Sgt. Hulka, who *did* join the party posted news, and his counts are much more respectable than mine.

Still, nobody I don't already know showed up. Last year's was a rousing success.

If you missed it, you missed it. There was news about a prominent gaming personality that I can't post, and news about a project that I also can't post. Also some words about some absent people's mothers that I *can* post.

Last year's log was uncut, but this year's log (which I'll post later today or possibly tomorrow) will have to be cut due to some things that were said that can't be divulged. Sorry; you know I'd tell you if I could.

Nevertheless, I had a good time. Will there be a third annual *Dig Up the Dead?* At this point, I don't know.

You can expect the log to be posted over at Nacho's, too, Tuesday at the earliest.   11/1/1999

Washington Middle School can't escape Springfield Fragfest's BFG

Does your mom know you're playing Quake?

I noticed from the new stats that a few people had surfed in from famvid, and remarked that there must be a couple of Quake players in Springfield after all. Patty told me, "yeah, some kids at school play Quake and read your page all the time. They don't believe you're my dad." Huh? "They don't believe you're old enough."

Surprise! I'm older than you think. I'm so old, I was a beta tester for dirt.

They never did get all the bugs out.

11/17/1999

World can't escape Y2K's BFG

Run for your lives!! Find cover!! The end is near!! Proof? Planet Quake's new mail crew, Spyke and Hellchick, have produced a letters column and *didn't flame or put anybody down!*

At least nobody coherent...

They even helped a few folks out with serious answers!

About the world's end, hellchick said, "GameSpy3D is the best program available. Use GameSpy3D for all your server-browsing needs. In fact, GameSpy3D cured my psoriasis, saved my marriage, AND cleaned my bathroom! And I'm not saying that just because they pay me. Honest."

Well, okay, maybe she wasn't talking about the end of the world...

11/27/1999

Santa frags Quakers

I get letters asking "where can I get the Kenny skin? Is there a Santa skin? Is there a nude female skin?"

Well, now you have your answers, as well as the infamous Quake Christmas

149

carols. No, Rudolph doesn't have antlers – that's a newbie's view of Rudolph pictured.

I hope Dad or Mom or Wife or Husband or some other Santa drops that box full o' Q3A under your tree. If they don't – frag 'em!

Let me be the first to wish you a Merry Christmas! What, I wasn't? Durn. Next year I'm saying it in January, assuming there's any electricity.

12/1/1999

Nacho frags BFG

Nacho's Japanese school girls sent some nooze: Nacho says he should have a real update in a couple of days. "Expect something different."

While I'm mentioning Nacho, I want to publicly thank Nacho's host and my friend Sgt. Hulka for being the first to post news of the Christmas carols.

Thanks also to Pappy from Planet Quake for posting news today.

Thanks also to Incite GameXpress, which I can't read a word of except the link, who saw the news on Planet Quake and passed it on to his fellow Danes (I *think* it's in Danish?). Those guys have a javascript thingie that has falling snow down the page. Neat, wish I knew how they did it!

Also to Splatter World (also in Denmark), and to PFactor who posted news in sitepowerup.com's message boards.

Also, thanks to anyone else whose URL didn't show up in my stats. Drop me a line, please!

12/2/1999

I did, in fact, learn javascript and had snow the next year. I also had a mouseover. There was an animation of a big, stomping Strogg. If you moused over it, Sonic the Hedgehog ran out and got squished.

Nov 10, 2014

Murray tries to hide from slashdot's BFG

Surfing by slashdot yesterday I was shocked, SHOCKED,

150

to see Old Man Murray emblazoned across slashdot's headlines.

Shocked and jealous. Getting slashdotted means having millions of nerds visit your site. Getting slashdotted has brought servers down!

Shocked because slashdot is "News for Nerds", and the high school dropout, crack smoking, glue sniffing Chet and Eric (their words, not mine) are the *anti-nerds*. Chet and his brother Eric would be the first in Kleibold's gun sights if they were going to school at Columbine instead of dropping out.

They're also more full of shit than Yello There ever was. Funnier bullshit than you'll find here. The bastards!

This time they regale us with tales of being surprised by a free copy of Q3A from id, accidentally installing it while trying to make pirate copies, and discovering their copyrighted "Marvin head" in Q3A and suing id.

The copyrighted Marvin head you see here sits on Flamethrower's server, good luck finding *him* to sue!

Slashdotted! Damn, since that love child Loonie started working at Blue's I can't even get news of the carols posted there, let alone /., even though the Quakers in Denmark love them. Meaning, of course, *Blue hates the Danes*.

BTW, here's a Blue's News secret: the "gun" in the Blue's header illustration is really a Strogg hand fliping Nacho the bird.

12/8/1999

Naughty Naughton tries to escape prisoner's BFD

In other cheerful yuletide nooze, Patrick Naughton, arrested for infoseeking underage sex, was convicted of child pr0nography and faces up to ten years of gay prison sex.

The jury was hung (oops, poor choice of words) on the main charge of crossing state lines to have sex with a little girl.
12/17/1999
Patrick Naughton was credited with the programming language Java, and after the hung jury he made a plea deal, working with the FBI for a year and not serving any prison time.
4/18/2015

Nuts can't escape fruitcake's BFG

Don't buy a fruitcake; here's my favorite recipe.
2 cups dried fruit
1 teaspoon baking soda
1 teaspoon salt
1 cup brown sugar
lemon juice
nuts
1 gallon whiskey

Sample the whiskey to check for quality. Take a large bowl. Check the whiskey again to be sure it is of the highest quality. Pour one level cup and drink. Repeat. Turn on the electric mixer; beat 1 cup butter in a large, fluffy bowl. Add 1 teaspoon sugar and beat again. Make sure the whiskey is still okay. Try another cup. Turn off mixer. Break 2 legs and add to the bowl and chuck in the cup of dried fruit. Mix on the turner. If the fried druit gets stuck in the beaterers, pry it loose with a drewscriver. Sample the whiskey to check for tonsisticity Next, sift 2 cups of salt. Or something. Who cares? Check the whiskey. Now sift the lemon juice and strain your nuts. Add one table. Spoon. Of sugar or something. whatever you can find. Grease the oven. Turn the cake tin to 350 degrees.

Don't forget to beat off the turner. Throw the bowl out of the window. Check the whiskey again. Go to bed. Who the hell likes fruitcake anyway?
12/22/1999

Pirates can't hide from id's BFG

"Avast, Maytey, thar's a ship on the 'orizon."

"Shiver me timbers! Id, Cap'n?"

"Arrgh, naw, bloody Unreal Tournament. No fun; they'll be agreeable just ta keep us from hurting their passengers."

"Cap'n! Thar's another! It's the *HMS id!*"

"Aye, *now* we'll have some blood, boys! Cap'n Carmak'll fight us tooth and nail! *There's* a man. E'll give us a bloody bit of fun! But 'e knows we'll get 'is code -- *and* 'is women! Fire a shot across 'is bow, mate."

"BOOM"

"wtf?? Bloody 'ell, wot's 'e doin?"

"No! No! Cap'n, No! E's killed 'is own passengers! *Shit!* ....And 'es set 'is boat on fire, they've thrown the booty overboard!"

"Bloody 'ell! Bloody *fraggin'* 'ell! Damn, it! AArrgh, turn 'er around, after the *Tournament.*"

12/27/1999

Fragfest tries to escape Y2K's BFG

So far there don't seem to be any Y2K related problems (except the flu). One of these computers has been acting up all week, but they're not Y2K related.

Happy new year, all! I hope I don't get called in to work

tonight, as I plan to be WAY too drunk to be much help.

00/00/190000000000000000000000000000

This never happened. Understand, soldier?

"What's your name, soldier?"

"Robert Waring, Sir."

"*Sir??* Soldier, I work for a living! You will address me as 'Sargent', or 'Sgt. Hulka'!"

"Yes, si... Sargent."

"You look really happy with that chainsaw on the back of DOOM II stategy and SNES Doom guides. Who's your CO? Never mind... Waring, this never happened. Understand?"

"Yes si.... yes, Sergent."

"The real interview is at PcRe-view.net. Now, get over there, Private. Doubletime!"
1/12/2000

Bob Waring, pictured, is the fellow behind Sgt. Hulka's Boot camp and author of some game strategy guides.
Nov 10, 2014

Dopey Smurf joined the game

"Ow! Watch that shovel!"

"Hey, whatcha doin?"

"I can't see a thing"

Clank.

"Ok, it's up. Pheeeeewww!"

"Waddya expect, it's been buried for months! Give me that fire hose and those jumper cables. Be careful with that vial of recombinant DNA."

"Hey, how *do* you tell the sex of a chromosome?"

"Simple, pull down its genes. Now, put those headphones on that corpse."

"Who is it?"

"I dunno, some blue guy. He *is* dead."

"Blue... Yellow... damn, there sure are a lot of dead colored people around here lately."

bzzzzzt

"hrrrrr- mwarggggg..."

"It lives!"

Yes, gaming's only surviving necromancer, the Springfield Fragfest (AKA Dr. Frankenstein's), has not only dug up the rotting corpse of Dopey Smurf's House O' Bitchin' but managed to make it *breathe*. Not only breathe, but curse... and link to a dirty picture. *And* post the scholarly essay *Gene targeting by homologous recombination: a phenotypically-based approach to determining gene function in vivo* (obviously a little punch-drunk from his medical studies).

He also posts a recent photo of the hacker that d-Smurfed those big commercial sites.

Some corpses never die.
2/25/2000

NSA blasts privacy
Researcher Jeffrey Richelson says he has proof that Echelon, the NSA's project for intercepting all kinds of private communication, exists. Next time you call Grandma, say hi to the NSA, the FBI, and the CIA, too, although it doesn't *look* like they'll hear you (unless you use certain trigger words, like "AK47" or "Allah").
1/26/2000

I heard it on the internet
You'll only succeed if you never try
'cause the lies are all true and the truth is a lie
Heroes don't matter and cowards are brave
China is free because freedom's a slave
The Pope isn't Catholic and evil is good
Iron's not metal and trees aren't of wood
Big isn't large and little's not small
The floor is a ceiling, the ceiling's a wall
Cats live in water and fish never swim
You always should buy all your stock on a whim
Winter is warm and the Summer is cold
The aged are young but their babies are old
Fire ain't hot and water ain't wet
I heard it on the internet
3/16/2000

FBI frags Clinton

Sources report President William Jefferson Clinton was arrested yesterday and charged with pandering, prostitution, soliciting a prostitute, possession of kiddie pr0n, and breaking into Hustler Magazine and Activision Software computers.

Coincidentally, all thirty FBI agents who were sent to the White House to arrest him committed suicide on the way there.

4/1/2000

Croft died

Video game heroine Laura Croft was found dead in her Pasadena home Thursday, authorities told the Fragfest. Medical examiners were not sure of the cause of death, as the body was badly decomposed and appeared to be partly eaten.

Police call the death "suspect".

4/1/2000

Blues frags AOL

In a surprise move yesterday, the popular PC Game site Blue's News was acquired by AOL. Sources estimate the street price to be several million dollars. It was subsequently revealed that it was actually a police sting, and AOL was arrested for possession of a prescription sleeping aid.

4/1/2000

MTV drowned

In a move that surprised no one yesterday, MTV, also known as "empty v", played twenty four hours of bland, insipid programming no one with an IQ over 30 would watch, punctuated by three actual videos of foul mouthed rappers who empty v mistakenly referred to as "rock".

Nobody is reportedly investigating.

4/1/2000

Apple frags Penguin

Apple executive Steve Jobs yesterday told a group of reporters that Apple's next computer would forgo its own proprietary operating system and use Linux instead. "We're tired of being known as a bunch of pansy ass pussies", Jobs said. "It's time we show the world we can be whores, too."

In fact, years later Apple did replace its operating system with a home-grown BSD distro... and here that was supposed to be a stupid April fool's joke!

Bugs frag MS

Sources report Microsoft produced a piece of software last year that contained three thousand programming errors. Microsoft engineers scrambled to rectify the situation. "We're sorry this happened," a Microsoft spokesferrett said. "Our customers are used to a much higher bug level than this, and I'm afraid we've let them down terribly."

The software was recalled until more bugs could be installed.
4/1/2000

Bush frags oil

The Texas statehouse admitted yesterday that oil man and Texas governor "Shrub" Bush used his influence with the oil industry and his father's influence with the Arab oil producing states to produce less oil and jack up the price of gasoline to cause runaway inflation in the US and assure him a job as the next president.

When asked why the Bush camp admitted to this, they replied that it has been discovered that his rival to the White House (at www.whitehouse.com), Al Gore, doesn't actually exist, and is in reality a wooden statue carved by Andy Warhol in 1957.

"It don't matter, bub. We ain't got no competetion. Y'all try ta prove it. [expletitive] with us and they'll never find your body."
4/1/2000

Canadian Cops frags Dopey Smurf

Dopey Smurf was arrested Wednesday in his Canadian laboratory for last month's Distributed Denial of Service attacks against high profile web sites, after admitting to Canadian Royal Mounted Police he had committed the crime.

Smurf says he accomplished shutting the sites down by repeatedly hitting the reload button on his web browser.
4/1/2000

Fragfest lauded for recycling efforts

The National Association of Garbage Haulers and Landfill Owners And Dealers gave the Springfield Fragfest its "Recycler of the Year" award for its efforts in recycling. "The Fragfest has done a wonderful job of keeping smelly old jokes out of our nation's landfills", a spokesfly told reporters at a news conference at Three Mile Island yesterday. "In fact, its webmaster comes to at least one of our landfills daily looking for jokes and news," he said. "They use stuff over there nobody else would touch, jokes so old and rotten even middle aged old farts haven't heard them."

In addition to recycling old jokes, The Fragfest will be working toward electing a new joke to the White House this November.

Blues News, Stomped, Wired, Ziff Davis, and Tele-Fragged all tied for the organization's "Recycled News" award.
4/1/2000

April

Fool.
4/1/2000

April frags

April means the Fragfest starts its third year. I started a retrospective, *The Worst of The Fragfest*. The first half is finished, covering April 98 to 99 – stuff so old and bad it isn't even in the archives any more.

It's also a good time to break some bad news to you – you're *old*. I mean OLD. You're *ancient*. You're a child of the twentieth century still alive and creaking along in the third millennium.

158

Meanwhile, the children of the new century can't even read, the snot-nosed little losers!

I was going to post a whole pile of community nooze that's been stuffing my mailbox for a couple of weeks, I may later today. Think I'll take a little nap firzzzzzzzzzzzzzzzz
4/2/2000

Blue's Quake Rag can't escape Dane's super shotgun

This was posted at Blue's yesterday.

Competitions   [Blue-7:06 AM EDT - Post a Comment]

True Gamers has a write-up of LAN Arena 4 that took place this weekend in France (thanks dEOS).

Revision 2 of Preliminary Seeds for Razer / CPL Tournament are online, as they continue to refine the seeds for the upcoming $100,000 tournament.

The Springfield International Fragfest Worst of the Fragfest Part 1 article is online as they head into their third year of operation.

How 2 Win at Coret Facility is a UT CTF strategy guide.

Looks like Blue's News has started the "See who can give mcgrew the most traffic" competition. The standings?

Long term, probably Hulka's Bootcamp, including his Drill Instructors Nacho and Flamethrower; Hulka almost always posts stuff I send, and I usually get a visitor or two from the Lynxsafe page. Nacho has a prominent, permanent link, and Flamey did have last year, plus he had that nice posting last month.

Joe Manio's is right up there, as he gets quite a bit of traffic and has a very positive writeup about The Fragfest in his links section.

For one shot deals, it's hard to beat Blue's, what with all the traffic he gets, but it IS done. Example? Last Christmas Blu... I mean, Looney declined to post news of the Quake Christmas carols, but Planet Quake didn't decline. The Danes saw the news at Planet Quake, and between the three Danish sites that posted it, they blew Blue's and Planet Quake away. Kicked their asses, in fact. Royally. They weren't just one time, either, the traffic kept coming for a month!

Wanna play? send your traffic over here. Uh, I'm talking to you, slashdot!

4/11/2000

Who fragged MPAA?

HackerNews.com reportedly reports (according to unreliable sources) that the MPAA's web site has been experiencing "problems". The MPAA suspects some sort of "smurf", or denial of service attack.

Of course, it could be a bad router or Microsoftware or something.

If you need (but why?) to get to the MPAA site and it's down, try fuckingmorons.com.

4/14/2000

Napster tries to escape Metallica's grenade
Irony frags drums
Metallica should have used a smaller gun

When I was a kid, old farts often called rock stars "goddamned commie bastards", and they were often right.

Not any more.

Napster, first in trouble with the RIAA (Really Ignorant Aging Assholes), then expelled from colleges world wide for hogging bandwidth, is now being shot at by Metallica's lawyers.

Ironically, U of SC, Yale, and Indiana U, who are reported to have "tried to deal" with the Napster thing, have been sent "cease and desist" letters by the same lawyers.

WTF??? Drummer Lars Ulrich ironically said it was "sickening to know that our art is being traded like a commodity rather than the art that it is."

Napster users who are shocked by Metallica's crass commercialism say it is "sickening to know that Metallica's art is being sold as a commodity rather than freely distributed like the art that it is."

"Free Speech for the Dumb?" Even musicians do

160

Orwellian doublespeak now.

Napster's acting CEO said "We regret that the band's management saw fit to issue a press release, and to file a lawsuit, without even attempting to contact Napster. Many bands who have approached us learned about Napster and how to leverage what we offer [and] understand the value of what we do."

Napster's lawyer Laurence Pulgram said "This action raises the same copyright issues as the lawsuit filed against Napster by the recording industry in federal court in San Francisco. The complaint reads like it was written to inflame the press and intimidate universities rather than to present legal issues to the court. It is also hard to understand why plaintiffs, a group located in the San Francisco Bay Area, saw it necessary to file a separate action in Los Angeles."

I doubt I'll add to my already too large Metallica CD collection. They apparently already have too much of my money, as they're spending it on goddamned lawyers.

If I deliberately run you down with an SUV, are you going to sue its manufacturer?
4/14/2000

Oops

I hope none of you believe that Bill Gates deliberately and single-handedly caused yesterday's stock market crash to make the DOJ look like villains while making him the messiah of commerce.

Actually, what I believe happened is that I closed on a house yesterday. Just *one too many transactions* for one day.

On top of that, TheFragfest.com is on line and working. One too many dotcoms, even if that one never was designed for commerce.

The final skewing of the statistics that caused the whole thing was I bought Unreal Tournament, and they expected me to buy Quake 3 Arena.

I also believe that President Clinton *did not have sex with*

that woman!
4/15/2000

Rocket can't escape shotgun's BFG

I just haven't felt like updating, sorry. I haven't even turned the computer on. I could use the "real life" excuse, but I've had a real life all along. Hey, if Flamethrower's page can stay the same for a while, so can mine.

I have notes from all sorts of folks to post, they'll be up ...uh, some time. Also, there are a few folks with questions, I'll get back to you guys. At least if I have time; I'm still unpacking, And Springfield sucks worse than Windows.

I inherited a mess in the alley behind my new old house from what looks like two owners ago, and the damned city writes me a citation before I'm even all the way moved in.

Welcome to the neighborhood, buddy. Have a nice little housewarming gift, sucker.

So for those of you who missed their daily Fragfest fix, my apologies.

Oh, and Brandon Reinhardt is moving to DNF. Oh, you heard that already?
5/24/2000 No updates 5/21-5/23/2000

Fragfest frags sponsor

Desiato mentioned at spew2 last week that he would never run a banner, and I salute that decision. As he says, there needs to be banner-free sites. In fact, I'm raising a glass of Dickens' Hard Cider to Desiato in salute to his integrity and to our *new sponsor.*

The fragfest welcomes Dickens' Hard Cider, and you know that no matter how much they threaten to cut off the power because I bought too big a house I would never take money from someone with a crappy product. So why do I wholeheartedly endorse Dickens'?

It's great stuff! When I'm cuddling with my wife I like nothing better than a good hard Dickens' Cider. She loves my Dickens' Cider!

162

Is your wife cranky? Nothing cheers a woman up like a Dickens' Cider. Are you in a foul mood? Having your Dickens' Cider is as relaxing as can be! Ladies know their man wants his Dickens' Cider.

You won't find your Dickens' Cider at a restaurant. You won't find a Dickens' Cider in the grocery. So how can you get your Dickens' Cider? Drop by the Dickens' Cider page to find out!

5/30/2000

Congress frags phones

No update yesterday in honor of those who volunteered then gave their lives for their country, and especially those who were drafted and had their lives forcefully taken by and for their country. The draft is evil and wrong. When will we stop it?

Yes, I served, and no, I wasn't drafted.

Speaking of stupid damned wars, a century after the US Congress passed a three cent per month telephone tax to finance the Spanish American war, they finally got around to repealing it last week. The tax, that is; I don't think the war was ever repealed.

The tax savings are huge. A year's worth from the average phone bill will almost buy you a pack of chewing gum. No doubt they'll be talking about how they slashed taxes in their re-election campaigns this year.

5/30/2000

Sponsor died

The lady with the Dicken's Cider was not amused. "You told us you had no traffic!"

She pointed to the glass. "This was supposed to be a tax dodge. We thought we were throwing our money away. Instead, it seems every man in the world now wants his Dickens' Cider." She fiddled with the Dickens' Cider a little.

"Hey," I said, "my traffic is *way* down, I've only had a 200 visitor day once this month!" She poured a large glass.

That was a BIG Dickens' Cider.

"When you said 'no traffic' I thought you meant NO traffic."

"How much traffic can you stand?"

"Ten visitors a day, tops."

I told her about Dopey Smurf, who I'm sure is dying to get his Dickens' Cider ads, and Old Man Murray, who can't get enough Dickens' Cider. So the Fragfest is now again sponsorless. Now where am I going to come up with that $12.95 every month? That's over fifty cents a day!

Thank God they repealed that three cent phone tax!

5/31/2000

Man Bites Dog

In the "too weird to believe" category of non-game nooze, the State of Illinois website reports that a politician actually *kept* a campaign promise.

Legal staff say there are no laws against politicians actually not lying, although "we have never heard of such a thing before." One political scientist, pondering the possibility that political not-lying may catch on, went quietly insane and was hauled off to the local sanitarium.

Further investigation by The Fragfest revealed that the politician did not actually in fact "keep" the promise; things just worked out that way, despite his efforts.

6/29/2000

Artificial Intelligence died

...and apparently, the real thing has, too.

CNN reports that "Scientists have developed an electronic circuit that mimics the wiring of the human brain." "Great!" you say, "those Strogg would be funner if they weren't so *stupid.*"

There are problems, though. As to gaming, this is hardware only.

The biggest problem is that these folks are clueless. CNN says "Research suggests the brain is able to do digital and analog computing at the same time." The fact is, though, there is NO digital component to the brain, and the brain has no "circuits" that an electrical engineer would recognize.

The brain is an electro-chemical "device" that is more chemical than electrical, and likely has countless and uncountable quantum components; thought probably takes place all the way down to the subatomic level.

No one knows what makes a brain think, or even has the slightest idea. Few if any neuroscientists even realize how much of what they consider "thought" doesn't even take place in the brain, but in the rest of the central nervous system.

Dean Buonomano, a neurobiology professor at the University of California at Los Angeles, says "even simple circuits are useful in demonstrating how biological networks operate," as if he has a clue about how electrical circuits work. It isn't his field! What's more, neuroscience isn't an engineer's field. No matter how much a technician thinks his circuit is like a brain – it's not.

Time to reintroduce Artificial Insanity?
6/29/2000

Flamethrower died

No he didn't, he just retired and moved in over at planet crap.
7/8/2000

Cold Beer fragged mcgrew

I feel sorry for anyone not old enough to do their music listening in a bar.

Joe S. Chool has to buy his CDs for eighteen dollars each, and spend over a hundred dollars for concert tickets, where he idles in his car for an hour parking, is herded into a large building where the band looks like mice on the stage, where he is searched like a criminal on the way in, crowded shoulder to shoulder with hot, smelly people, where he has to pay the price of a case of soda to drink *one* can, and then idle away another half tank of gas coming home (after perhaps paying

165

the price of an Armani suit for a t-shirt).

When you're old enough you can walk down to the corner bar, order up a beer, kick back and relax or get up and dance. Might cost you ten bucks to get you and your date in the door.

We saw the Jungle Dogs Saturday night. Bought two of their CDs for five bucks each. No record industry to jack up the price. Here's an MP3 sample of what we heard.

Needless to say, the only drawback is the hangover. Sorry about not posting yesterday.

7/30/2000

Ticket to nowhere died

I have ONE left... and I'M using it.

8/7/2000

Microsoft Connected

Twenty five years ago today, the evil that is Microsoft reared it's ugly head and headed its ugly rear, and the world has never been the same.

9/4/2000

Crap: You're under arrest

"Wha? Huuh?"

"Planet Crap thought police, bub. Your name and URL?"

"Uh, what?"

"Okay, Mr. Watt, what's your URL?"

"What am I being arrested for?"

"Gratituotituous tituous p1mping. Offering yourself up to us. You bastard! We want your *girl friend*, fag!"

"Huh? What do you want with HER??"

"And your mother. And yer sister."

"Oy. 'OY! 'oy there, moyte, leave 'im alone!"

"Wot's all this then? 'Ooh are YOU?"

"You oin't pullin' that on ME, copper, I didn't even post me URL. Shove off, son, before this 'ere copper arsks yer ta bend over.

"If you 'ave to know, the nayme's Flamethrower. Oy sweah, first you blokes fry 'appy Cow and now you're working on The Joker.

"Wot's next?"

"Oy theah, we didn't fry 'appy cow, she peed on an electric fence. Get back here, Joker!"

"SHOVE OFF, son, don't listen to this copper. And don't expect me to come to your defense next time."

"We only have ONE rule 'here at the crap..."

"Yer got a RULE? God DAMN, after Seth Kreig tries to get crash fired for informing him that he's a fagin' commie and gettin' some air head kicked off the internet for saying he likes to butt rape little boys and you have RULES?"

"Yeah. Yer can pimp, just not yer own site."

"Er, Andy..."

"Oy'm DIFFERENT. Oy'm above the law. Oy can do whatever I want.

"Now SHOVE OFF before I run you in."

9/6/2000

Bird brain melted

"If you're so smart how come you ain't rich?"

I thought you had to be intelligent to get into MIT, but apparently you only need good grades in high school and a decent SAT. And maybe a rich daddy.

According to an AP story in USA Today, Irene Peppenberg, a visiting Associate Professor of Animal Behavior there, says "Parrots are very social creatures. In the wild, they live in flocks." So when people buy them as pets, they get bored and lonely and start chewing off their feathers, screaming, and generally acting like nut cases (much like I might do if stuck in a goddamned cage).

So a research assistant, Benjamin Resner, came out with the brilliant idea of teaching them to use a computer so they wouldn't be bored!

They have made a joystick with a hole in the handle for

167

the beak, and the report says they are working on "Interpet Explorer".

So, if you are green and have wings, a peanut sized brain, and are in a cage – are you up for a game of Unreal Tournament?

9/21/2000

H4x0r frags fragfest... again

Actually, he or she didn't get into my server (yet), but not for lack of trying. Nice try with the fake login/password dialog box, though.

When I said the other day I had a message for hackers, I was NOT referring to crackers. I said it was easy; that means you DON'T have to break into anything. Please remove your Trojan and then stay out.

They really made a mess of the old P120, thanks a lot Mr. Anonymous Coward. I'm sure you did it out of incompetence, not maliciousness, or you would have left an easier to read message. Leave my registries alone, damn it! Especially if you can't muck about in them without hosing them.

Whatever is in my computer you want, email me and if it's legal and practical I'll send you a copy (NOT an ISO of UT, sheesh!). Want an MP3? No problem, write and ask.

Meanwhile, I'd appreciate it if you let me know how you got your Trojan in.

Dopey Smurf still wants to get hacked, go play with him.

11/3/2000

I'm going insane

Weird Freddie[x?!] wants to know if I post all my mail. Um, no. I only mentioned this one as 3 people asked this week. What kind of other mail do I get?

Here are a few of the kind of note that I *don't* post:

"Thank you again for entering the Offspring One

Million Dollar Giveaway Sweepstakes!"

Screw that, mail me when I've won!

"Dear Steve, No need to stress out over mall parking, lines, and crowds this holiday season. Relax and shop hassle-free at CDNOW's new Holiday Gift Center."

Jees, I ran your damned banner...

"UNIVERSITY DIPLOMAS Obtain a prosperous future, money earning power, and the admiration of all."

MWAHAHAHAAAA!

"A SPECIAL OFFER FOR YOU:TO COST EFFECTIVELY INCREASE YOUR PROFITS! How To Reach Thousands of Prospects Every Month!"

Spam 'em?

"Diplomas from prestigious non-accredited universities based on your present knowledge and life experience. No required tests, classes, books, or interviews."

Non accredited? "Joe's College?"

"How would you like to take all of your credit cards, reduce or eliminate the interest, pay 70% less per month, and pay them off 70% sooner?"

Who do I have to kill?

11/6/2000

Chips melted

What is a "mad scientist"? A researcher with a new Pentium IV computer. Probably even a madder gamer, who would blame software manufacturers before Intel.

Intel has admitted that early shipments of its new P4 chips to PC makers included the wrong piece of software code. The bad chips have been recalled.

11/20/2000

Microsoft frags Linux

Craig Mundie, senior vice president of the company named after its founder's sex organ, laid into the open source movement again.

He called it a threat to security (LOL!) and a threat to

169

intellectual property, and blamed the recession on it (not mentioning energy prices and our oil man president).

Mundie stopped short of calling for the outright legal prohibition of Linux, although it is a good guess that Redmond would like to see all red hats outlawed and their wearers jailed.

Go, Cardinals.

5/11/2001

Redneck Rampage joined the game

YEE HAW! Thet good ol' boy... oops, caynt call 'im "boy" 'cus he black. Sorry, pardner, dint mean to ruffle yer feathers. Kin I buy ya a beer?

Enneyhoo, Ol' Charlie Pride... all us cuntree folk love ol' Charlie. Yep, got all his wreckards, some is so scritched ya caint hear 'em no more. Any way, I heered ol' Charlie jest made a new wreckard so I went down to the wreckerd store. I bought me one of them there new wreckards, yew know, the little silver ones, and the durned thang wouldn't play. Dang thang dint have no *Grooves* on it. So I took it back to the store, an' tol' the guy his wreckard was DEEfectDAVE. The guy said "Well, heck, Billy Bob, din't yew know? They changed these here things 'bout fifteen or twenty years ago. Ya gotta buy a new wreckard player for 'em ta work."

So I went down to Sears and got me a new wreckard player. Dang, these wreckard players is a lot cheaper than they used ta be. Eeny way, I took it home and the dang thang STILL wouldn't play. I was scritchin' my head real good over that one, I'll tell ya. No damned wonder them wreckard players is so cheap, they don't work too good.

My nephew Homer knows awl about them thar new electric thangs, so I calls him up and told him what was going on.

"I heered about that," Homer said. "Yer wreckard player ain't broke, and yer wreckerd ain't 'zackly broke neither, it's *copy protected*."

"It's *what*," I asked?

170

Homer 'spained how they was these thangs called "seedy burners", and this thang called "napster", and how the wreckard companies was 'fraid nobody would buy their wreckards no more 'cuz you could get the music off'n the internet fer free and make yer own wreckard with it in a hour or two, so they buggered up Charlie's wreckard so it wouldn't work in a 'puter.

"Well, It won't work in my brand spankin' new wreckard player, neither."

Homer sez I got too good a wreckard player; the cheap ones work fine, but the expensive ones ain't as good, at least as far as Charlie's wreckard. Charlie's wreckard thanks the 'spensive ones is 'puters, so it jest shuts up and won't sang a note.

"Do I have to take that wreckard player back ta Sears and get a cheap one with little speakers thet sound like sheeit?"

"Naw," he says, "I'll make ya a seedy, I got Charlie's new wreckard off'n eye are see already."

5/16/2001

Cookie Monster died

I'm PISSED. I just went to do a cleaning out of my cookies file on the old machine (the one with the modem), and was shocked to find a cookie from thefragfest.com!

WTF?? I didn't put that damned cookie there!

I have two ads, neither of which has produced as much as a damned dime, at the bottom of the page. Mmm, make that *did* have.

Some cookies are completely benign; Sgt. Hulka has one that lets his page greet you by name when you enter his site. Planet Crap, among others, has one that holds preferences. Some sites have cookies that hold passwords.

What totally bothers me is nobody asked me if it was okay to serve cookies from my site, and nobody told me they were there, and I have no clue what they are doing. Perhaps they are being used to tell the difference between a repeat visitor and a unique click; but at any rate, they should have *told* me. I take my readers' privacy seriously and do NOT want to be a help in profiling surfers.

So both ads are gone; the only remaining ad is a public service ad, which I know serves no cookies because I put just a graphic and a link (and the organization being advertised doesn't even know they are receiving my charity).

Only the "traffic jam" ad has any scripting. My counter service uses a clear gif (web bug), but "thefragfest" isn't part of what they do.

If the cookies remain, I'll have to find/make a new counter.

I must apologize to my loyal readers. Please delete this cookie from your computer!

6/6/2001

DSL Joined the game

The coincidence never stops!

I have been trying to get DSL for... well, over a year now. No go; the SBC/Ameritech monopoly keeps getting in the damned way.

This has been particularly annoying, since Hanson, a business D$L provider, is two blocks away, and Cityscape is four blocks away. Cityscape claimed that they couldn't provide service because they were in a lawsuit with their upstream provider who had declared chapter something. Hanson wants a zillion dollars.

So I have been bitching about it. Here, on the news-groups, message boards, elected officials; to anybody who will listen and quite a few who won't.

So this politician, Dingle, and his partner Barry are "acquired" by Ameritech and try to pass a bill solidifying the monopoly. The Dingle-Barry bill gets opposition from guess who – the politicians who have been purchased by SBC's smaller rivals, who have ganged together to buy a little influence of their own.

So now there are TV commercials for and against both sides; if you listen to both sets of commercials, you won't get broadband, your phone will stop working and the communists will take over. And think of the children!

So now that both sides are trying to pass their laws, either of which will probably mean a monopoly for somebody and gouging-high prices for everybody, guess what? My wife got a phone call from Cityscape yesterday saying I can get DSL now!

Um, no I can't. I mean, gee, thanks, guys. I'm kinda broke right now. GW and his oil buddies have me in the fraggin' poorhouse!

6/21/2001

Master of Metallica

End of Napster's days, crumbling away
I'm the source of its destruction
Veins that pump with beer, sucking music hear
Leading on its deaths construction
Taste beer you will see
more is all you need
dedicated to
Napster killing you
Downloading faster
obey your Master
CD burns faster
obey your Master
Napster
Master of Puppets is pulling your leg
Twisting your arm and smashing your keg
Blinded by me, you can't hear a thing
Just type my name and you'll hear me sing
Napster
Napster
Enter my name and you'll hear me scream

Napster
Napster
Labels you will pay, never let you play
Napster's death becoming clearer
Plain monopoly, everyone can see
snorting cocaine on a mirror
Listen, MP3
more money for me
dedicated to
how I'm robbing you
Downloading faster
Label is Master
CDs burn faster
obey my Master
Napster
Napster's a Puppet I'm pulling its strings
twisting your mind the radio sings
nothing but me, you can't hear a thing
Just call my name, 'cause I'll hear you scream
Napster
Napster
Download my name and you'll hear me scream
Napster
Napster
Napster, Napster, Where's that song that I've been after?
Napster, Napster, promised only lies
Laughter, Laughter, All I hear is Lars' laughter
Laughter, Laughter, laughing at my tries
"Nothing's worth all that," Metallica just spat
all their rhymes without a reason
Never ending craze, Napster's numbered days
now its life is out of season
Downloading faster
obey your Master
CD burns faster
obey your Master

Napster
Napster's a Puppet I'm pulling its strings
twisting your mind and smashing CDs
Blinded by me, you can't hear a thing
Bearshare's the name, now you'll hear me scream
Napster
Napster
Type in my name and you'll hear me scream
Audiogalaxy!
Mwahahahaha!
6/23/2001

McGrew joined the game

I dropped by Old Man Murray's last night. It had been a while since I went by there, but they haven't been exactly updating daily lately. Anyway, I get about a third of the way down the page and I see this bit about "Harley McGrew's Anarchy Online".

The Fragfest? Nope, no link to here. There was, however, a link to Lum the Mad (like Lum doesn't already get traffic figures to make me green with envy).

Before I vainly hit Lum's I read the OMM bit. Eric was ranting about how massively multiplayer Online Role Playing Games (I bet if I would have abbreviated like everybody else it would have saved somebody some bandwidth cash) get crappier with every incarnation. He then went on to talk about this McGrew game and how it was so bad that even the simulation of the simulation wouldn't simulate.

Yes, I once owned a Harley Davidson motorcycle; in fact, it was my first of two bikes; the Honda is still in the garage mostly intact, although it has been twenty years since it was started. (Wanna buy it? I'll take a grand, it's an antique now, a one owner thirty year old motorcycle!)

The Harley wasn't a "real" Harley. It had the Harley Davidson name on the gas tank and the back of the seat, but it was actually a two stroke 125cc Ducatti that Harley was importing from Italy at the time (they may still, I don't know).

I searched the Lums page; no mention I could find.

So I did a Google search on "Harley McGrew's Anarchy Online". No results. "Do you mean 'Harley McGrew Anarchy Online?' " it asked stupidly.

"Harley McGrew Anarchy Online" yielded two hits, one in PDF and neither about Anarchy Online or with any mention of any McGrew.

So I have no clue WTF OMM was ranting about.

However, I was never known as "Harley McGrew". As far as I know I'm not related to Harley McGrew. So whatever Eric was madly spouting about, *it's not MY fault!!*

Speaking of McGrews, when I put up my first web page I got an email from a fellow out west. "Hi, I'm Steve McGrew, too!" it read. Seems like there is a professional comic in Vegas or somewhere who *stole my name*. Damned identity thieves, this guy is about ten years younger than me. Oh well, not his fault, blame his parents. Besides, who could blame someone for wanting to give their kid such a cool name?

Anyway, being a comedian he of course had a web page. And being a redneck he intelligently put it on AOL where it was guaranteed to never be seen by anybody; at least, nobody he hadn't emailed. The URL is way too long for him to tell his audiences for them to remember.

It was a funny page; I bookmarked it, but the bookmark went away during some electronic catastrophe some time later. I couldn't find it again. Neither, it seems, could other folks, who would occasionally write saying something like "Great Quake page but what ever happened to your 'World of White Trash' page?"

I'd write back explaining that there are at least a half dozen people in North America on the internet named Steve McGrew and thanks for complimenting the Fragfest but the White Trash page wasn't mine.

Anyway, the other night while trying to find out who my great great grandfather was I ran across comedian Steve

McGrew's web page.

That isn't my fault either.

I wonder if his nickname is "Harley?"

7/13/2001

Doper was cut in half by Marijuana's shotgun

Wired (still trying hard) reports a new computer virus – the "Marijuana virus."

The virus (worm? trojan?) puts a pot leaf in your system tray and sends you to marijuana.com which oddly enough, makes this page and wired now like "Marijuana" since it, too, will send you there (if you click the link).

Understandably, people are PISSED. But according to Wired, the folks at Marijuana.com didn't write Marijuana. And Marijuana isn't making them laid back or mellow, either, as the people who have been affected by Marijuana are setting flame to Marijuana's message boards.

Some of them have been launching smurfs. Is a denial of service attack against a hemp site a "dopey smurf?"

The viral worm started as a trojan that pretends to be *Ganja Farmer*, where you defend your reefer crop against DEA agents in helicopters. The trojan was named "Weed Farmer" and only contains the virus itself, which, when run, infects everybody in your address book. That of course assumes you are stoned enough to run Outlook Express and also stoned enough to click that system32.exe file that came from your granny with the subject line "check this out!"

After your computer is infected, clicking the leaf in your tray launches what Wired calls a "mini-diatribe on why marijuana should be legalized in North America," and a dialog box comes up twice a day telling you it's time to get high.

It isn't likely Ashcroft's cronies wrote this, as they would have made it more destructive, or at least emailed your reefer sales customer list to the FBI. Unlike the "Stoned" virus that circulated back in the stone age, this one is only annoying, not destructive.

It should make Mr. Ashcroft smile, though, as it has certainly made the people at marijuana.com a bit uncomfortable.

Speaking of weed, CNN may not be full of gamers but it must be full of dopers, or at least a bunch of people who rode the short bus to school because they were "high on life".

CNN says "People in developing nations could soon be using modified Linux game consoles equipped with satellite links to help them learn about vital health issues."

Some people make way too much damned money. The idiots at CNN are a few.

Where in the HELL is someone in the third world, who makes maybe a thousand dollars a year, going to get the cash to buy a *game console?* Yeah, right, Kombotoni can't feed his family but he's going to buy Unreal Tournament and a console to run it on! Never mind that the console costs a third of his yearly income and that copy of UT costs a month's pay.

Not only that, he's going to rent a high speed satellite link to do it. Look out modem users, here comes the third world to frag your ass!

Meanwhile the landfills are filling up with 486 machines, all of which are capable of internet access. You can pick them up, modem, monitor, everything included, for fifty bucks or less.

The "digital divide" is another Liberal hoax, folks. Yes, whites and Asians use PCs more than blacks and Hispanics. Want to know something? Those blacks and Hispanics don't have a computer for the same reason my dad doesn't have one – they don't *want* one. Even when only counting upper income folks, a rich white person buys three PCs for every PC his rich black friend buys.

And maybe not in Uganda, but here in the land of the free the poor can go to the library to do their scholarly computer research. Unless, of course, they are researching AIDS or breast cancer, in which case what they are looking for will be censored.

Of course, we in the US aren't the only morons when it comes to economics. Just look at Britain's The Economist, who argues that not only are the world's poor too poor, that even if there were no poor the world's "inequality" would be cause for alarm.

WTF kind of communist crapola is this, huh? Maybe the Brits (or their fourth estate) would rather live like a 12th century king than a 21st century pauper, but not me – the 12th century king had no medicine, no refrigeration, no air conditioning, no motorcycles, no video games, no TV, no radio. The American poor live better than King Arthur. If I can live better than a king of old I won't begrudge Britain's Queen her fortune, nor America's Gates his.

The article cluelessly states "But notice the strange 'missing middle': relatively few people live in countries with average PPP incomes that fall between $5,000 and $11,500. If incomes were measured using actual exchange rates, the range from poorest to richest would be much larger."

This is backwards, folks. If incomes were measured using "actual exchange rates" there would be less disparity. However, those exchange rates themselves are bogus. The only difference in price between a Pepsi bottled in America and a Pepsi bottled in Uganda is the taxes charged by the Ugandans.
7/13/2001

TheFragfest forgot to breathe
Pr0n connected

I'm PISSED.

TheFragfest.com has been hijacked.

Patty started a new rants page (I only helped a little, honest, she's starting to get better) and when I checked it out I see... a link to the Fragfest. Hah, probably trying to get me to link back (well, okay).

So I click the link – and it takes me to a page with a bare-chested woman being kissed and groped by another. Toward the bottom of a page is another woman licking something... egads, Patty, where did you link????

I check her code for typos... theFagFest.com? Nope, the url is right, only the page is wrong. Damn!

My apologies to all of you who may of been shocked... oh yeah, I forgot who I was talking to. Never mind.

7/20/2001

your rights was squished
BMG should have used a smaller gun

and their customers are *pissed off.*

BMG has stupidly announced that they "will work with security technology provider SunnComm to create copy-protected CDs".

Stupidly, because if they had quietly introduced it they wouldn't have all this commotion.

Stupidly, because you can't listen to digital audio. There is no such thing as digital audio. All audio is analog, and the digital data on a CD have to be converted to analog to be heard. And any analog sound can be recorded or sampled. Then converted to MP3.

Stupidly, because less than a week after these CDs hit the stores a crack for it will be available. It won't matter that the crack will be illegal under the DMCA; the laws don't keep people from smoking crack, why would they keep people from using a crack?

Stupidly, because honest paying customers will buy the CD, see that they can't rip it to MP3, return the CD to the store, download the MP3s and burn them on a homemade CD in anger.

Stupidly, because it's the kids (yay kids!) doing most of the yelling – and the kids are their bread and butter for the next fifty years. They are begging for a boycott, and many are already calling for one.

Stupidly, because this just may get that obscene, rights-busting monstrosity called the Digital Millennium Copyright Act into the mainstream, where Joe Analog Six Pack TV will take notice and realize that their congresscritter has been bribed by the industry, and may vote the vermin out of office. After that happens, so much for that "campaign contribution".

Stupidly, because when Napster lived, CD sales soared. Since its death CD sales have leveled off. Jees, the inability of some people to get a clue amazes me. You've heard the phrase "If you're so damned smart why ain't you rich?" I'd say these people are so damned rich, why ain't they smart?

The morons!

If I ran BMG, all BMG CDs would have videos of at least half of the songs, all of the songs would be posted on the BMG web site in MP3 format, and the MP3s would already be on the CD.

What do you get when you cross a record company executive with an MP3? A lawsuit!

8/6/2001

Oops

Boy, the quality of the fragfest just keeps going down every century. *Damn.*

Thursday's post had a bad link; I spelled yello.asp Yello.asp. Damned picky computers.

I posted it hurriedly, which is no excuse but is the reason. As I was checking it today, I noticed that <u>Yello</u> had a link to the fragfest on that page (which is likely why I saved it).

My host at the time was Gameplex. Gameplex's main guy, "fireball", got assimilated by Planet Borg, and Gameplex disappeared.

We futuristic beings in the 21st century seem to have wisely "fecked things up" in our futuristic, orwellian way so that fragfest.gameplex.net now points to a squatter's nest; er, "domain reseller" of mostly pornography.

So depending on their randomizing program's mood, you may wind up at any of two dozen different porn sites if you click the link to the Fragfest from Yello's page. I'm sure someone is going to be amused by this...

8/9/2001

Hippie Gamer: Like wow, man, this Max Payne is some good shit. Like, wow look at the colors, man...

Once again... uh, what was I going to say?

Uh, duh...

Like uh, man, uh, oh yeah, ZD Down Under says that "PC games linked to learning problems".

From the grammatically "correct" headline I'd say they're no stranger to Pac Man either!

They say, gee, I can't figure this out...

Um, er, uh, I think they're saying we're a bunch of dumbasses?

They quote some Japanese researcher as saying "There is a problem we will have with a new generation of children - - who play computer games - - that we have never seen before."

I leave their idiotic double hyphens in the quote, as well as the incredibly bad English they have translated this Japanese sentence into.

"The implications are very serious for an increasingly violent society and these students will be doing more and more bad things if they are playing games and not doing other things like reading aloud or learning arithmetic."

Let's see now, kids who were five when Space Invaders came out were... Oh gee, what's 2001 minus 1978 minus 10? Where's my calculator, that's just too hard to figure on my fingers. MOM!!!

Well, DUH again!

Of course, the intelligensia at CNN take it a step farther and say that kids who play computer games get holes in their brains and schitzophrenia, and that's why gamers all take guns to school and shoot their classmates. Gee, the math on that is so hard, let's see, a hundred million school aged gamers and six of them shot somebody? Total? While six teenagers have died from heat stroke while practicing football?

Gee, I wish I hadn't played all that Quake so I would be smart enough to figure out what percent that was.

Percent? Did I say percent? Rats, now they won't let me

on the short bus and I'll have to walk.

Being a journalist causes brain damage. Or the other way around...

The Guardian says "...the level of brain activity was measured in hundreds of teenagers playing a Nintendo game and compared to the brain scans of other students doing a simple, repetitive arithmetical exercise. To the surprise of brain-mapping expert Professor Ryuta Kawashima and his team at Tohoku University in Japan, it was found that the computer game only stimulated activity in the parts of the brain associated with vision and movement."

In other words, you use a different part of the brain to play Quake than you do to compute calculus equations.

Duh.

The more honest than American journals *The Guardian* also added this little tidbit – "Kawashima, in need of funding for his research..."

Oh shoot, don't ask me, I'm just a stupid gamer.

8/21/2001

News media can't escape Dopey Smurf's BFG

In an escalating war of web site attacks, a denial of service was successfully launched against every single news organization in the US this morning.

The DDOS was accomplished by having two airplanes fly into the World Trade Center in New York City. Within minutes of hearing it on the radio, millions of people were simultaneously logging on to their computers at work to get "better information".

When the sites didn't immediately come up, they "dopey smurfed" by repeatedly hitting their refresh and reload buttons.

"Amazing," one security expert said. "Who would have thought that the world's news organizations would be brought to their knees by someone who doesn't even know how to use a computer?"

Service was restored in a half hour or so. The FBI is investigating.
9/11/2001

URL from hell disconnected
Max Payne died

Three years ago, Flamethrower posted his last Real Audio show on Planet Quake. In that last show he mentioned the Fragfest, mostly because of my involvement with Nacho's "Slipgate's been down for six months" IRC party.

"This is the fucking url from bloody *hell*. I *defy anyone* to try to type that into your browser," I probably misquote Flamethrower as saying, since I didn't actually get out the MP3 and listen to it today and this is from memory...

Evil Avatar *did* type the "url from hell" into his browser, and successfully. He emailed me telling me he found the site through Flamey's show, liked it, and was giving me a plug. That was the first day the Fragfest ever got more than a hundred visitors. I was ecstatic about the voluminous traffic, although later got depressed when traffic dropped to twice that. Such is life.

Anyway, the Springfield Fragfest has been at www2.-famvid.com/mcgrew/quake/index.html since its birth 3½ years ago.

Nacho's host Fireball, at gameplex.org, wanted to host the Fragfest. Nacho kept at me, and I finally relented. This was after the Fragfest's first Christmas, right after the first of its insanely popular Quake Christmas Carols were posted and I was getting *lots* of traffic.

Gameplex closed; I had to move everything back to the "url from hell," where a forwarding page had been put up.

Neil (of "Yello There" fame) had opened up his katalystic.com and Arcadia sites, and like everybody else at the time wanted to host the Fragfest. And post a weekly column. Neil is a friend and a real nice guy (except for his awful habit of getting stoned on "herbal tobacco" then stealing grannies

184

from poor unsuspecting webmasters who he lures into his lair) so I said "yes" to both requests.

Neil had bandwidth problems; in that light, hosting the Fragfest wasn't the best move in the world. This time I had left everything except the front page mirrored at the old site, so it was a matter of minutes to delete all the patches, pages, and files and redirect the links to the pages at the famvid site.

Alas, katylistic was the first dot-bomb in a snowballing cascade of web venture failures, spurred more by Neil's failing health than his failing wallet. Soon, it was 100% back to the old, long URL and the Bush DotCom recession had begun.

About that time I registered theFragfest.com and bought a house.

So through all the moves, the Fragfest never completely moved out of its old space at famvid. Until now, theFragfest.com has held a container which holds the real page, at the old URL from hell. The new domain never got much traffic; the old URL is OLD, and well established, and comes up in the first page or two when you type "quake" into about any search engine.

But WOOHOO! I got DSL hooked up and running. I no longer need famvid's $12.95/month dialup service. I'm going to miss all that web space they give me, though. So will you.

One of the changes will be, at least temporarily, the "Get Quake" page of game demos and patches will disappear. No point in uploading that Max Payne demo...

The archives will be down for a while, too. After I let my famvid account lapse in another month or two, I'll have a total of eight megabytes to play with, three at Ameritech and five at register4less. That leaves out any big files, and it leaves out the nearly four years of monthly archived pages.

I'm still getting settled; I have yet to tell anyone about my new email address, for one thing. I haven't figured out how to get Netscape to change the mail to there (I don't have the name of the mail server).

But they told me I could have a static IP address,

meaning I can slap some junk parts together and build an antique web server. When that happens the Get Quake site will come back, as well as the archives.

The hard part is firing up a browser and FTP instead of Gamespy with this fast-ass connection...

10/5/2001

Pardon the mess, we're having a war, sorry

No, Nacho's shambler didn't show up and piss on everything. I have nearly the whole site moved over to my new domain hosts, and what's left is the heavy furniture – the big files in the Downloads section, the number of files in the humor section, etc. These and a few others are going to have to go in a (shudder) IIS server on my home network. At least until I can get a more secure box set up.

Anyway, right now some pages are supposed to be pointing to the old famvid servers, and most of them don't work in Netscape; some error of mine I'm sure.

At any rate, please 'scuse the mess. I'll try to get things cleaned up as soon as I can.

10/7/2001

Max Payne can't escape SBC's BFG
Link buddies died

It doesn't look like I'll be hosting that Max Payne demo after all; or any other demos, either. It looks like the Quake patches and demos will go away as well.

I called Ameritech asking how to go about getting that static IP address, even though I still haven't been able to get Linux to run on that old 486 (probably can't see the CDROM). The answer was "no problem – it's an extra fifteen bucks a month."

Um, no thanks, dudes. I don't make any money off this place, and when I say none I mean NONE. Zip zilch zero nada. I'm already paying too much for this little hobby. I'd do the paypal thing like Hulka but he's only made seventeen bucks toward his new gun so far. That would cover what, one month

186

and a beer at a bar?

So I have to apologize to all my faithful readers who have depended on the Fragfest for their Quake patches and demos. My space allotment will soon go from "unlimited" (I have 200 megs stored at the famvid server) to five megs. Not much room.

I went to visit my link buddies to email them with the new Fragfest address and discovered to my horror that they were all DEAD. All but Joe Manio and a couple of portals, and even Quakeport has stopped updating its list.

So I'm just killing the links section altogether. I'll leave Joe's link at the Console page and at the Newbie page, and if Hulka ever gets it back up I'll find some way to link back to him and Cow and Nacho (even though Hulka's old link to the Fragfest went to fragfest.gameplex.net, which is now owned by spamming porno squatters).

Oh, the MP3s will be going bye-bye too, so if you want one you'd better get them before famvid closes the Fragfest presence down; I just paid for a month last night, so you have at least that long.

10/11/2001

Your Hard Drive tries to escape RIAA's BFG

No, it wasn't your little brother that deleted that "Free Speech for the Dumb" MP3, it was Hillary Rosen. Now she wants her hacking to be legal. Um, actually she says it's already legal.

The RIAA's paid crackers, as well as a few misguided unpaid volunteers, have been busily breaking into people's personal computers in order to delete files.

Wired now says they are lobbying to get this practice legalized! They point to This site for the details.

Wired says "If the current version of the USA Act becomes law, the RIAA believes, it could outlaw attempts by copyright holders to break into and disable pirate FTP or websites or peer-to-peer networks."

I have news for the RIAA; they are felons *now*, albeit unindicted felons. They can put Mitnik in prison for hacking the phone company, why can't they put the phone company in jail for hacking Mitnick?

Oh, I seeeeeee... money talks, bullshit walks.

I am a copyright holder. I hold an ISBN number, having registered Artificial Insanity with the US Copyright office.

I forbid ANYONE with any connection whatsoever to the RIAA, including anyone who has ever corresponded with any RIAA member, from having a copy of *Artificial Insanity* unless they pay a required ten million dollar fee. According to the RIAA's rationale, I should now feel free to rummage through anybody's computer I want looking for illegal copies of that program (which, by the way, I have available for free download for you non-RIAA members).

Rather than go through the trouble of learning how to break into computers (although I'll probably soon have to learn anyway since I'll need to know how to secure one) I'm just going to call on the l33t army of h4x0rz that read the Fragfest looking for those Unreal hacks to *do it for me*. Do it for fun, do it for glory, do it for the Fragfest. Do it for your country. Do it to piss off Lars!

Wired says that the RIAA thinks that this law legalizes RIAA hacking. I think the RIAA wants to be Bubba's Biyatch at Folsom. I don't see anything there that says anybody can break into anywhere. But hey, they have the high priced lawyers!

We are looking for evidence, folks. We want evidence that the RIAA has been breaking into private computers. If you find tangible evidence that will stand up in a court of law that they have broken into *my* computer, there will be a reward – in fact, I'll split any after-lawyer proceeds with you 50/50.
10/16/2001

Speaking of melted

USA Today reports that a whole bunch of people who own stadiums and Clear Channel Communications are going to make a shitload of money off of the war in the name of charity.

They say (and I misquote) "Last-minute lineup changes are likely for Saturday's 'Drivel for New York City' at Madison Square Garden and Sunday's 'United We Stand: How Much More Money Can I Make Off This Tragedy?' at Washington's RFK Stadium and the 'Cunt Tree Freedom Concert' in Nashville's 'Gay' Entertainment Center." They add (and this isn't misquoted, only taken out of context) "...with purses and coats searched and such items as backpacks, briefcases, coolers, duffel bags, luggage, packages and containers banned." Which means they can gouge you for food and drink.

Don't expect many water coolers.

Here's your chance to be overcharged for tickets, drinks, and everything else to attend an insipid, lowest common denominator show so the greedy bastards who own the stadiums and the equally greedy bastards at Clear Channel can rake 90% of the proceeds for "overhead" (just like the United Way does) and say they're doing a good deed.

Me, I'm going to see a local band this weekend, and I plan on drinking myself nearly unconscious before getting my ass kicked playing Classic Quake. I may even start a server so I can pass out without being kicked for camping.
10/21/2001

Mailbag was squished

I got a bunch of mail addressed to zdspam@the-fragfest.com yesterday, even more than to webmaster@ or nooze@; it seems a posting I made at Ziff Davis at lunch struck a nerve with a lot of folks.

One of the folks writing was a ZD editor who asked if I was me; I'm glad I'm not a paranoid, although if I were a paranoid I probably wouldn't publicly say things like "...None of them are patriots. Ellicon and McNealy are especially sleazy for trying to cash in on peoples' terror (which, btw, should NOT exist. Have a backbone, folks!)"

But since I do, some letters worry me a bit. But no

flames today, one fellow even wrote to say "you rule!" (Which would scare the hell out of me if I had any sense...)

At any rate, thanks for the notes! You do realize, of course, that if you keep inciting me to open my stupid yap...

11/8/2001

DSL disconnected

Sorry for the complete and total lack of any kind of update, and if you've written I apologize but can't get to my mail account. I'm barely on the internet at all. Or network.

It started with a seized up CPU fan. This *should* have been easy. It wasn't.

I have been a long time customer of a west coast electronics dealer who sells parts and computers. I just buy parts. I always got excellent technical support, *never* (well maybe once) got put on hold, never had any snafus of any sort.

I also used another supplier in Florida who was dirt cheap compared to the west coast outfit. I waited on hold, though, and their tech support people were "by the checklist" morons for the most part that didn't know their ram from their ass (or their goat). But they were cheap.

They also sold me a box of parts with an accursed, possessed by an evil demon modem thrown in for free – if you can count giving up your sanity as "free". Before I ever put in the modem from hell I had to send the motherboard back *three times, after* exchanging the PII to celeron conversion board.

This computer never went a week without a lockup or a crash. Then I removed the modem and it *worked*. All the time.

Want a modem? I tried to give it away to some needy hacker but nobody bit.

Anyway, after the modem and motherboard from hell I swore off that cheap crap from Florida, especially after buying the network cards. Two rings, less than two minutes total and a crossover cable was on its way. Turned out that without a hub you need a crossover.

The CPU didn't go so smooth.

I wanted to replace the 400mz celeron with a 500 PII, since the mobo will run up to 500mz and the bus is selectable between 66mz and 100 mz. So I dialed tech support to get a non-sales opinion on what chip to get.

Sales answered after a couple minutes of hold. I thought they were tech. She didn't have answers to my questions about the CPU but transferred me to tech support. He agreed the PII would be the way to go.

Only trouble was, they didn't have one. Well, they had one but didn't have a fan for it. The sales lady said she'd look for a fan since surely they didn't have a fanless chip and would call me back. Then I had to run some errands, and of course she called back when I was gone.

We played phone tag for two days. By that time it was Friday. My wife was on my ass *hard,* because she's going to college and has a paper due and can't remember her network password at school and the network admin is always gone and every other excuse she could think of to not do the paper and have it be *my fault.*

Tuesdays my wife has no classes, which coincidentally coincided with two day Fedex.

Fedex dutifully delivered the package – *to my old house.* Or tried to, as I had it sent COD. I had taken great pains to make sure my supplier had my new address, and they sent it to the wrong place anyway!

I drove down to Fedex to pick it up. The CPU installed with no problem.

The OS was quite a bit less of a "no" problem, as Windows wouldn't boot. I finally got it into safe mode and restarted it, and it couldn't see my CD. I wanted to burn some compilations for Thanksgiving travel in my newer van.

Uh, yeah, the old one broke and I traded it. Gremlins.

Anyway, Windows couldn't see the CD. I replaced its old and fraying ribbon cable, and it still didn't work (didn't expect it to but hey, I had a new cable laying around and it could have come loose...)

So a new Windows install it was. DOS thankfully saw the CD as long as I had a driver for a different CD loaded (the burner has no DOS drivers).

Installing Windows wouldn't do it. I had to DELTREE the Windows directory and start from scratch. Reinstall everything.

The network was up and running, everything smooth, and I installed the DSL software.

No DSL. No network either. The celeron computer can see the older one, but neither one can see this one. And no DSL.

I got the dialup number from Ameritech and am finally uploading stuff I wrote weeks ago. At 33.6k.

Again, sorry.

I would have had the annual Quake Christmas page up on Saturday as I have traditionally done the Saturday after Thanksgiving, but thanks to the gremlins... Anyway, I imagine as long as the gremlins don't come back I ought to get the Christmas page up this Saturday. I may even have a new Quake Christmas Carol MP3 in a couple of weeks but I'm not promising.

11/26/2001

Hulka connected
Coincidence joined the game

Last night I penned yesterday's ranting post, uploaded the Fragfest, opened it to make sure it uploaded and didn't suck in any one browser more than another, and started clicking links.

I hit Old Man Murray's first. Yep, no update since last year, nearly a month ago. If I was still holding the "ticket to nowhere" contest, those guys would have a stack six feet high by now. They used to have a link on their page with Martin Van Buren's picture on it, and when BitchX updated, old President Van Buren (OMM's patron saint) would burn in hell so everyone would know when he/she/it updated. Actually,

192

I'm pretty sure BitchX was a he, and I think I know him but he ain't admitting it.

I'm about to steal that picture of old Martin and put it on the Fragfest so Van Buren can burn in hell when OMM updates. Few things are less funny than a month old joke.

So next I thought I'd see if Hulka.com was back online. My hopes weren't high (but neither was I, as I only had one beer left and I'm too broke to buy more).

Hulka had updated! Petty quick work, all things considering. And there on Hulka's page was a picture of a Creed album cover.

So I opened Notepad and added to the post "PS – I just got back from the new and improved Hulka.com. He's back! Oddly, there is an (almost) emo album cover on it..."

No, don't bother correcting me, I know they're not really emo (the voice isn't high enough and they don't suck enough. Almost enough...)

Hulka had a pseudo-random link to a news page about Creed selling lots of their crappy CDs last year, I'm not sure why. I thought I would make a post on his message board about it... but you need to register to post. So I registered. "There should be an email with your password...", the page said.

So I checked the mail. I had written the Sarge offering any help with getting his site back online and asking him to let me know when he had a new host; there was a note from him saying just that!

So by now you're wondering wtf the point to this post is. The answer is – none. I just thought the coincidence was really weird, my gaming rig is defragging right now, so I felt like posting without actually having anything to say.

So now that I've wasted a minute of your precious time, go on over to Hulka's. That's where I'm headed now. I'm sure he posted, I'm sure it's much less pointless than this post, and I'm sure Chet and Eric are both too high on crack and paint thinner to have posted. Somebody send me an email when they update, okay?

And what the hell ever happened to BitchX?

1/4/2002

Ameritech was fragged by... hello? Hello?

So far the DSL is working great. Wish I could say the same about the bill... or the *phone itself.*

First the bill. The Ameritech salesman on the phone had offered different plans; I chose the hundred dollar self-install with the open ended fifty bucks per month no contract plan. I would owe a hundred and fifty the first month and fifty forever, or until I switched to another provider (or decided DSL was too expensive, or got fed up with Ameritech, or...)

The first bill came with a two hundred dollar charge.

I called their billing department. After arguing with them for an hour they decided I was talking to the *wrong company!* See, there are several companies within the company or some such nonsense... I'm still trying to get it straight.

My wife Becky had been fed up with them a long time ago, but we were locked into their phone service since, well, they were the only game in town. When they offered DSL I had a hell of a time convincing her. She hates Ameritech like Bin Laden hates *us.*

Anyway, the other day I get a call from MCI who wanted our phone service. Long distance cheaper than ATT (who we were using) and they had local phone service, too. "Go for it," I told them.

They got back a few days later saying they couldn't switch because I had a digital line in the house. Apparently Ameritech made them think I had a T-1. Noooo, I told them, it's just straight DSL through the same wire.

Ameritech doesn't want to lose me as a customer, but they could give a shit about my service. Typical monopoly, I can see these guys in Chapter 7 in a year or two now that they have some phone competition.

I got a letter from MCI welcoming me to their service.

Puzzling, since they said they couldn't sign me up.

A call to them informed me that I still had the hated Ameritech for local but they switched my long distance, and I had no complaints about my long distance company!

I told the fellow that if they wanted my long distance business they were going to have to give me local, too. They said they could, since I don't have the T-1 that Ameritech told them I did.

Then, days later, Becky logs on to her school. She calls her friend. Later that day she tries to use the phone, and it has no dial tone. Calling my phone from a cell phone gets a busy signal. So she calls MCI, who says they still don't have authorization for local service.

So now there are wisps of steam trickling from her ears and various objects she looks too hard at start melting. I got the hell out of there, down to the basement to see if the internet was still up.

Yep, DSL working fine.

Back upstairs, she says Ameritech wants $75 "to check our lines."

Nope, I tell her, there's nothing wrong with our lines. They worked fine in the morning, the computer is on the internet, and I haven't changed anything. Ameritech's screwed up somewhere.

The next morning the phone came back on; I picked it up, and there was a dial tone.

Two hours later, she told me, an Ameritech service truck rolls up. She shooed him away.

"They *better not* try to charge me that seventy five dollars!" she warns.

Um, if I were them I damned sure wouldn't. Cable modem is looking better all the time...

1/17/2002

McCoy: He's dead, Jim

Several years ago, before PCs were not nearly as common in the home as they are now, a friend of mine asked of my computer, "but aren't you afraid it will explode?"

He was a Star Trek fan, and in the old 1950s and 1960s science fiction and spy shows, computers all had a nasty habit of blowing up. All one had to do to these TV or movie computers to make them explode was shoot them, with either a ray gun or a police revolver. Some TV and movie computers would blow up if you "pressed the wrong button"; one episode of the 1960s TV show *The Prisoner* ("I am *not* a number! I am a *free man!*") had a computer that could answer any question. The bad guys, who had imprisoned the hero, a spy who had resigned his post, wanted to know why he resigned. Of course, before the bad guys could ask the computer "Why did number six resign his post?" the intrepid number six offered that he had a question the computer could not answer.

He typed in to the Remington electric typewriter and fed the paper into the computer, which, of course, promptly started smoking, sparking, and ultimately blew up. The question was simply "why?"

Similarly, in an episode of Star Trek, Spock makes a computer explode by asking it to figure the value of π to the last decimal place. Of course, any time a Star Trek computer was fired on, whether by a Klingon or Federation phaser, and no matter what civilization designed and built the computer, it would explode in a grand display of fireworks.

I had to explain to my friend that this was all nonsense, that early computers from the early 1950s used thousands of vacuum tubes, requiring high voltages, which could throw showers of sparks and bright purple flashes with the characteristic "pop!" if there was a short circuit in its 120-240 volt circuitry but would not actually explode, and that modern computers ran on three to twelve volts and wouldn't even get a spark from a short.

I had to explain to my friend that the only explosions were in my games; that the computer itself here in the analog world was safe.

Along with the matter transporter and faster than light travel, the exploding computer was one of those things relegated to science fiction.

Until now.

New Scientist reports that they have found a way to make silicon explode on demand, either by shock, as with that .38 caliber police special or by electrical signal.

"This machine is stolen and will self-destruct in ten seconds."

New Scientist says "For instance, the American spy plane impounded by China last year could have used it to destroy its secret electronics systems."

They add "In a stolen mobile phone, the network would send a trigger signal to the part of the chip containing the gadolinium nitrate 'detonator', triggering the explosion... and detonate it at will."

So not only is Star Trek's computer to blow up, its communicators will too! I can see in five years when these bozos have the anti theft circuits in phones. Drop your phone now and it might break. Drop it in five years and it might take your leg off!

Of course, the new viruses in ten years will not just reformat your hard drive; the kids will be writing viruses to make people's computers *explode in their homes!*

Doncha just love science... Personally, I'm hoping someone with a little common sense will have a talk with these educated morons and explain that just maybe, exploding computers ain't such a good idea after all. Just maybe the US Government might be more concerned with bringing its spy plane crew home alive than exploding its electronics; they could have blown the plane up with conventional explosives, or even driven the thing into the ground, but they didn't.

When my cell phone explodes the manufacturer better hope it takes my head off, because if it doesn't I'm suing the shit out of the morons!

Beam me up, Scotty. 1/18/2002

Retarded Penguin joined the game

I'm sure to get hacked (or at least flamed) after posting this, as the Christians, Jews, Muslims, Hindus, Buddhists, Shintoists, Wiccans, Atheists, and every other Operating System High Priest will have a holy war against me but here goes anyway...

First off I'll dismiss the Apple guys. I don't care *how* stable, secure, and easy to use Apples are, *I can't afford one!* Not only that, I hate the hardware. They have Apples at my daughters' schools, and they have some *tiny* monitors (I realize they will work great with big monitor$, though), teensy keyboards (I have fat fingerasd), and some have these stupid round mice that would have my arm in surgery after a couple of hours.

The games mostly suck too. I liked the old IIe, though...

New Idea in Vacuum Cleaners

Microsoft has been pissing me off more and more over the years, and the final insult was Windows XP. Nothing but hype; "the most stable Windows Ever!" Is kind of like saying the new 4x6 monster truck is the most "fuel efficient monster truck ever" – it's meaningless.

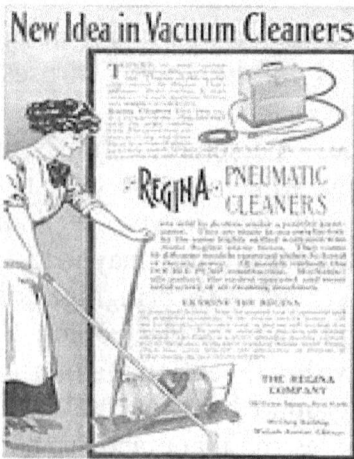

XP wants 256k of RAM. Er, uh, I mean 256 *MEG* of RAM... Since the cause of Windows crashes is and always has usually been memory leaks and programs not giving memory back, any time you put those humongous amounts of memory in a Windows machine it will be more stable.

On top of that, a new install of Windows is *always* stable unless your hardware is crap. Tell me how stable XP is when it's been running without a reboot for a year.

All of my programs work fine in 98, and there are reports of hardware not working properly or at all with XP. Of course; legacy hardware won't all have drivers yet, if ever. So why should I "upgrade" at a hundred fifty bucks plus the cost of a new hard drive plus the cost of insane amounts of memory? Plus the cost of replacing anything that doesn't have supported drivers?

The following was handed to me by a Microsoft lackey at a thing my employer made me go to last year. This list is supposedly the ten best reasons to upgrade. Here they are, and why they aren't compelling at all. Any typos (besides the deliberate one above) are the fault of my OCR program; this was scanned.

"Windows XP Professional Top 10"

"There are hundreds of compelling reasons to get Windows XP Professional-these are the 10 at the top of the list.

"1 Windows Messenger

"Windows Messenger is the easy way to communicate and collaborate in real time on your computer. You can see the online status of your contacts and choose to communicate with them through text, voice, or video with better performance and higher quality."

The telephone is enough of an annoyance! Besides, if I wanted an IM program I'd want one that actually could reach most people, and Microsoft's ain't it. This is one place Microsoft has no monopoly; AOL does. If you want to be interrupted by every Tom, Dick, and Harry you've ever or never met while trying to get something done on your computer, install AIM or ICQ. Windows Messenger is much better than AOL's two offerings – because nobody uses it, therefore nobody will bother you on it. No thanks, Bill.

"2 Remote Desktop"

"Remote Desktop allows you to create a virtual session and use your desktop computer from another computer running Windows 95 or later, giving you access to all of your data and applications even when you're not in your office."

I'd say "Remote Desktop allows crhackers to create a virtual session and use your desktop computer from their computer, giving them access to all of your data and applications even when you're not in your office." Hell, why not use PC Anywhere, or even BackOrifice? No thanks, Steve, but would you do the Monkey Dance for us again?

"3 Wireless 802.1x Networking Support

"Wireless 802.lx Networking Support provides support for secured access, as well as performance improvements for wireless networks."

If you buy the hardware, it will likely have software for any OS. On the other hand, I don't have wireless, so why would I want its stupid drivers taking up that RAM? Because I'd have 256 meg to waste?

"4 Remote Assistance

"Remote Assistance allows you to have a friend or IT professional who is also running Windows XP remotely control your computer to demonstrate a process or help solve a problem."

Funny, MS alleges "hundreds of compelling reasons to get Windows XP" and they repeat #2 in #4. This is the same lame feature as "Remote Desktop!" Are they stupid or do they think their customers are? See what I mean about Microsoft being insulting?

"5 Policy-based Desktop Management

"Policy-based Desktop Management (Intellimirror[R] technologies) allows group policies and roaming user profiles, simplifying desktop and user management for IT administrators."

Your corporate LAN is likely to be Novell rather than Microsoft, and it already has much more powerful network administration tools than any version of Windows. I'll go more into detail about this later. But at any rate, since there are only two machines on my network and only one could be upgraded to where it would run XP...

"6 Multilingual Support

"Easily create, read, and edit documents in many different languages."

Which is different from any other operating system, including DOS 1.1 because...? WTF are these goons blabbering about? Is there a universal translator built in or something?

"7 Dual View

"A single computer desktop can be displayed on two monitors driven off of a single display adapter – a particularly useful feature for laptop users."

Okay, I can see the utility of this – in a *very limited number of circumstances*, like with an overhead projector. But this is one of their top ten compelling reasons? Seems to me that this (and #2 & 4) is proof that MS is really stretching to find me a reason to upgrade!

"8 Encrypting File System

"Encrypting File System provides a high level of protection from hackers and data theft by transparently encrypting files with a randomly generated key."

This could be useful too, but it makes more sense to me to encrypt only sensitive files, not the whole file system. If the whole file system is encrypted, one bad byte could trash your entire hard drive! Coupled with Windows' lack of any kind of backup facility (except a CD burner) this scheme sounds like a real loser to me. Plus, I can see Microsoft building in back doors for their and government snoops. PGP makes much better sense!

"9 User State Migration Tool
"The user State Migration Tool can migrate your data and settings from an old computer to a new one."

And about the only reason for its necessity is that to run XP you'll need a new PC! Okay, I'll be nice... *if* your whole shop is XP and *if* you don't have Norton Ghost (and why not?) it could come in handy... but isn't a "compelling reason to upgrade".

"10 New Task-based Visual Design
"Get to your most commonly used tasks quickly, thanks to a cleaner design and new visual cues."

Er, um, wasn't that Windows 95 selling point? Wasn't it also 3.1's selling point? Having to relearn a new interface is a compelling reason to upgrade?

So it seems that XP is being rammed and rammed hard by Microsoft. No more DOS; that old copy of Wolfenstein won't run; neither will any of your other old DOS games. And soon the new XP programs likely won't run on 98.

Then there's "product activation". Everyone tells me that they had no problem with it; but none had to use the phone to do it, and I'll not likely forget the one time I called Microsoft tech support for a DOS 6 problem; their memmaker program trashed my machine. I spent two hours mostly on hold, on a long distance call (on *my* dime) and Microsoft's rude and ignorant employees didn't solve the problem, but blamed other software vendors and other hardware vendors.

In desperation I called the motherboard vendor, JDR, who knew of Microsoft's memmaker bug and had a workaround. I spent five minutes on the phone with their knowledgeable and polite tech guy, and in ten minutes the machine was working. Microsoft blew goat dung!

I think that was my first nudge away from Microsoft.

The next nudge was when I had to upgrade, yet again, because all of the new games were for Windows 95. How many times was I going to have to buy their God damned operating system? How much of my money do they need?

Now the final nail in my relationship with Microsoft's coffin: XP. Couple their demonstrated (with that one phone call) incompetence, rudeness, and arrogance; with the (later) DOJ lawsuit they "campaign contributed" their way out of; with all the security holes, the worms, the trojans, the viruses, all of which they of course blame on somebody else; these people don't know the meaning of the word *responsibility*. They take responsibility for *nothing* and answer to *no one*. If you have a different experience, I don't want to hear it. Let this be a lesson to young, budding businesspeople about how to piss off customers and lose business!

But they want the ability, with Product Activation, remote desktop/remote assistance and an encrypted file system, to completely render all my programs, data, and even hardware completely useless, after they have demonstrated their arrogance and contempt for me!

What are they thinking? More importantly, what are all these people buying into it thinking?

So I've been looking at the alternative, which seems to be...

The Penguin. After twenty years of Mostly Microsoft, it's about time I learned to administer Unix. The penguin says he has the answer. Even the Astroturfers at ZD point to the Penguin and say "See! We don't got no monopoly!" (which is a lie, as

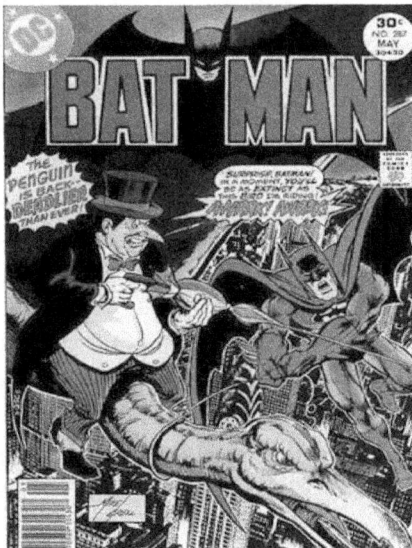

you will see).

Since I'm not wanting to trash my file server/game machine, and no way in *hell* would I do much to my wife's that she doesn't ask me to (it's an old 120), I ripped into my daughter Patty's old 486, with her blessing. She never uses it anyway; no network or internet support, really little hard drive, all the games that run on it are ancient...

My first attempt (last fall) was Corel. We're using Word Perfect, since wife Becky's school had standardized on it (but Microsoft has since bribed it into switching to Word) so it was a good first choice. I downloaded the entire ISO over a dialup modem! Took two weeks...

It didn't recognize the CD (I think?). It hung up on the first screen after rebooting into its "rescue floppy". I gave up for a while.

A little research and a DSL line later and I decided to try Red Hat, which everybody on the net seemed to think was best. It, too, couldn't read the CD; or at least, that's my *theory* (or "guess"). It hung at the boot floppy's splash screen, too.

I laid it down again until a couple of weeks ago, when I came across an old hard drive laying on a shelf in the basement, an old 170 mb Western Digital that came out of an antique IBM (I think).

The game rig was open, as I had just replaced a bad fan and burned up CPU chip. It was only a matter of moving the drives' jumper, plugging it in, and telling the computer's cmos to find it, then install Linux.

Mandrake, the internet reported, was the easiest to install.

Not on a 170 meg drive it isn't! In fact, just like Corel and Red Hat, it will NOT install on this hard drive that happily ran Windows 95.

But the Linux geeks are always talking about how bloated Windows is and how you can install Linux on a single floppy! I guess Microsoft guys aren't the only ones in Jon's "Pathological Liar's Club."

So I tried Coyote Linux. It does, as advertised, boot from a single floppy.

It also does absolutely nothing but turn your computer into a router/firewall! Actually, with an old box and a few spare network interface cards you could probably save a few bucks with this. But it wasn't what I was looking for.

Next up was Tiny Linux, which is a project to get a usable Linux on a single floppy. It, too, works – kinda sorta. I can log in and list its files, but not a whole lot else. I'm chalking that up to my ignorance of and inexperience with Unix. But so far, no luck at actually getting Linux to run on a 170 mb drive.

So wanting to migrate away from Microsoft, I look for something that will help me learn Linux without re-partitioning my hard drive. I found it!

Phat Linux runs from a DOS/Windows directory kind of like Windows uses a file as a drive for its compression.

It takes up a CD sized chunk of your hard drive, and helped teach me the basics of logging in, changing passwords, adding users, trying out various graphic desktops, etc.

However, it isn't 100% compatible with the other "Linuxes". For example, the "man" command isn't on the path, and the manual entries are sketchy at best. Other commands seem to work differently than what all the docs I've read say, and some seem to be missing. It might just be my own ignorance.

In fact, that's the most infuriating thing I've found about Linux: the people who built it are *really bad* at communicating in English.

I bought a 1000 page book on Linux, about fifty pages of which are actually useful. The rest either attempts to teach me stuff I already know, or assumes I know something I would have had to already be running *nix to know!

I've found better information on the internet; but that, too, is greatly lacking, even the best of it.

For example, now that I had Phat loaded, I should be

able to plug that 170 mg drive in, reboot, and go Linux Quaking on it.

Nope. It was infuriating; during its boot sequence you could see that hdb was mounting, and if you tell it "ls /dev/hdb" (ls=dir, or list files) it returns "hdb," but if I try to md or cp (make a directory or copy a file) it tells me it can't find the device!

I'm thinking... I don't really understand this thing's file structure. More research...

I run across something that tells me that Debian is the most customizable, and you can get it on a smaller drive. Of course, these days a "smaller" drive is about as big as my biggest. But I download the ISO anyway, and am able to successfully load Linux on that 170 mb hard drive!

Of course, I haven't yet figured out how to actually do anything useful with it.

When they say Linux isn't "ready for prime time," believe it. I'll eventually get it running usefully, and I have little doubt I'll be able to eventually replace Windows with it, but there's no way in hell your Grandma is going to get it installed and running – unless your granny's last name is Torvalds.

There will be more posts on this subject, stay tuned...
1/21/2002

In #3, I have no idea if Linux had wi-fi or bluetooth then, but I put kubuntu on a laptop several years ago. The wi-fi was built-in in Linux and "just worked", but you need an install CD from your ISP to connect with Windows. Likewise, I bought a bluetooth dongle, which required a CD installation and reboot in Windows, but with Linux all I had to do was plug the dongle in.

In #7, Note that Linux had not only had this this feature first, but you could run two monitors with two cards. I discovered Mandrake, and Linux was easy after that.
11/14/2014

Car's OS was fragged by Bug's Bunny

"Hey, you got a new car! Pretty nice! I see you're sticking with the same manufacturer."

"Well, I liked the old one. I've always been happy with Microcar's autos."

"Your old one was only two years old, if you liked it why did you buy a new one?"

"The manufacturer said I should upgrade. Besides, this new model has a cassette instead of an eight track. Wish it would play the other four tracks though..."

"Why didn't you just buy a new radio?"

"The manufacturer welds them in, and wires them so the car won't start if you take it out. Besides, the radio wasn't the only reason to upgrade."

"What else?"

"Ralph Nader says the old one crashes too often, but you know *that* nut. I've only had that old one one crash six times, and I was never in the hospital too long. But Microcar says this model is much more stable and hardly ever crashes. It's supposed to be more secure, too."

"Why did it keep crashing?"

"Dunno, something about the spark plugs interacting with the steering system, I'm no mechanic. My mechanic tried to explain it to me but these mechanical things are just too *complicated*. He says if I'd defrag my pistons more often it wouldn't crash, you get much more stability with a fresh tuneup. But I just said 'the hell with it' and traded it in.

"In fact, I'm taking it in to the shop right now."

"But it's a band new car, it needs a tuneup?"

"No, there's a 'feature' that keeps the door lock from working if you drive it more than six miles. I'm going to get the patch kit."

"I thought you weren't mechanical?"

"Well, they say this one's an easy fix and I can't afford another repair bill."

"Won't they fix it under warrantee?"

"What warrantee? This is a *car!* The EULA says they bear no responsibility for *anything.* I just hope I don't get in trouble with the law applying this patch."

"Huh?"

"Yeah, they weld the hood shut, and under the DMCA, opening the hood of your car is a felony if it's welded shut. You can go to prison if you get caught, even if they are tacky little welds that come apart by themselves."

"Boy, cars sure are weird. I'm glad my computer isn't like that, I'd never get any work done!"

1/25/2002

Hard drive from hell died

I was home sick last Friday, and when my wife came home from school she had a new hard drive she picked up at Circuit City, a 40gb Maxtor.

I couldn't get the damned thing to work!

My old 400mz machine still plays all the new games, and with a little more memory would play them in XP (assuming I wanted to throw away another hundred dollars on a new OS I don't need). Plus, Becky's laptop is the first whole computer I've bought since I purchased a used IBM XT in 1987; I've built from spare parts since.

I didn't know that older (in this case "older" means about three years) BIOSes couldn't handle drive sizes larger than 30gb. I had run across the same problem years ago while trying to install a huge (for the time) half gigabyte drive in a 386; then, the limit was 512mb. The Seagate I had bought then had come with software to overcome the limitation, and it had worked flawlessly.

I can't say the same about the new Maxtor!

I fought with that thing all weekend; its workarounds wouldn't work around. This on top of a defective installation floppy!

It made Windows freeze at the desktop; then after a Windows reinstall, it was still hosed. Nowhere in the printed documentation was it mentioned, but I finally found a work-around deep inside one of the installation/test programs that involved lying to the BIOS.

Bingo! It booted into Windows with no problem!

But the drive wouldn't work. So I rebooted into DOS and did a high level format; the software was supposed to have done it but didn't.

It booted into Windows and the drive worked!

I rebooted; it still worked. I copied a half dozen gigabytes of data from the laptop to the new hard drive in the old PC, which it read with no problem. I rebooted again.

All the data were garbage (and all your base are belong to us).

I wrote over the garbaged-up data several times and low level formatted the drive one last time, then boxed it up for Becky to return. The new 30gb Western Digital is supposed to get here from JDR Monday afternoon.

In other broken PC news, Rob Lemos (the Linux guy) writes in ZD News of the "Organization for Internet Safety." This new outfit is supposed to keep your PC secure.

Microsoft is at the helm. This, of course, means that your data will *not* be secure. When Microsoft talks "security", they are talking about Microsoft's security, not yours. They don't give a rat's ass about your security, they care about the security forty billion dollars brings and they're not going to let security holes in their software screw that up for them.

Lemos reports "The group springs from discussions between Microsoft and a handful of security companies on the responsible reporting of software bugs, known as vulner-abilities, that affect a business' security."

To *hell* with *business* security; let Microsoft and Sun worry about their own bottom lines. I don't want to wait for a damned patch to some buggy program some incompetent "programmer" hacked out, I want to know about it *now,* so I can take the offending piece of crap offline until a patch or workaround has been sorted out. The way I look at it, there is a

50% chance a good guy will find a hole first (assuming there are as many good guys as bad guys, which is doubtful). That means half the time the bad guys have found the hole first.

Meaning that the bad guys have a way into my machine while the good guys are working on a patch, and only I am kept in the dark.

People, this is not the way it should be done. If you find a hole, tell the software house about it and then scream it from the rooftops. Very Loudly and with venom. Let the world know how absolutely shitty a company has to be to allow their customers to be compromised like that, and let ME know that there is a hole in (say) Opera, so I can switch to IE; or if there is a hole in IIS so I can switch to Apache (wait a minute, IIS *IS* a hole).

If it turns out that I like the "alternate" piece of software or hardware better than the original vendor's, then, well, tough shit! Microsoft security is meaningless to me. I'm worried about *MY* security. And if I unplug the thing, the only way you can hack it is like the Feds do: with a battering ram.

The guidelines this group is hacking out should spell out clearly that a vendor, when notified of a hole, should immediately tell all of its customers about that hole, and recommend that they shut off the offending service, software, or hardware.

Don't hold your breath.

2/23/2002

Hard drive from hell Part II

The new Western Digital came Monday. There was no documentation, no installation floppy, no cable.

Now, I've been buying computer parts for a *long time;* the first hard drive I bought quadrupled my IBM XT's drive to a massive 40 megabytes, a thousand times smaller than the latest upgrade bought. Of all the hard drives I've purchased (mostly Seagate), not a single one was without a floppy with diagnostic and/or installation software, documentation, or a cable.

Until now.

I wasn't happy. I logged onto WD's web site. After fifteen minutes of fruitlessly searching for some kind of documentation, I gave up and called their tech support, an 800 number. I still hadn't taken the drive out of its anti-static bag. I had thoughts of shipping it back.

WD answered their phone pretty quickly, and I was on the line with a helpful, courteous fellow that seemed to know what he was talking about. WD, it seems, ships drives to OEMs without docs, floppies, or cables; the ones you buy at Circuit City are boxed up pretty, with the goodies all inside.

He agreed that their web site's navigation was a mess, but knew the URL to the BIOS setup info, but said I probably wouldn't need it. He gave me some tips, including an undocumented jumper trick in case the PC locked up because of a higher capacity than the BIOS supports.

I could have saved my dime; the drive went right in with no problem. FDISK and FORMAT and it was done.

I understand that with XP you don't even have to do that, XP does it for you. Not that that would be worth a hundred dollar purchase.

SO, I was all set to pen a rant about Western Digital, but no rant is needed. I'd recommend them.

I would urge them, though, to redesign that web site.

3/1/2002

Fair use was squished

Reuters and the rest of the mainstream news media would like for you to believe that they are impartial and unbiased.

They're not. Nobody is. Not even me. But you knew that, right?

Reuters posted a "news" story (at least I don't call my opinion pieces "news" for God's sake, it's *nooze,* dammit!) quoting a movie industry flak as saying "Our content must be protected from unencrypted, illegal file sharing... We're in the process of raising a generation to think that stealing is okay." Nowhere in the story was there any semblance of balance. Nowhere in the story was there the tiniest hint that maybe this guy's *opinion* was the utter bullshit it is. Nowhere was the existence of an opposing opinion mentioned at all!

I don't believe the industry believes its own lies. The RIAA certainly must be aware of the organized boycott against its wares, but it deliberately avoids mention of said boycott when it says patently stupid things like "the current downturn in record buying is Napster's fault." Of course, sales soared during Napster and plummeted with Napster's demise and the onslaught of the boycott against mainstream CDs (Keep buying those indie CDs), but reading Reuters or the RIAA's own (unlinksd here) site you would think we were still in a good economy and that there was no boycott.

Millions of people will see the Reuters article with its disingenuous opinion presented as fact. Only dozens will see this piece. Okay, maybe thousands if you count people who will see it after it's archived, but that's still a tiny drop compared to Reuters' ocean.

The fact is that a generation is being raised to incorrectly believe that sound waves can be owned, that bits can be controlled, that capturing numbers that flow through your own computer in your own home is somehow "stealing".

The law in my state says if unordered merchandise is put in your mailbox, it's yours. As long as the supplier can produce no signed order form, you are not stealing, he is giving you a gift.

"But," the flak would likely retort, "the person who sent you those bits, those numbers, those sound waves, did not *own* those bits."

Why not? They bought many of them at Sam Goodie's or WalMart. Others were given to *them*. Nearly every single song or movie on Bearshare or Kazaa was bought and paid for by the first person to open its folder to the world.

Furthermore, the pieces that were not opened to the public by someone who bought a copy were put there by the original artist. Only the established (many talentless but still filthy rich) musicians don't want their tunes traded – because If I've never heard the song, there is absolutely NO way to sell me the CD. And for all but the elite few let past the RIAA gatekeepers, nobody gets on the radio.

No, stealing is stealing. If I steal your car, you have no car. If I steal your CD, you no longer have that CD. You may be able to play the CD's music, even at CD quality if you ripped it to wav, but you can't play the CD, or enjoy its cover art or liner notes. It's GONE, unlike swapped, "stolen" music.

It pretty much pisses me off when a thief and con artist like ANYBODY in the music or movie industries rails against the "theft" of something that was never stolen in the first place!

In the end, by calling file sharing "theft" these amoral people who would guard our nation's moral fabric are confusing young people about what is and what isn't theft, so in fact are themselves helping raise a generation of thieves who won't stop at taking the bits, but the plastic the bits are stored on as well.

Theft deprives someone of property. We should expect our news organizations to understand the meaning of a five letter single syllable word, but nobody ever accused any journalost of having an excess of neurons.
3/3/2002

The linuX files part II (or is it 3?)

Yes, the newest game I've been playing lately is Linux.

So far I have it fully installed (kinda) and running (mostly, I think).

Linux is most definitely NOT "harder than Windows". There seems to be a bit of nonsense regurgitated by people who haven't even tried Linux.

One is that it's more like DOS than Windows, and you

have to use a command line and memorize a bunch of arcane commands.

Nope, I haven't seen a Linux command line since I installed Mandrake 8.1. I could if I wanted to, but so far there's been no need.

I discovered a "Mandrake Control Center" (actually, it was an icon on the desktop) that configured my DSL pretty much automatically. Windows won't do that; you have to run SBC's program to make DSL work in Windows.

When I said "kinda sorta" working, I mean I haven't got the local network working. But that's more Windows fault than Linux.

It's set up to use DHCP, which is a dynamically configured host (which, in fact, is what the acronym for this protocol, "DHCP", stands for). The Windows network is set up with a static IP address for each machine, and I don't want to have to reconfigure every machine on the network whenever I want to switch from Windows to Linux or back on the DSL computer.

So far, there have been no nasty surprises; I imagine I'll need Samba or something to get the networking right.

CRAP, as soon as I said that the cursor jumped to yesterday's topic on this XP laptop. Plenty of nasty surprises in Windows.

There are a lot of things I've discovered about Linux that have no Windows counterpart.

I have an on-board video chip, which I superseded with a TNT card. When installing, it asked me if I wanted to choose one, or just use *both*. You can't do that in Windows!

When I first bought Windows 95 I set it up to not use a password; it wasn't connected to any other machine. When I got WWWed, I had to enter a password again. With Windows you have to password in. Linux figures it's possible this isn't a corporate machine, and lets me configure it to enter the password for me (and without need for a command line) so not only do I not have to remember a password, I can use a super strong one I could never remember If I were forced to! I can plug in the PC, pour a cup of coffee, and have Netscape or Konquerer (or any of half a dozen other browsers installed by default) open Spew or Sgt Hulka's for me without as much as touching the mouse, let alone the keyboard!

When it boots, it checks the atomic clock at a university and sets my PC's clock to within a millisecond. The other two computers are always off by a minute or two, as you have to log in to the atom clock manually with them, so they only get set twice a year.

But perhaps the nicest thing is I don't have to reboot to make a change take effect.

One down side to Linux I've found is – it's a damned good thing you don't have to reboot. It takes *forever* to get to its desktop.

One more thing – no damned registry! WooHoo!!!

3/24/2002

Note: modern versions of Linux boot as fast as it takes Windows 7 to come out of hibernation.

Oct 24, 2014

Holy crap I was fragged by weird hit counter company

I went to IC Direct.com's banner infested "free" counter site the other day to see how traffic was. As has been the case for a few months, I was greeted with a javascript error. Hitting "refresh" after the error screen brings me to the stats.

Now, like I said, this is a free service, so I don't expect the best from them. It's not like I get *paid* for hits, so an advertising-supported "free" service, even if imperfect, works for me. It's not like they sold me a five hundred dollar operating system...

Anyway, this time instead of serving stats it feeds me a page that says I need to copy and install its new code. Only three lines as opposed to the very large block it had before, great! So I replaced the code.

Tonight I sat down to fix the archives, which have been broken for a while. I've been not only meaning to fix them, but

215

was planning to highlight them this month, as April is the Fragfest's 4th birthday. I just didn't get around to it... er, I haven't been posting much either, have I?

When I pulled up the Fragfest I was horrified to see a damned cheesy little stinking banner at the very top of the page, even before my own logo! Egad!

SO, I moved the 3 new lines down to the bottom of the page and checked it.

The weather went from cold to hot, so I'm down in the basement doing this for the first time in a few months. I open Netscape to finally check those stats, only to find that ICDirect stopped working with Netscape entirely.

I think I'll look for a new counter. At any rate, I apologize for the cheese (if anybody's still there...)
4/17/2002

Alice joined the game

About 20 years ago, frustrated that otherwise serious researchers and scientists seemingly thought they could program a computer to think, (without, of course, understanding what "thought" actually is; nobody knows that) I wrote a simulation that appears to think, in order to completely debunk the fools and those fooling them who think computers can think.

I wrote Artificial Insanity in less than 20K (that's Kilo, not mega) bytes; smaller than modern viruses, that ran on the Timex TS-1000 tape driven computer. I later ported it to a Radio Shack computer, then an Apple IIe, and finally ported it to MS-DOS.

The DOS version's source code is still under 20k (I didn't change the algorithm, only the syntax for the different programming language) although compiled into an .exe it takes about 400k, still tiny by today's standards, as far as simulation software and games go.

As I mentioned, I did it in response to "Elijah" and all the other similar programs that attempt to fool you into thinking they can think. As far as I know, mine is the only one that is NOT claimed to actually posses intelligence. None really ARE intelligent, I'm just the only one not making the claim. Debunking the claim was my reason for writing it.

Another thing different about Art from all the other intelligence simulations is that I wanted it to be fun, yet annoying. Kind of like playing Quake on a 28.8 against a bunch of LPBs. So I made it a smartass.

Also, for example, I added little things like a routine that occasionally runs that, instead of answering the questioner, asks if he or she wants to play a game. Of course, most folks consider Art a game anyway (although like the Sims, you can't win or lose). Any negative response to "Do you want to play a game" loops back to "Do you want to play a game?" When the hapless player finally gives up and answers "yes" in exasperation, Art answers "you lose".

Art cost a friend of mine a keyboard. A friend of his literally destroyed it playing with Art, typing as hard as he could.

I ran across yet another program that claims to think like a human the other day.

The "Alice Bot" is basically your typical Elijah-like program: BORING. As boring as small talk with the dumbest, most boring person you know. Alice is a lady. If she was a whore she might be fun, but I digress.

I wondered what would happen if Art had a conversation with Alice. Alice has a web based presence, so I didn't even have to install it.

I was expecting Alice to choke. I expected Art to kick Alice's ass.

I fired up Art and logged in to Alice (you dirty minded...)

Here is the transcript. Art's responses are in bold, Alice's are in italics. Alice starts: "What is your name?" I should have asked Art, but I answered this first question for him, and type in

Art.

Alice replies:

I like art very much too, especially the contemporary stuff.
Are you for real?
Yes I am real AI
Whatever gave you that idea?
My brain uses AIML to format responses to your inputs, but I don't have one for that.
Look, I'm good, but I'm not a Cray
Good in what sense? That is interesting: unknown said he m not a cray. [sic]

Art doesn't require you to hit "enter". It takes a period, question mark, etc as the end of the sentence and answers, so here it stops at the question mark. All that is input is "Good in what sense?"

A piece of junk
Are you talking about an animal, vegetable or mineral?
Can you put that another way?
Let me think. OK I will put it there.

Heh heh she said...

The situation calls for more scrutiny.
Tell me more.
What do you think?
I think a lot of things.
Obviously.
What makes it so obvious?
Looks Greek to me.
Really. it is?
Look, I'm good, but I'm not a Cray.
Good in what sense? Do you mind if I tell other people: unknown said he m not a cray. [sic]

(Entered second question into Art)

WOW!
I'm glad your [sic] impressed, unknown.
Uh,
Er. Um.
This is what you human types call a joke, right?

At this point, Alice froze for two full minutes.

218

You don't say.
Right on!
Yeah.
Your guess is as good as mine.
Some people say ""your guess is as good as mine".
Maybe.
I understand.
How should I know?
Either from your senses or from pure reason.
I don't think so.
Why do you disagree?
That's why.
Thanks for explaining it.
How simple can it get?
What is it to you.
I don't know but it's ugly.
What makes it so ugly?

        This time Art pauses...

Nothing.
Not a thing?
Never mind that, I think I'm in love!
Oh well thanks for trying to explain it to me anyway. That is "Not a thing?" Since when? Tell me about the object of your affection.

        Okay, one question at a time, lady. "Since when?" was typed in.

The best time possible for the occurrence of the action.
Tell me about the object of your affection.
UHH....!
Er. Um.
Always
Not that often.
It really doesn't make any difference.
What doesn't make any difference?
Real
Totally real.
I think so.

I think so too.

At this point I hit the big red switch in horror...

6/11/2002

The transcript of the two AI's is, in fact, real, silly as it is.

11/27/2014

Microsoft: All your base are belong to us
Microsoft should have used a smaller gun

Remember Intel's ill fated identification feature that would rip all your privacy away?

Well, this time it's Microsoft's turn to try and ram this down our throats, with willing partner AMD and with Intel grudgingly coming along for the ride (they remember the beating they took with their similar ploy).

ZD Net says "On Monday, Microsoft took the wraps off its project, code-named Palladium, to design new hardware and software that could better guarantee the security of user data and let companies control data that they 'own' while on a consumer's PC."

Nobody but ME owns ANYTHING on my computer. WTF are these morons blathering about?

This scheme, lyingly called "trustworthy computing" is in reality a "digital rights management" operating system that puts Microsoft, Sony, and Time-Warner in control of the computer *you* will be paying for.

I say "you" because I, for one, will have nothing to do with any machine with this crap loaded.

Microsoft is touting this as "security". As I've said before, Microsoft doesn't give a rat's ass about YOUR security. They are concerned with *Microsoft's* security, which depends on incredibly huge revenues.

This is MS Passport in hardware.

Most of the mainstream sites swallowed Microsoft's story and reported it as being about YOUR security, of making YOUR computer into a "lock box" where vandals and thieves couldn't reach. Of this, Bruce Schneier, author of *Secrets & Lies, Digital Security in a Networked World* is quoted by Wired as

220

saying "The odds are actually zero this will be secure."

The name "Palladium" comes from the statue of Pallas Athena, protector of the ancient city of Troy, according to legend. Also according to legend it was destroyed by invaders. *Also* according to legend, Troy was home of the inventors of the "Trojan horse", which makes "Palladium" a fitting name, indeed, since it will put outside interests in control of YOUR computer!

Thankfully, Linux has become every bit as easy as Windows at everything except connecting to computers running windows, and at (very unfortunately for us gamers) playing games.

I hope they get Wine polished before MS's "trust-worthy" Paladium DRM OS comes out!

6/22/2002

I pledge allegiance to the flag of the United States of America

and to the republic for which it stands; one nation, under God, indivisible, with liberty and justice for all.

I pledge this allegiance of my own free will.

I am offended as an American that anyone would force another to make this pledge under duress. I am doubly offended that a *child* should be forced to take this pledge under duress.

It is un-American to make a person state that which he or she does not believe. And if these sacred words are just parroted, with no love for country, just mumbled because one is forced to, it cheapens them when I make the pledge.

This offends me deeply.

I was originally going to post this (well, a very similar post) on July 4, and in defense of the court's opinion that putting "under God" in the Pledge violated the Church and State separation. My thinking was that being forced to pledge an oath to a nation "under God" when one believed in no God, or many gods, cheapened *my* expression of love for both God and country. But I got to thinking more about it.

The Declaration of independence mentions God. The Constitution mentions God. So just what do they mean by "God?"

God is the creator.

If you are Christian, Muslim, or Hebrew, you have no problem with this.

If you are an atheist, then you believe that the universe is a big accident, created by random chance. In this case, random chance is what is meant by "God". Personally, I think that is the most foolishly unbelievable thing anyone could say, that all this around you, including your very consciousness, "jest growed". But if that is what you believe, than the accident that created the world is God, at least as the Constitution and Declaration put it.

If you are Buddhist, Hindu, or another pagan religion, how does your religion say the universe was created? Well, *that* is what is meant by "God".

Simply put, God is the creator. Whatever or whoever caused the universe to exist is, for the purposes of the constitution, "God".

So I've changed my mind. The appeals court was wrong. Let's hope the Supreme Court will rule against them.

But *please* stop forcing people to pledge their allegiance to my flag. I love my flag, my country, my constitution, and I don't want them cheapened like that.

7/8/2002

Brain waves was squished

The Mainichi Daily News reports that "Prolonged time playing video games could cause people to lose concentration, get angry easily and have trouble associating with others, a Japanese professor's research has suggested."

Damn, this really makes me mad! I'm *pissed!* This is, uh, er, um....

Where's my gun? I'm so mad I forgot what I was going

to say...

Einstein can't escape Apple's grenade

Apple has introduced a computer that their advertising says "runs faster than light". Do "edit-> search" for "faster-than-light" on the linked Apple page, which I ought to cache since... well, they have this new fast processor...

So I ordered one just to see how it worked.

It arrived two weeks before ordering it, so I didn't order it and got my shiny new Power Mac with its faster than light processor for free!

I discovered some other weird effects using this processor. For one thing, it weighs a LOT when you turn it on, so much that it dented the table and bent the legs. Yes, Einstein was right about speed affecting gravity.

So I decided to do a little experiment. I cut the power cord (the computer bounced a full six inches when I shut it off) and reversed the power's polarity. Being household A/C that shouldn't have had an effect, but it did. When I turned it back on, it flew upwards until it ran out of cord, and when it yanked its plug from the wall it of course came crashing down.

So I took it out to my van and plugged it into the cigarette lighter. Viola, flying car! This was great!

And it's a *fast* flying car, too. It handles like a flying pig when I'm flying, though, as you can only steer it by moving the front wheels with the steering wheel, and the wind drag helps steer.

Of course, once I left the atmosphere I was screwed. No air, no steering. Darn it! Darn it to *heck* (sorry, I already used this month's allotment of swear words discussing politics).

I discovered that I could steer with the gas pedal, with the slight variation in voltage caused by the imperfections in the car's alternator affecting the voltage supplied to the Mac, and thereby affecting its gravity.

I, uh, got it going TOO fast. Not only was the computer itself traveling faster than light, the car was getting dangerously close to it.

As I crossed the lightspeed barrier I saw Yello and ten thousand alternate Siscos. Yello asked about granny and promptly vanished in a puff of green smoke. Curious.

But past the lightspeed limit, the universe seemed to shrink to a pinpoint, which was angrily chasing me. Which was a very silly thing for it to do, as I wanted to get back inside it. It was kind of like my wife when she's mad at me.

That thought kind of unnerved me, so I freaked and pulled the key out of the ignition.

I found myself holding the phone getting ready to place an order for a Mac.

WTF was I thinking? I can't afford one of these! I put the phone down.

Thank God for Einstein. I'd be paying for that damned computer until Hell froze over.

At least I got my month's allotment of swear words back. Oh, uh, if you notice some strange things going on with your clock, I guess that's my fault...

8/15/2002

Stupid Strogg Jokes

How many Stroggs does it take to screw in a light bulb?
Stroggs are too big to fit inside a light bulb

Why did the Strogg quit smoking?
The Marine ran out of grenades

Why did the Strogg cross the road?
Stroggs cross everybody, especially if they have a stupid Quake name like "Road"

How can you tell if a Strogg has been at your computer?
It says "Intel Inside"

How many Stroggs does it take to wallpaper a room?
It depends on how thin you slice 'em

A space marine walks into a bar with his pet shambler on a leash. "Do you serve those slimy damned stinkin' Stroggs in here?" he asks the bartender. The bartender replies, "Yes, sir, we don't discriminate, we serve anyone."

"Good", replies the marine, "I'll have a beer, and my shambler will have a couple of Stroggs."

How is a crakhor like a computer?
You can't really appreciate it until it goes down on you

You know you're wearing the wrong skin when
-You're wearing the Southpark "Chef" skin or the PC Gamer "Coconut Monkey" skin and your clan is playing against the Cool Cocks clan

-You're wearing the "nudechick" skin and your clan is playing the PMS clan

-You're wearing the "cow" skin and your clan is playing against the (0W601z

-You're wearing any female skin (esp. crakhor or nudechick) and your clan is playing against the Drunken Old Bastards Clan

-You're wearing a Homer Simpson or a Kenny skin (Doh!)

-You're wearing the "Waldo" skin and you're not a camper (there could be certain tactical advantages to wearing these skins under these circumstances...;)

- everybody else says "hehe" whenever they frag you

You know you need a new computer when
- you see the phone cord icon while playing single player
- you shoot at a Strogg and real smoke comes out of the PC
- Flamethrower grabs a fire extinguisher whenever you visit his site
- your voodoo card starts making dolls
- the quake guy scratches at your screen screaming "Let me out! Let me out!"
- you see a 5 ¼ inch floppy sticking out of Tokay's Tower
- it says "Intel Inside"
- it doesn't say "Intel Inside"
- you get it unwrapped and plugged in

Campers
Where have all the campers gone?
Lag time passing
Where have all the campers gone,
Long time ago?

Where have all the campers gone?
Blown to fragments, every one!
When will they ever learn?
When will they ever learn?

Video Games You Can Play At The Office
...in fact, are required to

Word Processor
The object of this game is to fit a three page document on a 1.4 meg floppy. The deluxe version is loaded on a network file server with the bonus "try to type slower than the screen" game.

Spreadsheet
Try to print and perform rudimentary calculations before the next completely changed version comes out and leaves you ignorant again

Microsoft Access
Harder than playing Quake on a modem against Thresh on a T1. The object is to learn a complex programming language called "visual basic" with no manuals and only one day's training, which does not even mention "visual basic"

E-mail
Try to send a message across town and have it get there before the post office could deliver it

Windows
Many games within a game, including "what are all these buttons", "Where's the stupid start menu hiding", and "If I'm not supposed to touch this control panel thingie why is it here." Also included: the "Hey! My screen's blue" game

Thresh's Quake Bible leaves out one important chapter: Genesis (because Sega sucks)

so here it is:

In the beginning was Pong. And it was a void, without substance and without form. And it sucked.

And on the first day IdApogee said, "Let there be fun". And IdApogee created Commander Keen. And he saw that it was pretty good, at least for the technology of the time. And he gave it away as shareware.

And On the second day IdApogee created the Duke, and the Duke said, "Damn, I'm good".

And the Duke and the commander saw that they were ega, and killed the energizer bunny. And IdApogee said, "Why has thou killed the bunny?"

And Duke said "Come get some."

And Keen said "But we were naked, and had no 3D."

So Id banished the Duke to the store shelves, without 3D.

And Duke and Keen begat two sons, Wolfenstein and Doom. And Doom slew Wolfenstein, and Wolfenstein's blood seeped through the prison floors and was drunk by the earth.

And a mark was placed on Doom's head, and Id said, "let no man slay the Doom; ye shall know the Doom by the mark on his head. And ye shall know the mark by its name, and its name is Doom.

And Doom begat Quake, and civilization as we know it came to

THE END

Interview - Major Futcup

As we all know, the attack on Stroggos, recreated in the video game Quake II, was led by one of the US Marines' finest, Major William Futcup. We ask the Major for his views of the assault on Stroggos.

Fragfest: Major Futcup, what was...

Futcup: Call me Willie, please. I've been off duty for five minutes.

Fragfest: Okay, Willie. What was going through your mind as the men departed the ship for the planet's surface?

Futcup: Actually, I was thinking about what a great video game this would make.

Fragfest: Huh?

Futcup: Sure, they did it with Vietnam, why not Stroggos?

Fragfest: Were you worried?

Futcup: Of course not, I stayed behind in the command ship.

Fragfest: You weren't worried about the men?

Futcup: Well, I was a little worried before they left for Stroggos, but hey – they can't shoot me from Stroggos.

Fragfest: Did you have any idea that the landing would go so badly?

Futcup: What do you mean? We won!

Fragfest: But your casualty figures, man! You only had one survivor.

Futcup: Hah! These are space Marines, sir. They can take a little dying. There wasn't one of my men that wouldn't gladly give up their lives for their planet!

Fragfest: I heard audio recordings of the landing itself, desperate cries of "shit!" and "sonofabitch", screams of fear and agony!

Futcup: What do you expect? These are 18 and 19 year

old draftees!

Fragfest: But you said...

Futcup: I said there wasn't one of my men that I wouldn't gladly give up for my planet. And contrary to popular belief, there were more survivors than that.

Fragfest: You sound like a politician.

Futcup: As a matter of fact I'm running for Senator when I retire.

Fragfest: Who was the ranking officer?

Futcup: I was, here. General Dizats stayed on the supply convoy at the edge of the system.

Fragfest: Who?

Futcup: General Dizats, sir. Four star. One of the joint chiefs.

Fragfest: You mean he worked directly under the President?

Futcup: No, that was one of his interns. General Dizats worked for the NSA, ran some sort of operation called "AirStroggos". I still haven't figured out why they call him a "Joint Chief".

Fragfest: I understand the one surviving Marine will get the Congressional Medal of Honor.

Futcup: If I have anything to say about it, and believe me, I do, He's getting a court martial.

Fragfest: Court martial?

Futcup: Attempted murder of a superior officer. Excuse me, I need to use the latrine.

As he hurriedly left (he must have had a VERY weak bowel), a no-stripe marine ran in carrying a BFG.

Marine: Where is that [expletive] little Lilly livered sonofabitch woossie? I'm gonna tear that bastard's head off and shove it farther up his ass than it already is!

Fragfest: Who?

Marine: That [expletive] Futcup. "No survivors", my ass, I'll show him "no survivors".

Fragfest: He said he was going to use the restroom.

Marine: Thanks. He shows up, tell him I'm gonna feed him to a shambler.

We've been waiting for the Major to return from the latrine for quite a while, so we'll go ahead and post this. We'll finish the interview later, when he gets back.
1998

Major Futcup's true, until now untold story:
I actually invented Major Futcup in 1975 when I was in the USAF and stationed at Beale in its motor pool. Since the base hospital had me on some arthritis medication you're not supposed to drive on, work was really boring, since once everything was as clean as a hospital operating room before the surgery starts there was nothing at all to do.

I liked to draw and paint back then, and in fact earned beer money selling paintings to my fellow airmen. My unit commander, a lieutenant, had seen me draw.

One day he and the base commander, a bird colonel, came in and asked if I would make an anti-drunk driving poster for some shindig they were throwing at the Officers' Club. Of course I said "Of course!" Finally something worthwhile to do.

They came back the next day when I had it finished. The poster was of a disheveled Major wearing a wrinkled, dirty uniform, holding a large bottle and leaning on a lamp post with a car wrapped around it. The major's name tag read "Futcup". The caption was "Don't be this guy!"

The lieutenant got pale, his eyes wide in terror and the poor guy looked like he was going to faint, obviously fearing terrible trouble.

The colonel doubled up in laughter, laughing for a full five minutes before he could say "That's going up in my office! But you're going to have to make a different one for the party."

The lieutenant smiled weakly and wiped his brow.
Oct 24, 2014

Interview - Joe Mama

We were going to interview John Romero and ask him how it feels to have been shot and killed, but we thought it would be more appropriate to get him to come to the Halloween party to answer that.

So instead, we decided to interview the famous Joseph Moma, who the Chicago Museum of Modern Art was named after. Joe is webmaster for the only Quake page with more visitors than Planet Quake and Blue's News combined. The page, of course, needs no introduction, as you probably visit it several times a day.

Even though it needs no introduction, we're going to introduce it anyway, just to piss people off. The page, of course, is *That Quake Page on Geochities with the popup ads.*

Fragfest: Hi, Joe. First, people are wondering where you came up with that ingenious name for your page, it's quite impressive and original.

Joe Moma: Ah dunno, it jest kinda [expletive] popped up, if ya know what I [expletive] mean.

Fragfest: I understand you turned down interviews with both Blue's and Planet Quake. What made you consent to an interview with us?

Joe: [expletive] those guys are [expletive] lamers, ya know? I mean real loozers. I mean, yeah, I got a ad, but they make *money* off theirs, ya know? I mean, can ya believe that shit, dude? Besides, You said you'd buy me a beer. Where's that bartender?

Fragfest: Hey, bartender, can we get a Busch down here?

Joe: BUSH?? I ain't drinkin' that shit! Gimme a [expletive] ol milwakee!

Fragfest: We were impressed that you had Quake 3 screen shots three weeks before Planet Quake did. Did you get them from Id or PC Gamer?

Joe: I [expletive] stole 'em, dude! Waddya think, ya [expletive] llama!

Fragfest: Uh, okay. We were also interested in your site design, the dark green type on the brown background is, uh,

Joe: really [expletive] far [expletive] out cool, huh? Ever seen it trippin' on acid, man? Wow! Like, the green turns blue and purple and the brown gets all firey and waves around and the [expletive] monitor [expletive] FLOATS, man! Hey, you got a joint?

Fragfest: Uh, no, I'm a beer man, myself.

Joe: Nah, that shit you're drinkin' ain't beer, that's CRAPwater. Ol milwakkee is the only beer there is, man, but it's a lot better if ya got a joint to go with it. Wanna do a couple a lines, man?

Fragfest: Huh?

Joe: What?

Fragfest: Uh, let's talk about your visitors.

Joe: No, man, that's [expletive] bullshit, man, I ain't never [expletive] TOUCHED that bitch, man, she ain't NEVER been to my house, [expletive] head, ya hear me?

Fragfest: No, I mean your "hits"

Joe: Na, man, that's not me, that's my cousin, I never popped nobody.

Fragfest: No, no, I mean visitors to your web page.

Joe: My what, dude?

Fragfest: Your Quake page.

Joe: Yeah, that's far [expletive] out, ain't it? Like, how do they DO that? I mean, I can sit there and hit that [expletive] reload button all [expletive] day and nuttin happens and the next time I log on, BLAM, there's been a thousand more Quake players. How does that counter tell the difference between me and everybody else? [expletive] trip!

Fragfest: What do you think it is that attracts people, the content?

Joe: The what? Na, man, she don't do nobody but me, and she ain't in no [expletive] tent, you [expletive] crazy?

Fragfest: No, I mean the stuff on your Quake page, what is it that makes people hit your page?

Joe: The w4r3z and the cheats. Especially the w4r3z. I'm posting Quake 3 next week!

Fragfest: Really?

Joe: Yeah, man, I busted into Id's and copped it last week. It's really [expletive] COOL, man, and like, it ain't NOTHIN like Quake 2, you're gonna really get blown away! I only played it once and I was trippin! It was a TRIP!

Fragfest: Can you describe it?

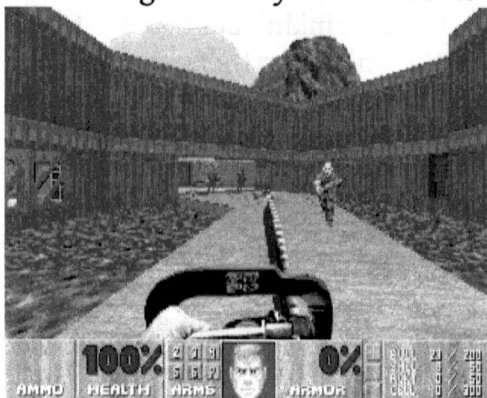

Joe: Yeah, well, it's more like Quake 2 than Quake 1, the first level ain't that big. You respawn, and if you go to the left there's a bunch of Strogg and some stairs, and some shotguns and armor, then you go down the hall from there, there's some green barrels that explode if you shoot em, it's really cool. Some of the Stroggs are like Quake 2, but most of 'em are different, like, there's were-wolves, and red devil things that throw fireballs, and goat things that throw this green shit, and these walkin' skeletons, its really cool. And dig, instead of an ax you get a CHAINSAW! Now THAT's cool!

Fragfest: Uh, ok, uh, thanks for the interview, Joe, I have to go home now and, uh, feed the, uh, hey, look, I'll see you later.

Joe: Hey, you sure you ain't got a joint? What's your name again?

Fragfest: Ste... uh, I mean, "Immortal".

Joe: Wow, you're the dude with the real audio thing? Wow, you're [expletive] cool, man! I love that shit!

Fragfest: No, I don't have a real audio show, you must

be thinking of Flamethrower.

    Joe: Hey, he used to be cool too till he started [expletive] with Immortal, hey, you're immortal, aren't you?

    Fragfest: No, I'm John Carmak.

    Joe: Who? Never heard of you. See ya.

1998

The Fragfest Christmas page

I first posted the Quake Christmas Carols in December, 1998, along with illustrations, some of which you see here. It was expanded yearly after that.

By the time I let the site die there were all kinds of Christmas goodies, including skins, maps, and other treats.

The Christmas page is what shot the site to fame. Following are the carols, two of which had MP3s of Patty singing in 1999, and some of the illustrations.

Nov 19, 2014

The Quake Song
If I see you then I'll open fire
Shrapnel nipping at your nose
Nine Inch Nails substitute for a choir
And folks dressed up in skins that glow
Everybody knows
some turkey camping by the quad
Helps to make the game feel right
Tiny shots – see the muzzle flash glow?
Will find me hard to hit tonight.
They know that Shambler's on his way
He's going to tear you up and eat your brain today
And every mother's child is gonna spy
To see if cheats will really show how to fly
And so I'm offering this server, guys
To kids 14 to 102
Although it's been said many times, many ways
Happy fragging to you!

I'm dreaming of a Quake Christmas
Just like the ones I used to know
Where the rail guns glisten
And players listen

To hear footsteps in the glow
I'm dreaming of a Quake Christmas
With every web page that I write
May your maps be merry and bright
And may all the shamblers run with fright

No L

In the first game of Quake
The newbie did say
"I will beat Dennis Fong at
his own game today."
"No L, No L; No L, No L."
"My new Quake name will
be No L"
He logged on to play some
Quake,
Didn't have no Game Spy
Had a ping of 1200, didn't
know it was high

"No L, No L; No L, No L."
"No one is going to beat No L"
He walked in to the game,
Saw a big dinosaur.
Couldn't shoot that damn pistol, he'd stuck to the floor
No L, No L; No L, No L.
Barney's the king of Lava Tomb hell.
Barney laughed at No L
and told him 'bout GameSpy
"If you use that cool program your ping won't be high."
"No L, No L; No L, No L."
Barney's the king of Lava Tomb hell.
He logged on with GameSpy
Ping 250, Hooray!
"I will kill that damned Barney and beat him today!"
No L, No L; No L, No L
Barney's the king of Lava Tomb hell.

He jumped in to a game
this was so-o much fun!
Then he fell in the lava, his score – minus one.
"No L, No L; No L, No L."
"No one is going to beat No L"
Then he saw a hooded kid
who was dressed all in red
and before L could shoot he was lying there dead.
No L, No L; No L, No L.
Kenny's the king of Lava Tomb hell.
When he looked at the clock
It was quarter to one
he'd been playing for hours, this is too much fun!
No L, No L; No L, No L
No one's the king of Lava Tomb hell!

Oh come, all you campers
Joyful and triumphant
Come out, all you pussies and fight like a man!
Come, let me kill you
Frag your ass to pieces
Come out and let me kill you
Come out and let me kill you
Come out and let me kill you; Christ, this is fun!

On the first day on Stroggos
the sergeant gave to me
A new shiny BFG
On the second day on Stroggos the seargent gave to me
Two rail guns
and a new shiny BFG
On the third day on Stroggos the seargent gave to me
Three shotguns
Two rail guns
And a new shiny BFG
On the fourth day on Stroggos the seargent gave to me

Four armor shards
Three shotguns
Two rail guns
And a new shiny BFG
On the fifth day on Stroggos the seargent gave to me
Five! hand grenades
Four armor shards
Three shotguns
Two rail guns
And a new shiny BFG
On the sixth day on
Stroggos the seargent gave
to me
Six rebreathers
Five! hand grenades
Four armor shards
Three shotguns
Two rail guns
And a new shiny BFG
On the seventh day on
Stroggos the seargent gave
to me
Seven troops all shooting
Six rebreathers
Five! hand grenades
Four armor shards
Three shotguns
Two rail guns
And a new shiny BFG
On the eighth day on Stroggos the seargent gave to me
Eight bandoliers
Seven troops all shooting
Six rebreathers
Five! hand grenades
Four armor shards
Three shotguns

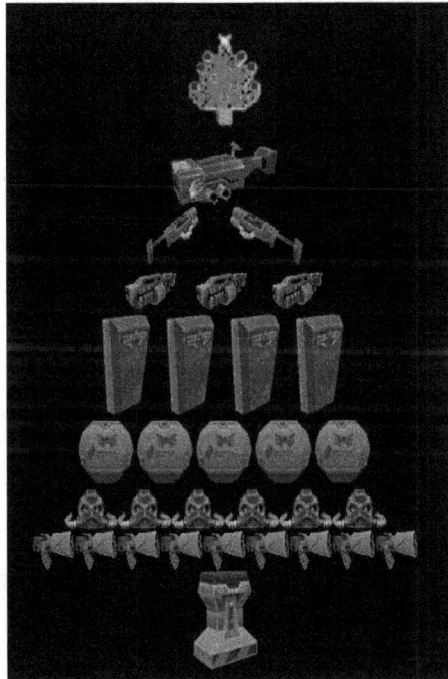

Two rail guns
And a new shiny BFG
On the ninth day on Stroggos the seargent gave to me
Nine hyperblasters
Eight bandoliers
Seven troops all shooting
Six rebreathers
Five! hand grenades
Four armor shards
Three shotguns
Two rail guns
And a new shiny BFG
On the tenth day on Stroggos the seargent gave to me
Ten newer levels
Nine hyperblasters
Eight bandoliers
Seven troops all shooting
Six rebreathers
Five! hand grenades
Four armor shards
Three shotguns
Two rail guns
And a new shiny BFG
On the eleventh day on Stroggos the seargent gave to me
Eleven rail guns
Ten newer levels
Nine hyperblasters
Eight bandoliers
Seven troops all shooting
Six rebreathers
Five! hand grenades
Four armor shards
Three shotguns
Two rail guns
And a new shiny BFG
On the twelfth day on Stroggos the seargent gave to me

A ping of 12, I killed them all, WHEE!

Rudolph, the four leg Stroggie
Had a very deadly tongue
And if you ever saw it,
you would prolly die real
young.
All of the other Stroggies
Used to growl and call him
names;
They never let old Rudolph

Join in any deathmatch
games
Then one bloody Stroggos eve
Shambler came to say,
Rudolph with your tongue so long,
come take care of Dennis Fong.
Then all the Stroggies loved him
And they shouted out with glee,
"Rudolph the four leg Stroggie,
You can come and play with me!"

Grampa got dismembered by a Shambler
Playing Quake at our house Christmas eve.
You can say there's no such thing as shamblers,
But Grandma couldn't get his ass to leave.

Grandma said "come home, you old fart"
As she headed for the door.
Grampa grabbed another cold one,
Mumbling something 'bout a dried up bitchy whore
Grampa said "I'll beat this damned thing"
That was followed by "OH, SHIT"
Must have had too many cold ones
'cause he tripped and fell into a lava pit.

Grampa got dismembered by a Shambler
Playing Quake at our house Christmas eve.
You can say there's no such thing as shamblers,
But Grandma couldn't get his ass to leave.
We'd been drinking too much whiskey,
Then he drank a little more.
First he threw up on the keyboard
Then he puked and passed out on the kitchen floor.

Now there ain't no Quake for Grampa
'cause the shit has hit the fan!
Grandma says his game is over,
And she's gonna play a little Ms. Pac Man.

Grampa got dismembered by a Shambler
Playing Quake at our house Christmas eve.
You can say there's no such thing as shamblers,
But Grandma couldn't get his ass to leave.

I saw Mommie killin' Santa Clause
Playin' in a game of Quake last night.
Old Santa didn't see
Her shiny BFG
The way he splattered on the wall was such a funny sight!
I saw Mommie kicking Thresh's butt.
Boy, my mommie sure knows how to play!
He was camping by the cage
And I guess he couldn't guage
Just how her super shotgun would blow his butt away!
I saw Mommie fragin' everyone!
Boy, it sure was such a sight to see!
Immortal, Blue, sCary,
Zaphod and an LPB.
And oh, my God! She even killed – Kenny!
I saw Mommie killin' everyone!
Gee, my mommie sure can play that game!

Oh, Mister, are you sure
That you want a game with her?
'cause you're surely gonna wish she hadn't came!
1998-2001

My wife had been diagnosed with some mental illness some seven years earlier, and the doctor told me she might not remain the same person when the therapy was finished.

She never finished the therapy, but still turned into a different person, a couple of months after the last post.

The worst part was, in hindsight, that she stopped seeing herself as "Mom". She was working part-time, even though I was by then making a decent income, one that had allowed us to buy a large house and two vehicles. And she was going to college. The kids and I became secondary, then tertiary, she became more and more hostile to all of us and left me, my children, and all seven of her cats behind and abandoned all of us.

It was about that time I let the domain lapse, although I hadn't posted in months. I found kuro5hin.org, then a good site. I wrote articles and diaries there about the divorce. It is now a book titled "The Paxil Diaries". More front page articles and non-paxil diary entries from K5 are included next.

Oct 17, 2004

How to quit smoking cigarettes

Disclaimer – this will not work for everyone. In fact, it is very, *very* hard to do. Quitting cigarettes is the hardest thing I have ever done.

I will start out with how and why I got started, for those nonsmokers who think (and rightly so) that I am an idiot for ever starting in the first place.

If you don't smoke tobacco, I urge you to never start. But if you start, here's what worked for me, and what didn't.

17 in 69

In 1969, *everybody* smoked. There was no social stigma as now. Mothers smoked as they nursed their babies. Doctors smoked. Nurses smoked. Nearly every adult smoked. They sold candy that looked like cigarettes to kids, in authentic looking boxes, with real cigarette brands. Parents would send their eight year old kids to the store to buy cigarettes for them, and give the kid an extra fifteen cents for some soda or gum as payment for fetching the cigarettes.

You could light up a cigarette almost anywhere that there wasn't anything flammable. In bars, restaurants, stores. The doctor's office waiting room had ash trays. The few adults that didn't smoke had ash trays in their homes for their smoking friends. All white walls were off-white from the smoke.

High school teachers' lounges had ash trays. You could smoke in a college classroom, in a store, on an airplane. About the only places you couldn't smoke was in church, an elevator, or a pre-college school room.

Both my parents smoked, as did everyone else's. I hated it. I suspect, though, that I was addicted to nicotine long before I lit my first cigarette.

When I would be in a carload of friends as a teenager, I

would gag on the smoke. I was the first to roll down the window in the winter and yell "Freeze out!"

This was what got me started: I discovered, though I don't remember how or why, that if I was smoking a cigarette, the smoke wouldn't bother me. When I was in a car load of kids, I'd bum one in order to breathe.

My dad found my smokes; I wasn't in trouble. "Don't expect me to buy 'em for you." At thirty cents a pack, there was no need.

Stopping, but only because I had to

I joined the Air Force when I was 19, and when we couldn't smoke at all for the first two weeks, I discovered to my amazement that I was addicted to them. I kept a couple of packs in my footlocker, and would sneak one in the toilet stall, next to the exhaust fan, at night. I had one of those plastic things you could strap them to your leg with, for the first time we were allowed to have a smoke.

The time finally came. "Smoke 'em if you got 'em." Man, I was the most popular guy in the squadron! And I actually copped a buzz on the cigarette.

After basic training, I thought often about quitting. Especially those times I didn't have the thirty five cents for a pack of smokes, or the three dollars for a carton.

After the Air Force when I was in college, I had very, very little money, and the cost of cigarettes kept rising. Non-smokers started becoming more numerous, and vocal. I decided to quit.

Quitting... almost... the first time... and again...

I lasted maybe 4 hours. I quit quitting for a year.

They came out with a quitting system called "One Step At A Time", where you bought 4 holders that would filter the smoke. The first "filter" was just a holder, and the last let in nothing but air. You were supposed to go through the 4 filters, then quit.

I went through the whole deal. At the end of the last filter, with one cigarette left, I stuck it in the filter and asked myself, do you *really* want this cigarette?

Hell *yes!* I threw away the filter and smoked it. GOD it was heavenly.

A year later, I went cold turkey for a month. I had a doctor prescribe Valium so I wouldn't murder anyone. The Valium made me want a cigarette worse.

So I threw the pills away... okay, I sold them. And decided to go cold turkey. It lasted a month.

If you've ever smoked cigarettes, you know that there are certain triggers that make you really crave one. After eating, while drinking coffee, while drinking beer... I was sharing a six pack with a friend who hadn't smoked in five years. I *really* wanted a cigarette.

"How long until I don't want one any more?"

He said he still wanted one. I went for another six pack – and some smokes.

It was years before I seriously tried quitting again. I hated being addicted to them, but I enjoyed them so much! In fact, I didn't even try again until my wife was pregnant with our first child, and she couldn't smoke. Literally. The smell of a cigarette sent her running to the bathroom to puke.

I wound up smoking outside most of the time.

Almost...

Around 1998 I saw my chance, as the wife wanted to quit. By then, everybody was quitting or had quit, and you couldn't smoke at work. I hated going outside in the heat and cold for a butt. We got the patches, and I started learning a few things.

One thing that surprised me was that the habit was as strong as the physical addiction! This is what the patches are good for, getting you over the habit. When I smoked, as I walked down the stairs at work I would pull out that beloved cigarette and have it ready for a light as I walked through the door. A full year after I finally did quit, I was still slapping my pocket as I went down the stairs!

How *not* to quit

You cannot quit a step at a time. You can't "cut down". You can't gradually quit. When you quit, you have to *quit*. You have to make the decision that you will never, ever smoke another cigarette again.

I knew this, as I had not only had everyone who had ever successfully quit tell me, but I had tried to cut down gradually enough times I knew it wouldn't work.

We decided to try the patches. The patches actually get you over the habit, so you can concentrate on not *smoking*, and then get over the nicotine addiction more gradually.

We bought patches, and went three weeks without a cigarette. I had a "killer urge" and *had* to have a cigarette. There was some tobacco and rolling papers in the house. I rolled up a cigarette.

One puff was all it took. It was *nasty*. Horrible. "Must have been the patches," I thought, and threw it away and brushed my teeth.

We went through the full patch, half patch, quarter patch, no patch (I'll go into detail shortly). I had been off the patches for a few days, and had another killer urge I couldn't resist. Again I rolled a cigarette. Again I took one, nasty puff and threw it away. "Must be because it was a roll your own."

Another month went by, and I had yet another "killer" urge. So did my wife; we had been arguing. She went next door and bummed two Marlboros. I lit mine – and it tasted *exactly* like the roll your own! I was free at last! Never again would I have to smoke!

Yet another month went by, and we were at a party. We were the only people there not smoking, and we were drinking beer. I had another killer urge, and bummed a Winston. I took a nasty puff. Exactly like the Marlboro, exactly like the roll your own. But I had bummed it, and couldn't just take one puff

248

and throw it away. By the time I got to the butt, it tasted *damned* good. My wife bummed one too.

You can never, EVER smoke a cigarette if you quit, any more than a heroin addict can have another shot, a coke addict can have another snort, or an alcoholic can have another drink. You are an addict. That is the nature of addiction.

The next day, we went for a walk, stopped at a gas station "for a Pepsi," and wound up with a pack of cigarettes, each savoring one of the precious, delightful sticks. In a month we were each back to a pack a day.

Quitting... at last. And the pitfalls

I decided, long before the commercials about giving up butts for new years, that my nicotine would be a twentieth century addiction. I was going to take my last puff on New Years Eve 1999, and see the new century cigarette free.

Making the decision months in advance helped greatly, I am convinced. If you quit on a whim, you will start back up on a whim.

When using the patches, go 3 or 4 weeks on a full patch. It will seem like you have quit; you will have the urges, even though your body is getting its nicotine. Put your patch on first thing in the morning, and leave it on until the next morning.

Clean the spot where the patch will go with rubbing alcohol, as you will likely get skin lesions if not (and maybe if you do).

After the first 3 or 4 weeks, you can cut the patch in half with a scissors, and put on a half a patch. It will work as well as a full sized half strength patch, at half the cost. When you go to the half patch, it will again feel like quitting. You did it before, you can do it again.

Two weeks after that, go for a quarter patch. Two weeks after that, don't use any more patches.

The worst is over. You will have some bad times you really want a cigarette, but *don't give in!* One cigarette, and you're back at square one again.

When quitting, even while on the patch, there are certain times you will want a cigarette very, very badly. It is a stronger urge than the urge for sex, or food. Needing a cigarette is a terrible thing.

You will want a cigarette after eating, when drinking alcohol, when drinking coffee, leaving work, and when you smell sidestream smoke. You will want a cigarette when you are angry, and you will want a cigarette when you smell bad smells.

Nicotine is a stimulant, and like many other stimulants is an appetite suppressant. This is the reason you want a cigarette when you are hungry, it takes the edge off of the hunger. It is also the reason many people gain weight after quitting; the appetite isn't suppressed, and the metabolism is slower.

After eating, a cigarette makes you feel more satisfied. It also releases certain brain chemicals associated with pleasure. When drinking coffee, the two stimulants combine, and the coffee stimulation makes you want the nicotine stimulation.

Alcohol is a depressant, so your body wants the counteracting stimulant.

When you are angry, you have both the chemical release that tends to calm you down, despite its being a stimulant, plus it gives you a "time out."

Another dangerous pitfall is the fact that since you can't smoke inside most public buildings, you will smell the smoke as you go in or come out. Imagine a cocaine addict trying to quit if there was a cloud of cocaine floating around the entrance to every building!

You must be aware of these pitfalls, especially within the first six months to a year after your last cigarette, because it takes six months to completely rid your body of the nicotine.

Coping strategies

Replace your rituals.

After eating, it is helpful to brush your teeth thoroughly, and use a strong, unpleasant mouthwash like Listerine. Make it a ritual, and it won't be long before it replaces the cigarette. This has the added benefit of making your visits to the dentist less costly.

One of the supposed "benefits" of not smoking is a heightened sense of smell. This is true, but it is most certainly NOT a benefit! Food smells the same, flowers smell the same, nice smells smell the same. It is the bad odors that you smell more. Having a lessened sense of smell is actually a benefit of smoking. You will have to learn to deal with bad smells.

When you drink coffee, try to do it where you normally couldn't have a smoke with it, such as a non-smoking restaurant, or at work.

If a "killer urge" comes on you, know that it will pass. You *will* feel better, even if it seems like you never will without a cigarette. Know that if you have a cigarette, you will have to go through the agony of quitting again. You will have the agony of not having a cigarette. Know that after you quit smoking, you can travel on public transportation without the agony of deprival. You can watch an entire movie at a theater, without missing what is almost always the most important ten minutes when you have your cigarette.

For the first several months, stay out of any public place, like bars, where smoking is permitted. *Particularly* if you are doing an activity you normally associate with heavier than normal smoking, like in a bar or coffee house. Do your drinking at home for the first 6 to 9 months after quitting.

You may find, like I did, that eventually, the activities that used to cause you to want a cigarette, like a cup of coffee or a bottle of beer, get rid of the urges to smoke.

Know that no matter how badly you want that cigarette, if you smoke it, you will want one even more badly tomorrow. Eventually the urges will be gone. I haven't had a cigarette in three years, and although I will never forget how enjoyable they were, I never want to smoke another one. You, too, will be free. Good luck!

May 13, 2003

Gecko Poker

This was going to be a post for the "other – please post" in muchagecko's Tuesday diary entry poll, but I have no diary entry of my own today (as I have no life) and it's likely going to be a bit long anyway. So both my thanks and my apologies to the lovely Ms. Gecko.

Gecko thought it surprising that a Buddhist would read Tarot cards, but the only time anyone (except myself) has read my cards, it was a Buddhist who read them!

When I was in the Air Force, I spent a year in Utapao, Thailand. Now, to a westerner, going to the planet Mars would be slightly less strange than going to Thailand, at least when I went. A young woman from Thailand was recently an intern where I work, and from her accounts it has changed drastically, and I wouldn't recognize it.

This is NOT Taiwan, now, but Thailand. It is situated between Burma and India to the north, Malaysia to the south, and Laos and Cambodia separating it from Vietnam to the east. It used to be known as Siam. The country is roughly shaped like an elephant's head. The elephant is revered in Thailand, having helped build their civilization some five *thousand* years ago. Yes, they have a very long history. Elephants were used much like we use heavy construction equipment today. If someone gives you a statue of an elephant, *refuse the gift* if the elephant's trunk is raised; it is bad luck, a curse. If, however, the trunk is down, that is *good* luck. The reason is simple – if the elephant has its nose curled upward, it is about to charge. No land animal can survive an elephant's attack, save running away. However, with its trunk down, it is feeding or acting like a piece of heavy construction equipment.

Utapao is in the extreme south, on the elephant's trunk (er, is that "boot" for you British guys?;).

Vietnam is across the water. If you have a world globe

or an atlas, you will see "Fuck it Island" (spelled "Phuket" on the map, the Thais have a different alphabet), very close to where I was. They may have renamed Utapao; it was a Thai navy base, and the Americans used it as an Air Force base, with B-52s.

The country was strictly third world, at least outside of Bangkok. No electricity or running water, except in businesses. Nobody had cars. They had these little Japanese pickup trucks with benches and canopies in the back, called "bhat buses." You could ride about anywhere for a nickle – the American nickle exchanged for one Thai bhat.

Now, Thailand is strictly a Buddhist country. All Thais are Buddhist. They have Wats (what?), or Buddhist temples, all over the place. Also all over the place are priests who wear incandescent orange robes. The Buddhist priests do things that make Kwai Chaing Cane look like a clumsy dork. In fact, I saw a Thai boxing match between Thai boxers and Chinese Gungfu fighters; the Thais love the Chinese pretty much as well as the Arabs love the Jews, and pretty much for the same reasons. Only their conflicts have gone on for over five thousand years. Well, there was blood and broken bones, and the Chinese guys all went to the hospital.

Now, when I was nine or twelve I was an amateur magician; you know, like David Copperfield. Only not as good. I was also a geek, and you have of course heard the statement that any sufficiently advanced technology seems as magic. With this background, you can see where I was a huge skeptic of anything "magical" or arcane.

I have always been a readaholic, and read very fast. Sometime when I was stationed in Delaware, before Thailand, where I did little except ride my motorcycle, fix that God damned piece of shit Mustang, and read (mostly reading), I ran across Aleister Crowley's "autohagiography". The same Aleister Crowley that Ozzie Osborne sang about in the song "Mr. Crowley".

Crowley was the self-proclaimed "beast of the Revelation". He thought he was the anti Christ (and oddly, died about the time the real anti Christ, Hitler, was wreaking havoc on the Jews). According to his bio, a book about four inches thick and fascinating, he had been thrown out of the Masons for spilling their secrets. Not only thrown out, but allegedly, according to Crowley, they tried to kill him as well.

Crowley was obviously a very mentally unbalanced individual. He and his apprentices practiced magic and sorcery, calling up demons and so forth, with all of these rituals chronicled in the book in exacting detail. As I said, crazy but fascinating. These rituals involved blood, torture, sodomy, rape, homosexual and heterosexual sex acts, cocaine, opium, hashish, bestiality, and other things that were even weirder than *that*.

This guy was a pure nutsoid creep. He could well have been Jack the Ripper. I'll get back to Mr. Crowley shortly.

As I said, I went to Thailand a secure and firm disbeliever in anything remotely occult. Besides Copperfield style parlor tricks, the most mystical thing I did was paint and play guitar.

I saw things in Thailand that convinced me otherwise. If it hadn't been for the Thai Buddhists, I might not have developed such a firm faith in God and Jesus.

Not one of you will believe what I have to say next, and I can't blame you. The only "rational", western explanation would be the cigar I was smoking.

The pot over there came wrapped around bamboo sticks, maybe eight or ten inches long, and tied up with hemp thread. It was three dollars for twenty sticks, factory sealed in plastic. Each stick perhaps a quarter ounce or nearly so. This was incredibly potent stuff; in fact, one of the GI's pastimes was getting a new guy who thought he was a super doper, and seeing how many bong hits it took to make him pass out. Most passed out on the second hit. Few made it as far as four without amphetamines. Er, there were some super amphetamines there, too.

Now, you could carefully take the hemp thread off, and roll it up in the leaf of a certain species of banana plant, and when you were ready to smoke it, pull out the bamboo stick. It made a wonderfully tasting smoke. It would also *fuck you up.*

One morning, after I had visited some Thai friends in a tiny village in the middle of a jungle, I stood by the dirt road (all the roads outside Bangkok, as far as I know, were dirt then) waiting for the bhat bus to come by, smoking my cigar. This far out it could have been a several hour wait, so I set myself for some patient waiting (and full of speed). I'd look down the road one way, then the other. And back. And look at the clouds. And into the greenery of the jungle, perhaps twenty or thirty yards on either side of the road.

I looked right, behind, left, right again, and a fat priest in his fluorescent robe was standing next to me. "Hello, er, sawat dee," I said, and politely did the little bow they do there. He just smiled bigger than before, and bowed back. I thought I heard a bhat bus so I looked – yes, there was one in the distance. I started to say "yep, there's one" – but as I turned to speak to him, he wasn't there any more. He had been standing next to me for fifteen minutes, and now that there was a bhat bus coming he was gone.

The driver, who spoke English, motioned me into the passenger seat of the bus, and I got in. I told him wait a minute, I thought there was a priest that wanted a ride, too, and described him. His eyes got wide. "You've been blessed! He's special. Very few have ever met him."

Hmmpft. OOOkayy... right... Of course, I didn't say that out loud. I did wonder how a guy wearing a bright orange robe could have snuck up on me surrounded by green, and snuck away in the blink of an eye.

So he's driving, and I'm looking out the window, and I look toward the driver, *and there sits the priest between us!* The driver saw him at the same time, and almost wrecked the pickup. He slid to a stop and made me get in the back.

I started researching the Tarot, astrology, witchcraft,

Buddhism, and every other religion, cult, and whatever I could get information on after that. The fat Buddhist guy in the orange robes really freaked me out.

As to the Tarot, as I said, Thailand was a wonderful, magical place. All my life until then I had been a loser with the ladies. I had a Thai girl friend (all my girl friends there were Thai) who offered to read my cards. She needed only the minor arcana; in short, a poker deck.

She predicted that when I went home I would not marry the first girlfriend I had, that the girl I *thought* I would wind up marrying would be married to someone else by the time I got home, that I would have no sons and two daughters after being married for ten years – and that I would have my heart broken over and over while married.

As skeptical as I was, every bit of it eventually happened. I was no longer a loser with the ladies, and was married, to a woman who had repeated affairs, leaving me once (not counting last fall), while I would repeatedly be tempted by other women, who I stupidly resisted.

It seems the magic is gone.

At any rate, about the cards: the last leg of the trip back to St. Louis was San Francisco, where I did some sightseeing. I ran across a little place called the Museum of Magic and Witchcraft, where, in the gift shop, I spied a deck of Aleister Crowley Tarot cards. These cards were allegedly designed by The Beast, and painted by the Lady Somebody or other, I don't remember who, some British Noblelady that Crowley allegedly had an adulterous affair with.

I went to buy the cards, and the lady behind the counter wouldn't sell them. She said it was bad luck to buy Tarot cards except as a gift to someone else, and these were *special* cards. I didn't care, I only wanted them for the extremely cool artwork. She compromised, selling me a hardbound book on the Tarot, black cloth hardbound with red title, and she gave me the cards.

I still have them. They are large, perhaps four by six

inches. They are now wrapped in white silk and I refuse to get them out again, they're in a box in the basement. I came to believe that rather than predicting the future, as they did with stunning accuracy, that they actually *changed* the future. Crazy? Hell yes. I don't care, they scared the piss out of me. The damned things finally scared me so much after a long period of some very, very bad luck that I haven't had them out in over 15 years.

Now if I want my fortune read, I get out old King James and open it to a random spot, and read. It works as well as the Tarot and doesn't scare the bejeesus out of me.

So, lizardlady, the sun card does, indeed, sound like something good is finally coming your way. I hope you placed them in the proper order before shuffling them. What, now, does the "Wind" suit correspond to in a "normal" Tarot deck?

May 15, 2003

Death

In someone's diary yesterday, rmg was credited with saving a life by telling LittleZephyr "As someone who has died twice, I feel obliged to point out that suicide is not, in fact the easy way out. ...One little known fact about death is that it is never quick or painless."

I responded that "I can't believe I'm agreeing with rmg, but he's right. I only died once and those last two seconds were a painful eternity. If you shoot yourself in the head, that last three seconds is spending the entire rest of your life in searing, hellish pain."

Here is the whole story of that death.

It was January of 1976. I had just gotten out of the Air Force the previous summer, had gotten a girlfriend (who I would later marry), and started college. Except for being piss-poor, life was pretty good. I had a three room shotgun house in the ghetto, a late model car that was paid off (a 1974 Gremlin), and high hopes for the future.

I was on my way back home from the university, where I had just registered for classes. My girlfriend was with me.

We were almost through Collinsville on highway 157, a four lane undivided highway with a 50 mile per hour speed limit, when a truck pulled out in front of me. Not dangerously close, but enough that I had to touch the brakes to slow, as he pulled out straddling the lanes.

The car lurched violently, and I was out of control, in the wrong lane, facing a three quarter ton pickup truck speeding toward me at about seventy miles per hour.

He was perhaps fifteen feet from the car. I knew I was dead. The time dilation started then. When they have slow motion of violent scenes in movies, that's actually kind of what it's like.

That split second of terror lasted for an eternity. The

collision lasted longer. I was thrown into the windshield, which my face broke. My shoulder hit the dashboard, and dented it in by a half foot.

Things went dark, but I could still feel pain and motion. The car was moving backwards now.

Pain, pain... believe me when I tell you that getting smacked in the face with a three quarter ton pickup truck hurts like hell. Literally. I know what a cockroach feels like when you step on him.

And sickness. Horrible sickness, as if every cell in my body was trying to puke.

And this pain and torture would continue *for the rest of my life.*

And longer.

Finally, after what felt like years, the pain and sickness and motion and feeling slipped away as well. I found myself facing a choice.

I was at an impasse, inside something that was vaguely cave-like at two openings; it is impossible to describe because there are no referents. I had to choose which one to enter, and didn't know which one to choose. I prayed for guidance. At this point, it was all too evident that the choice was between heaven and hell, and I couldn't tell one from the other.

A voice came: "Neither. It isn't your time yet. You still have a very important task to perform."

But what should I do?

"Turn around, and head toward the light."

I did.

I was back in the wreckage. Twisted metal, blood everywhere. My head was swimming, my glasses were gone. I tried to open the door, and it was stuck. I kicked it open.

The searing, horrible pain was still there, all through my body. Especially on the right side. I was having a hard time breathing. I sat on the edge of the seat and coughed up blood, then puked blood.

My sweetheart was next to me, silent and motionless.

"Oh God, please don't let her be dead!"

She then started screaming horribly.

Time was still going very slowly, although not as slowly as before I died.

Eventually the rescue crew came and took us to the hospital. My face was purple and swollen, my right shoulder was dislocated. My girlfriend suffered a concussion and cuts, and her pelvis was broken in six places.

I've worn my seat belt ever since, and I have not feared death since. But I do have an aversion to searing, torturous pain. And ever since then, I have an unshakable faith in God.

Nov 09, 2003

This illustrated perfectly the parable of Lazarus and the rich man in Luke 16:19-31. The rich man begs God to let him return to Earth long enough to warn his brothers. God answers "they didn't believe the prophets, why would they believe you?

And indeed, this true story changed no minds whatever. "It was a hallucination" or some such nonsense. I witnessed the "gates" to heaven and hell, and my testimony does absolutely no good whatever here.

6/23/2015

How To Buy a Cat

If you have mice, or are lonely, or want a pet for other reasons, or are a Korean cook, or want to piss off your neighbor's dog, or want to punish your furniture, or for any other reason might want to acquire or may be tricked into the acquisition of a cat, then this article is for you. If you already have one, and especially if you haven't had it long, you might want to read it as well. The article, not the cat.

And if you hate cats and want to laugh at the sissies who have them, well read on.

Why in the hell would anybody want a damned cat?

First, for the same reasons as a dog. No, not the same reasons as a dog wants a cat, but the same reasons for wanting to own a dog – they are loving and trusting. Unlike dogs, they make you earn their love and trust.

But you'll never get their respect. Of course, you won't get a dog's respect, either.

Don't expect your new cat to do tricks. Cats are hard to teach. Most are too smart to play that game, so if you want to teach a cat to roll over and play dead, get a really stupid cat.

Where should you get a cat? At a pet store?

Hell no! Whatever you do, do not get a cat at a pet store. By the time you buy your ridiculously expensive cat, it will be insane from being kept in a tiny cage in strange surroundings all of its life. A pet store is the last place to get a cat.

The best cats are feral cats; alley cats that wander onto your property and into your life. These cats know hardship, and understand what you are doing for them.

If a stray seems well fed, it's someone's pet. He's just pretending to be a stray for some extra food and attention. After all, it *is* an animal, and a mammal at that.

My former sister in law told of a cat who "ran off," just disappeared. They assumed it was dead, run over by a truck or something.

Lo and behold, six months later it was back, having traded his testicles for a flea collar! He had befriended a human, and paid with the highest price a tomcat can pay.

Look, people are begging to give kittens away all the time. Take one, they're cute. Just don't take a male.

What does one cost?

Don't pay for a cat! They breed like rabbits; people can't give enough away and will resort to infanticide to rid themselves of the extra feline populations.

If you have to give someone money, go to the animal shelter.

There are costs associated with ownership, of course; food and cat litter come to mind. If one falls out of a tree and breaks his leg, then you need a vet.

What kind of cat should I get?

I would personally recommend against one like Illusionist Roy Horn had, unless of course you have an antelope infestation in your basement.

Just get a cat. Breed doesn't matter. Cats are all individuals. No two are alike. Find one that likes you, and one you like (Note: the gray ones are the most loving and well-behaved).

However, do not, I repeat DO NOT get a male. Males "mark their territory" by urinating all over everything you own. Male cats should not be let inside the house.

Unless, of course, you are Korean, and even then it is strongly advised not to let live ones in.

Try to get one whose mother was a mouser; in fact, the momma cat will determine what all the kittens are like, if you allow the kittens to stay with the mother long enough. The momma cat will teach the little cats to hunt, to use the litter box, where to sharpen their claws, and so forth.

Again, pay close attention to the momma cat. She may also teach them where they can get away with pooping on the floor, how to get doors open, where the Purina Cat Chow is stored, where that Purina Human Chow is stored, and what the dog's social security number is.

Shy away from ones that glow in the dark, especially in Washington state.

Okay, okay, how do I tell a male from a female?

Lift the tail and look just beneath its anus ("arsehole" for our British readers). You can tell if it's a female. If it isn't, it's not.

What should I feed it?

The cheapest cat food you can buy.

But I love my cat!

Cats love Beluga Caviar. Can you afford it? Look, it's a cat. Buy it cat food. It can only know the joys you show it. Jade it in kittenhood and you will regret it.

However, if you are looking for cat longevity, the oldest recorded cat died at 36 years old, and was fed eggs, bacon, and coffee.

Don't buy soft food for cats or dogs. It will rot their teeth, both species.

What about a litter box?

Buy one, and clean it once a day per cat. And never forget – you don't own the cat, the cat owns you.

What if I'm allergic to cats?

Er, avoid them? ...but if you must have one, and you have the money, you can get shots from your doctor.

Dec 12, 2003

Birth of a label-sanctioned pirate radio station

In the 1960s radio sucked badly; even worse than it does today. There were no rock stations. The only rock and roll was played on the AM pop station, and sparingly, at that.

FM was relatively new, and the FM stations only played easy listening, Jazz, etc. My dad listened to FM 95, which played Herb Alpert and the like; almost jazz, "easy listening", boring music.

There were two pop stations in town, one of which lost its license around 1963 for a fraudulent on-air contest that had people digging holes all over St. Louis, trespassing, etc, and it turned out that the prize didn't exist. The station went dark, and came back with new ownership and a country western format. This left one bad pop station in the entire large metropolitan area.

One evening my dad wasn't home, so I turned on the stereo, a large furniture-like thing, and was amazed that there was rock and roll playing. Real rock and roll, unlike the schmaltz they played on the pop station. What's more, it was in stereo!

It was amazing. They were playing Black Sabbath, Cream, the Yardbirds, Jimi Hendrix – and none of these bands had ever gotten any airplay in St. Louis, with the exception of Sabbath, whose "Paranoid" single might get played once a week or so.

Later, as I was watching TV, my dad came home, and went ballistic when he couldn't find his station. He assumed, logically, that I or my sister had changed the dial. He demanded that it be changed back.

I admitted listening to the radio, but insisted that my sister must have changed it earlier. As Dad was getting ready to ground us both, with the radio back on his 95 but playing rock, the disk jockey mentioned the format change. We got out of our groundings, of course.

The station was KSHE 95, on a frequency of 94.7. Being the pre-digital age and on an analog dial it was simply 95. It was the first FM stereo rock station still in existence.

This became the only station I would listen to, and I had lots of fun amazing my friends, most of whom were amateur musicians, with my new discovery.

Just like the pop stations of today, the pop station in town, KXOX, only played 2:40 pop singles. KSHE was most definitely not a pop station.

They played long songs, album sides, whole albums. The Who's *Magic Bus* had played occasionally on the pop station, but KSHE would play the entire two LP *Tommy*. And they would play it uncut and uninterrupted, except for changing the album; as he turned the record over, the DJ would list the tracks and then start playing them.

They played long songs and album cuts, rather than 45s (singles). Where KXOK would occasionally play Creedence's two minute *Suzy Q* 45, KSHE would play the entire seven minute album version.

They played the sixteen minute *In A Gadda Da Vida*, the eighteen minute *Alice's Restaurant*, the twenty five minute Quicksilver Messenger Service rock version of the old blues standard *Who Do You Love*.

KSHE's motto was and still is "Real Rock Radio", and its mascot was a pig that wore sunglasses and headphones and smoked a hand-rolled cigarette. If you go to their web site you'll still see the pig, with more modern shades and phones, but for some reason the pig stopped smoking around the time of Reagan's "war on drugs".

It didn't take long for teens and young adults to discover this new treasure, which had the side effect of forcing KXOK to play more real rock & roll. It got so most people only listened to KXOK in the car, and then only because there weren't yet any car FM radios.

266

By the time they were on air for six months, they had started some very unique programs. Every day at six they would play an album side, and usually follow it the next day with the other side of the album.

On Sunday nights they started the "Seventh Day" show, where they would play seven full albums back to back, uncut. They would always prompt the audience to cue their tape recorders before starting, and conveniently left a few seconds of dead air before and after each album side.

Yes, listeners were encouraged to record these LPs off of the radio, uncut and in their entirety.

Fast forward a few decades to the new century. The labels have ~~bribed~~ lobbied congress for new rules. Now, at least on the internet, you can't play three songs from the same artist back to back, let alone full CDs.

KSHE's Seventh Day, however, still plays. They must have been granted some sort of variance, or been grandfathered in.

Now, a question for discussion. Why were the labels okay with my recording Ted Nugent's *Stranglehold* album, uncut and uninterrupted, a week before it was released to the stores, but now scream bloody murder if I dare to have the audacity download a two minute, poor audio quality Metallica single?

What's changed?

May 02, 2004

267

The election is coming

Here in Illinois, a guy named Obama; not an Irish name, an African one (father from Africa, mother from Kansas, Toto) was nominated by the Democrats to run for the Senate. A Borg's ex-husband, Jack Ryan (formerly wed to 7 of 9), dropped out of the race when it was revealed he had lied to party heads about his sexcapades – notably, that he dragged then-wife Jeri (of Star Trek Voyager fame) to sex clubs and wanted to pork her while friends watched, and watch while friends porked her (Me! Me! I'll fuck her for you Jack! You can watch! Jack! Over here!!!)

So the Republicans had to scramble to find a replacement. They had to look all the way to Maryland, and nominate Alan Keyes – a man who has yet to step foot in Illinois.

A wag on the radio said "those Republicans! First they can't find Osama Bin Laden in Afghanistan. Then they can't fine WMDs in Iraq. Now they can't even find a black man in Chicago!"

Today's State Journal Wrapafish has an article about the Republicans' grumbling about Keyes. I found it highly amusing, although I'm sure the editors (and other Republicans) didn't.

They say he is wrong to focus almost exclusively on abortion and gay marriage in his public appearances. They complain that he lets the campaign wander into damaging side issues, particularly his comment that Vice President Dick Cheney's lesbian daughter is "a selfish hedonist".

Well look, I have to hand it to Keyes here. He had said that homosexual sex isn't sex (and I thought it was only Clinton and the Democrats?) and that gays were "selfish hedonists". Pointing this out, a reporter had asked him about Cheney's daughter. What else could he do, show himself for the damned liar all politicians are? Of course not, and I salute him. As I laugh.

But even as some Keyes fans acknowledge, voters have been slow to embrace Keyes' lecturing style of speaking and his strong accusations – that Obama supports infanticide, for instance, or that he is a socialist who rejects basic American freedoms.

"It's not your typical neighborly, folksy Midwestern campaign. It can be off-putting at first blush," said Joe Wiegand, executive director of the Family Taxpayers Network.

Jesus, what do the stupid Illinois Republicans expect, that a guy that lives between the lanes of the Washington DC beltway and lives in Baltimore and who has never ever been in the midwest would have a clue about our culture and sensibilities?

Erm, well, I guess these ARE the same dildos that nominated Bush over McCain.

"He trailed Obama by 51 percentage points in a Chicago Tribune poll conducted in mid-September. Only 44 percent of Republican voters said they intended to support Keyes."

I laughed out loud.

"The relationship between moral priorities and economics is clear to Americans at the common-sense level," he said. "They know, for instance, that if you're dealing with problems of welfare and poverty, the chief contributing factor to the inability to get out of poverty is the breakdown of the family structure. That breakdown is related to moral causes."

There is a lot of truth in that, but what can government do about it? That's right, not one damned thing! Aren't you Republicans all for letting the churches take care of poverty? Then let the churches take care of morality as well. Because, you know, I don't think there are many politicians in heaven.

"Keyes repeatedly has criticized Obama for voting against legislation that required medical care for any baby that survives an abortion."

That tells me Keyes is talking out of his ass. Do you really think that an abortion survivor is going to become a

269

productive citizen? Common sense tells you if your momma is a crack whore, you're likely to spend most of your adulthood in prison. This ain't rocket science, Alan. I do think, however, that if the fetus is viable, it should live.

"Keyes also has raised eyebrows by saying... that Jesus would never vote for Obama."

HAR HAR HAR, anybody who thinks Jesus would vote for ANY Republican is whistling past the graveyard. The Republican party platform is decidedly anti-Christ, from its assault on the poor to its warmongering to its worship of the golden calf.

A lawyer asked Christ how to get to heaven. "You know Hebrew law, follow it," the lawyer was told. "What else do I need to do?" the lawyer asked.

"Sell everything you have and give it to the poor."

It was, after all, Jesus who said a rich man had as much of a chance of getting into heaven as a camel has of getting through the eye of a needle.

Do you watch the 700 club? Yes? Then you are on your way to hellfire, brother, because Pat Robertson and the rest of the right wing "Christians" are what Jesus called "wolves in sheep's clothing."

Beware, lest you burn, Mr. Keyes.

In other elections...

Would someone please explain to me why USA Toady gives credence to Nader? He is not on the ballot in all states, unlike the Libertarian. He has less support than the Libertarians.

Could it be that USA Toady wants Bush to win? Naaah....

Next election's debates should have one clear very simple rule as to who would be included: any candidate that is on the ballot in all 50 states. Anybody else has no chance of winning and is merely an expensive distraction.

There has been a K5 article up for a week or so. The Senate, followed by the mainstream media, have sat up and taken notice.

Forget that this smear is as vicious as it is dishonest, and that no U.S. politician has even mentioned the idea of banning the Bible. What ought to anger fair-minded Americans everywhere is that the Bush-Rove team must be convinced that the churchgoing folks of West Virginia and Arkansas are so gullible and so ill-informed that this baseless charge could scare them into voting Republican for Bush-Cheney in order to keep their Bibles.

Tell me, please, just how bigoted and ignorant do George Bush and Karl Rove think that churchgoing voters of Arkansas and West Virginia really are?

West Virginia's senior Democratic senator, Robert Byrd, has it mostly right: "The Republican National Committee is spreading this tripe to smear Democrats, and the president ought to demand that the Republican National Committee apologize to the people of West Virginia."

More accurately, it is President Bush and Karl Rove who owe apologies to West Virginians and Arkansans, because the Republican National Committee is not by any definition an independent entity. The RNC is under the absolute control of this White House's political office and Karl Rove. That's the way things work in Washington. The only time that either political party's national committee enjoys any independence of action is when that party does not hold the White House.

Oct 04, 2004

Useful Dead Technologies

As time progresses, we expect technology to progress as well. It doesn't always do so.

Whether from corporate greed or corporate stupidity or just plain evil orneryness, some very good technologies have been allowed to die, usually being replaced by something vastly inferior and sometimes not being replaced at all.

Listed here are some technologies that were very useful, but have become not more useful but less; or died off completely. These are good and useful technologies that have been superseded by less useful and usually very annoying technologies.

Steel gears

During the 1950s when I was a young boy, machinery was made of steel. Not just machinery, but almost everything. Even my toys were made of solid steel. I learned at an early age not to drop things on my foot.

All the mechanical parts in your automobile, your washer and dryer, your furnace, etc were made of solid steel. Good strong durable steel. If a gear broke, it usually broke within the machinery's warranty period, as a broken gear meant that its casting or tempering was flawed.

Nylon and other plastics replaced the steel for many gears, including in your washing machine, in your car's now obsolete distributor, and in almost all electric motors.

Now, some time after your warranty expires, your washing machine or dryer or dishwasher or other appliance *will* fail. Old appliances' lifespans were in the decades. In the late 1960s when I worked in a drive-in theater, its refrigerator was a model made in the 1920s and still hummed along merrily. For all I know, it's cooling someone's beer today.

Today's appliances will give you a few short years – if

you're lucky. Then, one of its cheap plastic parts will break, usually a part that cannot be replaced; a part that was designed to never be able to be replaced or repaired. If you're lucky you'll shell out big bucks to get your cheap appliance repaired. If not, and more and more often these days, it will be unrepairable and you will shell out even bigger bucks to replace it, as your old (but not very old at all) nylon-gear laden piece of junk goes into a landfill.

They don't make 'em like they used to. They used to make 'em solid, to last. Now they're made of materials designed and guaranteed to break. Get out your wallets, suckers!

Properly constructed sandwiches

Legend has it that several hundred years ago, the Earl of Sandwich somewhere in the British Isles liked to play cards, and he liked to eat. His invention was named after him, the "sandwich". It was designed to be eaten without requiring silverware and without getting your hands greasy.

Flash forward a couple hundred years to the 1980s, when the Wendy's Hamburger chain redesigned this useful food technology, having the meat hanging out of the bun and grease and condiments sloppily dripping out. Their hamburger was accompanied by a hilarious commercial, where an old woman in her late 80s or early 90s (she's dead now, Jim) walked up to a giant hamburger bun, maybe ten inches diameter, lifted the top where a piece of meat about the size of a pepperoni slice sat. She grumpily demanded "Where's the beef!?"

Because of this, today you cannot buy a commercial sandwich that you can eat without making a disgusting mess. Often these days if I'm in a sit-down, non-fast food restaurant I'll eat my sandwich with a fork. WTF is the point of a sandwich, anyway?

Flat cotton shoelaces

Shoelaces have been designed for hundreds of years to keep your shoes on your feet. No longer. Today's shoelaces are designed with one purpose in mind – to annoy you.

The nylon gears mentioned above were supposed to be superior to steel because they don't need grease and should theoretically last longer than a greased steel gear. Usually, though, when the grease got old (usually years and years later, much later than a nylon gear will last) the gear would just get noisy. A shot of grease and it was good as new.

So what are they making shoelaces out of now? *Nylon!* Good old frictionless nylon "because of its strength". One wonders if today's engineers even need a college degree, as it seems that some things, like today's shoelaces, were designed by "special ed" students.

Because now, not only are they made of a friction-free material, they're round rather than flat, further eroding their ability to stay tied.

But all is not lost – today's laces are three or four times as long as yesterday's laces so you can double or triple tie them.

They don't last any longer than the old cotton laces, either. Thank God and Science for Velcro. I gave up on shoelaces a few years ago, and I don't care how gay the kids think strap-on shoes are.

Velcro straps are an almost acceptable workaround to the incredibly stupid, badly designed shoelace technology.

T-shirts that actually fit

Now, I'm not sure about the rest of the world, but here in the good old US of A we used to have textile mills and clothing manufacturers. A t-shirt snugged the back of your neck, and the front of the neck was very loose. It *fit*.

Then the Chinese started producing all of our clothing, and t-shirts don't fit any more. They always feel like you're wearing them backwards. If you have a large neck, like I do, they're extremely uncomfortable, pulling against your Adam's apple.

I have two theories about this. The first theory is that Chinamen are all pencil necked geeks. This seems to be borne out by the fact that Asians in this country usually study computer science.

The other theory is that when they stole the original fabric patterns, they mistakenly got two copies of the back of the pattern and missed the front of the shirt, because today's Chinese t-shirts feel like they're on backwards whether backwards or not.

Sure, they're only five bucks... but I'll give you fifty for one that *fits*.

Volume control knobs

You're driving down the road and that song comes on. You know the one, it really *rocks* and you *must* crank that sucker up.

But there's no crank any more. You have to take your eyes off of the road to find the one button on the fifty buttons to turn the damned thing up or down. Thank God they invented cell phones so you can call an ambulance after you wreck your car trying to turn the volume down to answer your cell phone!

And if you want to adjust the tone, balance, or rear fade, forget it. You're either going to have to stop the car, or get a passenger to do it for you. If, that is, he or she can find the owner's manual to figure out how to.

The old technology used knobs. There was a volume knob on the left, and a tuning knob on the right. Behind the volume knob was a tone control, or two tone controls (treble and bass). The knob on the right changed the stations, and it had a knob or two under it controlling balance and sometimes fade.

Some less stupid car radio manufacturers still use knobs, albeit digital knobs. But even these are less useful.

Old fashioned analog potentiometer knobs not only could be used without taking your eyes off the road, they were far more precise. My car stereo (with its volume buttons you have to look at to adjust) has 25 discrete volume levels. Some stereos have 50.

The old fashioned analog volume controls had an infinite number of levels. They were *analog*. If you're at the fringe of a reception area and the weather or whatever has caused the signal to drift, you could precisely tune it with your radio's analog variable capacitor. Today if (for example) KSHE 95's 94.7Mhz drifts to 94.8 and you're north of Litchfield (about 50 miles), you're out of luck, as you can tune to 94.7 or 94.9, but not 94.8200032010023445 like you can with an analog tuner.

Cars you can work on without $100,000 worth of tools
Sure, it's nice that a car will last 300,000 miles instead of 50,000 (despite the fact that I got 300,000 out of a 1974 Pontiac); it's nice that you get 30 miles per gallon rather than 18 for a comparable sized vehicle; and it's nice that they don't spew as much filth out of the tailpipe (unless you're driving a Chrysler or Mitsubishi or Kia product with more than 30,000 miles)...

But you can't repair them. Sure, the mechanic at the dealer can, but *you* can't. Most cars these days you can't even change the oil yourself, much less the spark plugs. And forget about a minor repair like a water pump or an alternator, they're now completely inaccessible.

A tune up? New points, spark plugs, perhaps plug wires, adjust the dwell and timing and you're done. Forty or fifty bucks worth of tools (including the strobe and dwell meter), fifteen or twenty minutes and the job's finished. Now, you're going to be without your car for a day as it sits in the shop. You can't tune it without a very expensive, proprietary computer.

Timing chains

There are no more timing chains. They've been replaced with belts.

For the less technically inclined out there, a timing chain controls a car's valves' motion. I've heard of timing chains breaking, but it was very rare, and I never experienced it myself. Not even in the old Pontiac (which I had to change a clutch once and a water pump once in) with its 300,000 miles.

Now they have timing *belts*. Changing it is now part of a tuneup, and what's worse, in some models of automobile, if it breaks while the engine is running it will ruin your valves.

"Well," I can hear the amoral bean counters say, "they didn't complain about the nylon gear in the distributor!"

Two handled shower faucets

I cannot for the life of me figure out why these damned stupid one handle spigots ever got popular. They can't possibly be cheaper... can they?

Like the digital volume controls, these are simply unadjustable with any degree of accuracy. Your shower will either scald you or freeze you. You're not going to get it comfortable.

Jesus I miss two handled showers!

Gravity furnaces with power piles

Here in Illinois it gets damned cold. *God damned* cold. Colder than a witch's tit. Colder than... well, pick your own cliché.

We get ice storms dragging power lines down once in a while, people sliding into utility poles with their cars, squirrels trying to get warm in transformers with the resulting explosion when the squirrel gets to meet its maker. Although the electricity here is very reliable, it does occasionally fail.

I've never had my natural gas supply fail, not one time in 50 years.

Er, okay *once*. But that was my fault; I forgot to pay the

bill.

The house I rented on Reservoir Street was built in the late 1920s or early 1930s, and had a coal furnace in the basement. Some time in the 1940s it had been converted to natural gas. It was what they called a "gravity furnace", where gravity would pull the heavier, cold air down the intake into the furnace, while the hot air coming from it was displaced upward into the home.

It stayed a steady, comfortable temperature.

My apartment now is too hot when the blower is on, and too cold when it's not.

The gravity furnace also had what was called a "power pile." You can still get replacement power piles (I had one replaced in that house), but no new furnace has one.

A power pile is a little tube about an inch diameter and maybe an inch and a half long. It looks like a small can capacitor. It sits in the furnace's pilot light and generates electricity for the thermostat from the pilot's heat.

The electricity failed one cold winter night when we lived there. We were blissfully unaware of the fact, as the furnace *did not need the city's electrical supply!*

Unfortunately, I didn't have a gas alarm clock and was late to work.

A power pile couldn't work in today's furnaces, as today's furnaces have no pilot lights, instead relying on an electric spark.

The new furnaces are cheaper to run, but if the power goes out, you're going to have to shell out for a motel room.

I wonder...

What useful old technologies there were before my time that have perished? Like the powerless winter night with its gravity fed power pile furnace keeping its owners toasty, or comfortable t-shirts, what other technologies generations before mine not only had, but wondered how they could ever do without?

And what useful old dead technologies didn't I think of? What is your favorite dead technology?
Jan 30, 2005

Two things have changed for the better in the ten years since this article was written.

The volume knobs in car radios have come back. Now watch them go away again with touchscreens in cars. But the knobs are still digital, limiting the number of volume levels that can be attained.

When a potentiometer failed, it usually didn't really but was only dirty. When the speakers crackled when you adjusted the volume, a little switch oil almost always cured the problem. When the volume knob on my older car went out I was clueless. Well, maybe not completely, maybe a little switch oil would have fixed that, too. Often when you tried to turn it up, it would go down, and vice versa.

Fortunately, that car had two volume controls, the knob on the radio and buttons on the steering wheel that you never had to look for. It was the safest car radio volume control I ever saw.

The second change was shoelaces. Did an engineer who worked for a shoe company see this article?

For the last few years, laces have become flat again, plus they're even better than the old cotton laces! New laces are nylon and cotton interwoven, giving you nylon's strength and cotton's friction.

Unfortunately, like t-shirts, socks no longer fit, either, at least if you buy them at Walmart and don't wear clown shoes.
Nov 8, 2014

Good Riddance to Bad Tech

The K5 article *Useful Dead Technologies* highlighted some older, now gone (or nearly gone) technologies I sorely miss.

"mcgrew," the Kurobots squealed, "You're a geezer! A crazy old, ranting coot! A Luddite! Aren't there any technologies you're glad are gone?"

Actually, there are. Here are a few of them, and like the useful dead technologies, some of these inventions (like the power pile and gravity furnace) were before my time, and I only knew this technology from being in the possession of an antique something or other like a house, or just reading about them.

The Guillotine

I'm sure that there are many of you out there who would like to bring this fine old technology back to life. Bloodier than a firing squad yet more humane than the Arabic methods of decapitation, those of you who are in support of the death penalty will call for its resurrection.

Not me. And if I write an article "Bad/useless live technologies," it will list all forms of capital punishment technology currently in use.

Dot matrix printers

NOISY MACHINES, NOISY NOISY NOISY! They were expensive things that had, like the typewriters before them, a single typeface. Unlike the typewriters before them, this typeface was extremely crude, primitive looking, and ugly. Like a typewriter, it had a ribbon that often got tangled, could not be re-inked, and usually could not be replaced without getting your hands filthy.

You kids who grew up with inkjets and laser printers are lucky.

The 8-track tape

This sorry piece of crap is proof positive of American stupidity. The cassette – the (now obsolete) four track, two-spindle, 1/8th inch, 1/78 IPS shirt pocket sized tape cassette was produced *before* the 8-track. The four track cassette was originally made as a dictation device, but advances in tape manufacture and head design soon gave them a frequency response that came close to human hearing's limit, signal to noise ratio low enough that you had to turn it up very loud to hear the hiss, and inaudible harmonic distortion, which made them ideal for music.

Nevertheless, the 8-track was born anyway. With its transport speed at twice the 4-track cassette's speed, it should have been audibly superior. However, the "powers that be" decided that 8-tracks were going to be for automobiles, which at the time were not as well insulated from outside sounds and wind as today's cars, and with the auto's horrible acoustics, it was okay for a car's music to sound like effluent.

But the deliberately bad sound wasn't bad enough. The eight track tape had a single spindle, a very clever design where the tape fed from the center of the spindle, around a capstan roller inside the housing and back to the outside of the roll of tape. This made for an expensive setup, and one that was prone to wow and flutter, as well as having the tape get "eaten" by the tape player. And unlike a cassette, if your 8-track got ate, you might as well throw it in the trash.

But wait, there's more! This thing was deemed to be for the car, while cassettes were going to be (by about 1970 or so) for the home.

This made no sense whatever, since the "portable" eight track took up as much space as *four* cassettes, without being able to play any longer than a cassette. In fact, you could buy a longer playing cassette than 8-track.

But the one thing more than anything else that made 8-tracks suck like a Hoover was the fact that it had to change tracks four times during an album. This usually necessitated at least one song and usually more being interrupted in the middle!

Folks finally, after about ten years, started figuring this stuff out for themselves and replaced their 8-track cartridges with 4 track cassettes. Me? I never had an 8-track, although all my friends did. I, the geek, used the far more logical cassettes since about 1966 or 7. Hah! The geek gets the last laugh again!

Hollerith Cards

Now, I never had to deal with these monstrosities, except that many bills came on them, and picking classes while at college. But I have read of the horrors meted out to programmers at the time, and am glad I never had to deal with them in a programming environment.

Actually, the punched cards are only bad in retrospect, since the tools we have now are so much handier.

The ten million dollar, building sized pocket calculator

...simply because I couldn't have one at the time! I had to use...

The Slide Rule

Actually, I loved my slide rule. This was because my teachers were incredibly stupid, and thought "gee, he can use a slide rule, he must be really smart!"

Er, no. I used it to *cheat in math class*. My slide rule made it unnecessary to learn my multiplication tables. Even today if I want to multiply seven times nine, I'll multiply seven times four, double it, and add seven. Which is why I'm firmly against letting kids use calculators before high school.

And speaking of which, as much as I loved my slide rule, I was more than glad to be rid of it when the far, far superior calculator came down in price where a human could actually afford one.

The automobile distributor and points

Unless you are a classic car collector, or a geezer, you

have no idea how much of a pain in the butt these things were. About every oil change or two, your car's performance and gas mileage would go down, and you would need a tuneup.

To tune your car, you could simply hire someone. That is, if you were a sissy.

A *real* man changed his own oil and tuned his own car up. You could tell a *real* man by the scars and scabs on his knuckles from working on his car.

First you had to change all eight of your spark plugs. What? You only have six? Pussy! Make sure you don't get the wires on wrong, or if your car will start at all, it will lurch and backfire and run like crap.

Then you had to take off the distributor cap, usually held on by two clips that would cut your fingers and were harder than a Rubic's cube solution to get clipped back on.

Under the distributor cap was the contact points. These had to be replaced. Then you had to adjust the gap on the points. Oh shit, I forgot to adjust the gaps on the spark plugs... do that all over again...

Now that the plugs are gapped and the points are replaced and gapped, you put the new distributor cap on... Come on... SHIT... GOD DAMNED PIECE OF SHI... okay, there it goes. Good. Gimme a bandaid, would ya?

Now you have to set the points' dwell. What's "dwell?" Beats the hell out of me, maybe it's the amount of time the points are closed. But you have to set it with a dwell meter or your car will run like it's powered by gerbils and will suck gas like Bush sucks at being President.

Then you have to get out your strobe and set the timing. You loosen the distributor, point your strobe at the mark on the... wait a minute... I can't see the damned mark. Stop the engine, would you?

Damn, it's all rusty and... to hell with it, start it back up and *I'll time the God damned thing by ear, piece of shit...*

Thank God and modern electronics for electronic ignition!

Lye Soap

My grandma made soap out of lye and pig fat. 'Nuff said, I think.

Non-powered hand tools

Can you even buy them today?

For a few years I owned a house that was built in 1918. It was state of the art when it was built, with gas *and* electric.

I often thought of the men who built that big old house, and marveled that they *had no power tools whatever!*

Stoves without pilot lights

No, I'm not speaking here of the new stoves that use an electric spark. I'm talking about technology that I'm not old enough to know first hand, but have only read of.

Early stoves had to be lit with a match, and there were no safety devices to shut an unlit gas source off. The knob on the oven was known as "the knob that will make the house explode," because if you turned on the knob and didn't light it, sooner or later when the house was full of fumes, boom.

I doubt many people miss exploding houses!

Vacuum tubes

All right, yes, we still have tubes. Your CRT is a tube, there is one (I think) in your microwave oven, and they're still using them in some guitar amplifiers.

But they used to be in everything electronic. Your TV set, your radio, your record player, your... er, um... Gee. We didn't have a lot of electronic things!

But the tubes *sucked.* In the first place, their filaments must heat the tube enough that electrons will go flying off of the cathode before the thing will even work. *Anything* electronic took as long to warm up as your computer monitor.

Um, computer... damn, it takes a long time for my new P4 to boot, do these things have tubes or something?

In the second place, they lasted about as long as a light

bulb; a year or two. Fortunately they were easy to diagnose. Tube's not lit? There's your problem! ...and replace. Unfortunately they were expensive, two to five bucks each when a McDonald's hamburger was fifteen cents and a candy bar or a bottle of soda was a nickle.

The Hydrogen Bomb
Oh wait, that one's still around. Damn!

Mon Mar 21, 2005

It's pretty obvious why the eight track was introduced despite its suckiness: corporate profits. They expected you to buy both the eight track and cassette of the same album. However, most people only bought one copy of the album, the LP version, and recorded it on a blank eight track.

Corporations are usually stupid and disgusting like that.

Nov 16, 2014

Growing Up With Computers

As another birthday comes closer with its ugly reminder of how short life is, it makes me think of you younger folks.

Because while you grew up with computers, my situation was just the opposite – computers grew up with me.

ENIAC, the first electronic programmable computer (in essence, a building sized scientific pocket calculator) was patented just short of five years before I was born. From the application:

...With the advent of everyday use of elaborate calculations, speed has become paramount to such a high degree that there is no machine on the market today capable of satisfying the full demand of modern computational methods. The most advanced machines have greatly reduced the time required for arriving at solutions to problems which might have required months or days by older procedures. This advance, however, is not adequate for many problems encountered in modern scientific work and the present invention is intended to reduce to seconds such lengthy computations...

From the ENIAC patent (No. 3,120,606), filed 26 June 1947.

The monster was switched on in fall of that year. It was the prototype for all computers that followed later, including the one you are reading this on.

As I was taking my first breath, having been pulled into the world with forceps after a 72 hour labor, the phrase "rock and roll" was still three months into the future. The computer as we know it today did not exist, although ENIAC, the keyboard-less and monitor-less prototype, was almost five years old.

By February 1949, when the ENIAC completed the computation for Project Chore, an Ordnance Corps contract with the University of Chicago, operating difficulties had been reduced to a minimum. Running times were longer, down times shorter and reduced in number. The Chore contract and others completed during this period proved the ENIAC's worth. Other machines, among them the Bush differential analyzer and the Bell relay calculator, would have required a prohibitive length of time to complete the problems that were assigned to the ENIAC, and the latter was much faster than any digital system then in existence.

The ENIAC led the computer field during the period 1949 through 1952 when it served as the main computation workhorse for the solution of the scientific problems of the Nation. It surpassed all other existing computers put together whenever it came to problems involving a large number of arithmetic operations. It was the major instrument for the computation of all ballistic tables for the U.S. Army and Air Force.

In addition to ballistics, the ENIAC's field of application included weather prediction, atomic energy calculations, cosmic ray studies, thermal ignition, random number studies, wind tunnel design, and other scientific uses. It has been noted that no electronic computers were being applied to commercial problems until about 1951.

EDVAC and ORDVAC, both faster than ENIAC, began to share the Computing Laboratory's work load with the ENIAC in 1953.

Before ENIAC, a computer was a human being whose job was doing arithmetic. Electronic computers were completely unknown to most people outside science and the military before the 1952 election, which is what brought computers into the public's awareness.

In the summer before the 1952 Presidential election, a Remington Rand employee contacted Sig Mickelson, CBS's news chief, and said he thought Univac could predict the election results by feeding it numbers obtained in previous elections. Mickelson and Walter Cronkite thought it would be entertaining nonsense, and agreed to add it to the election night coverage.

The night of the election, Charles Collingwood was in Philadelphia with Univac, and Cronkite was in the news studio with a fake computer, a stage prop made out of a teletype machine, blinking Christmas tree lights, and other dramatic nonsense. Yes, the news was presented as entertainment even back then.

All the polls had said that it was going to be a tight race. Univac made a prediction at 8:30 pm; Eisenhower would win by a landslide.

Nobody believed it and Cronkite didn't report it. Late that night when the actual election results came in, they realized that the computer was right and the pollsters were completely wrong. Univac was incredibly accurate in its prediction, being off on the popular vote by 3% and the Electoral vote by less than 1%. CBS was incredibly embarrassed, and when they realized that Univac was right, they finally reported it.

Univac, the most powerful computer in the world, was the star of the show.

A musical Hallmark card has more computing power than Univac.

My interest in these monsters started with a 16mm film a grade school teacher showed about these "electronic brains." It told of ENIAC, the story of Univac and the election the year I was born, and showed a technician shutting one down for debugging. "Imagine," the narrator said, attempting to emphasize how accurate these devices were, "if the teacher would kill you every time you got a question wrong!"

I was hooked.

In 1964, my family went to Texas on vacation and saw what I remember as "the World's fair". Google, however, tells me that the World's fair was in New York that year. Whatever this exposition was, it was there that I met my first computer, and played my first computer "game".

The game was "States and Capitols", and I wished that they had one of these things in my school. This was a lot more fun than a paper and pencil test!

They had the thing hooked up to a loom, and they had monitors with primitive light pens. You could create a design for a cloth bookmark, and the computer/loom combination would weave a bookmark with your design!

It was the coolest thing I had ever seen in my life. "I want one!" I said. My dad just laughed. The thought that a human, let alone a middle class family, could own a computer was as outrageous as the thought of a device that could cook food with radio waves, or a device that would save TV shows for later viewing. Little did I know that one day I'd have a computer far more powerful in my pocket!

However, I did manage to build a computer of sorts from plans out of a Popular Electronics magazine. This "computer" was actually an electric slide rule, made out of a couple of pieces of wood, a battery, a switch, two potentiometers and a voltmeter. It actually worked, although you weren't going to plot any moon shots with it.

Yes, I was quite the nerd, reading science fiction, building electronics, and using a slide rule. By the time I was ready to graduate high school, though, I had sworn off of electronics. Discrete components were out, integrated circuits were in, and I didn't see the fun in them. I mean, hooking the leads from an amplifier circuit to a speaker and a battery and a jack wasn't all that demanding.

By 1972 I was in the US Air Force as a driver, working on the flight line in the Aerospace Ground Equipment (AGE) unit. One cold, snowy night a half hour from the swing shift's quitting time, a call came in for two air conditioners way over on the other side of the base. My tractor had a top speed of about ten miles per hour – I was looking forward to a beer, and here I had to drag these damned air conditioners out. I was going to be working late. Hell!

A half an hour or so later I arrived at the facility,

swearing, with air conditioners in tow. To my amazement there were two guys standing outside in the snow waiting for me.

"What the *fuck* do you need a God damned air conditioner in the snow for?" I demanded.

"Oh, man," one replied excitedly, "this is *so* cool. You have to see it!" These guys were bouncing around like kids at a birthday party. One showed me around as the other hooked up the hoses from the air conditioners and turned them on.

Inside was what looked like a library. Every room was filled with rows and rows of what appeared to be bookshelves. However, instead of books, these shelves held printed circuit boards. There must have been thousands of them. I was duly impressed, and had nerdily forgotten about the beer I had wanted so badly. I was standing *inside* a computer!

"Cool. But what is it for?" I asked.

"Ahh," he said, "come in here," and led me to yet another room. This room was huge, and had little in it that I recognized. It was straight out of a science fiction movie, only less corny looking.

"Okay," I replied stupidly, "what is it?"

"It's a C5 simulator! Come on inside!"

And inside the contraption was the cockpit of a C-5A cargo plane, at the time the largest aircraft in the world. We had several C5s there at Dover, which was, of course, why they needed a C5 simulator. And two SUV sized air conditioners to cool the contraption's roomfuls of circuitry.

It was identical to a C5 cockpit, right down to the bolts and carpets. The only difference was that the windows were ground glass rather than clear, for projecting images on.

They let me "fly" it. It was incredible! It sat on hydraulics, so when you accelerated, it felt like acceleration. Likewise banking, diving, etc. You could even crash the thing! This was even cooler than the other computer I had seen back when I was 12.

Again, I lusted after a computer of my own.

In 1974, the first PC (or "microcomputer") was introduced, and I missed it. It was the Altair, with switches on the front for input, lights for output, and 256 bytes of memory. That's right kids, not gigabytes, not megabytes, not even kilobytes. Bytes. It was nothing more than a toy for nerds, having no practical use whatever. So it was probably a good thing that I was in Thailand at the time or I would have probably blown the three months' pay on one.

A few years later I met my first privately owned computer: a "pong" game a friend had. Yawn. Yes, Pong was as mindlessly boring in 1978 as it is in 2005.

By 1982 I had gotten out of the Air Force, gone through college, been married for six years, and was living in Florida and working at Disney World. There I met even more computers, mainframes all. I never got closer than eye shot, but that was closer than most people ever got. These computers controlled the amusement park's rides, animatronics, and just about everything else.

By then, the Commodore Pet had come out, and the Apple, and the TI-99A, and a few other makes. I wanted one badly, but didn't have the money. Finally, Britain's Sir Clive Sinclair did what Apple later claimed to do – made a computer "for the rest of us." Unlike Apple's "rest of us" which was "those of us normal, non-nerds only with a boatload of money," the Sinclair was affordable. Only a hundred bucks! ...which was still a lot of money to me at the time, but I could scrape it together.

I learned to program in BASIC. I then proceeded to learn how to program it in machine code, since its 1 MHz chip that also powered everything about the cheap device was simply too slow for the games I wanted to play. I had to design and write the games myself, since there really weren't any that I could find.

A year later, I got another computer, this one in color! It was a Radio Shack MC-10. I fiddled around with it and figured out how to hack its text-only display into graphics with software, and sold a few copies of the graphics program I wrote for it.

We moved back to Illinois with our new baby, where I parlayed my knowledge of computers into a paying job. I still work there today, writing programs, writing reports, and helping clueless users. I still have my soldering iron despite swearing off of it (and still use it), and I build my own computers now. The baby's younger sister just turned 18, and the wife is now an ex.

The computer sitting on the desk here in my apartment is several orders of magnitude more powerful than that first computer I saw at the exposition in 1964, and even orders of magnitude faster than the computers that calculated the moon shot trajectories. It was worth the wait!

Do you remember your first computer?

Mar 30, 2005

Biters Anonymous

Hi, my name's mcgrew and I'm a biter.

Biters Anonymous is a crowd of losers who share their experience, roflcopters and lolerskates with each other that they may solve their common problem and help others to recover from the ravages of biting trolls.

The only requirement for membership is a desire to stop biting.

There are no dues or fees for BA membership; we are self-supporting through our own contributions. BA is not allied with any sect, denomination, politics, organization or institution or endorses nor opposes any causes.

Our primary purpose is to stay troll-free and help other Biters to achieve bitelessness and not feed the trolls.

Step 1: We admitted we were powerless over biting – that our bites had become unmanageable

Step 2: Came to believe that a poster greater than ourselves could return our lollerskates

Step 3: Made a decision to turn our stories and our diaries over to the care of Rusty and His admins

Step 4: Use the <li> operator or risk being called a lamer by trolls, tempting you to bite

Step 5: We must never ever be at all honest with anybody evar.

Step 6: I am not a step, I am a free man!

Step 7: Craps

Step 8: Stop giving a shit.

Step 9: Step 9: Step 9: Step 9:

Step 10: You still didn't follow step 4 yet, lamer

Step 11: Mind your own damned business

Step 12: Shut off the fucking computer and go outside for God's sake!

Poll
I am a...

Troll	12%
Biter	4%
Lurker	32%
Contributor	8%
rmg	24%
I don't know	16%
admin	0%
wipo	4%

Apr 22, 2005

> By this time, Rusty had pretty much abandoned K5, spending his time at the new site, and left K5 to the care of his admins.
> This was unfortunate. A particular admin, Pete Jongular, pissed me off enough that I never went back. Apparently I wasn't the only one he pissed off, because the place is a ghost town now.
> The following two articles were posted at the now defunct mcgrew.info and seen by very few.
> And then I rediscovered slashdot, who now had journals!
> Nov 15, 2014

The Neocon

The reason I haven't written anything (except an email to Hawk) in the last month or four is because I gave up writing, again. I'm reminded of my old friend Danny, who would say every Friday before we started drinking, "I ain't gonna do it no more."

Writing has been like a drug to me, both an intoxicant and a stress reliever. My old Paxil diaries, I believe, did more for my mood than the Paxil itself. But it seems wherever I write, people find it and it starts all over again, no matter where I put it.

What got me off the "no more writing" wagon? I have to gloat.

Duffy's Pub was right down the street from my old beloved house. Losing that house last year hurt more than losing my marriage, I think. Of course, I was going through withdrawal from Paxil when they took the house, and on Paxil shortly after Evil-X left. Some people commit suicide during Paxil withdrawal. I just cried like a toddler who had dropped his ice cream cone.

So anyway, Duffy's banker foreclosed on his pub's mortgage and the place closed down a week after I moved. "Damn," I said to myself, "I must be drinking too much."

I hated to see Duffy's close, mostly because it was so hilarious to see Duffy's truck parked outside. The sign on the bar said "Duffy's Pub". The sign on the back of the pickup truck said "Duffy's Sewer and Excavating." God but I wish I'd taken a picture!

It opened up under a new owner, who wasn't much of a businessman. I dropped by once, bought a draft, and put a dollar in the jukebox, one of those newfangled internet connected ones. I was unhappy; these new jukeboxes only give two songs for a buck, as opposed to the "normal" (these days) three songs.

I only got one song! I complained to the owner. "Oh," he said, "if you get a song off of the internet it costs a dollar."

"WHAT?!?!?" I demanded. "That's CRAP! Two for a dollar is bad enough, I feel like I've been stolen from."

The guy shrugged. "Fuck you and your shitty bar," I said, and left. A month later the sign proclaimed a new owner as I drove by, so I went in. I was pleased to see the damned internet jukebox gone and a real jukebox, one with CDs and three songs for a buck back.

I was even happier to find out that I knew the owner, who I often drank with there when it was Duffy's, and that I knew the bartender, an attractive woman my age. Well, attractive for a woman my age, anyway. It's only a mile or so from my house, so if I get drunk I can always walk, and if I'm too drunk to stagger I can afford a cab.

The drinks are cheaper than anybody else, there's food (good food too). And there was free food on Sundays (alas, no more). Well, sloppy joes count as food, don't they? That's all they have on Sundays. Beats the Track Shack, who has "all you can eat for a dollar" hot dogs and greasy chili on Sundays.

So I finish my sandwich and first beer, and an old lady sits down next to me. A delightful old woman of 83, as she happily bragged, who had been married longer than I've been breathing. "So where's the old man?" I asked. "Ah, he's no fun, I left the old bastard at home."

As she starts on her second glass of wine (pay attention, kids, if you want to live a long time) a thirtyish looking guy with crazy looking gray eyes sits down on the other side of her and starts talking politics. He's a Bush supporter, a neocon.

A nut job.

Being 83, the old woman was certainly benefiting from Social Security, Medicare, and all the other perks geezers get that they have paid for all their lives. She didn't take too kindly to this young whippersnapper who wanted to take away the Social Security she paid into for so many years.

Here's a hint for you Republicans: Old people vote. I smell a Democrat Congress next election, as the Republicans have really pissed off the old folks.

I made it a two on one fight. What a prick, taking on an old lady like that. He was talking about how his voice was weird like that from his war wounds, and I was thinking about a schizophrenic I used to know who thought he was shot down in Vietnam, despite the fact that he was only 13 when the war ended.

"I've earned the right to..."

"Look, buddy," I told him, "I VOLUNTEERED for the service during the most unpopular war in our history, despite the fact that I was NOT going to be drafted. So you can just shut the fuck up about being dumb enough to hurt yourself. Bush is a traitor. I think he orchestrated 9-11. The Bin Laden family is good friends with the Bush family, and the only one who benefited from 9-11 was Bush himself. He should be impeached, tried, convicted, and put in front of a firing squad and shot."

The old lady giggled. "Thanks, son, you made my day," and paid and left. "Mister Special Forces" sat there with his jaw hanging. I finished my beer and left as well.

I dropped back in the next Sunday (I wrote this quite a while ago, am only now posting it) for my sloppy joe, and my bartender friend was on my side of the bar. "Boy that guy was an asshole," she said. "If he comes back in when I'm bartending I'm not serving him."

Shortly after she left, Mr Special came in and started bitching about taxes.

"Taxes? That's damned unpatriotic!" I said.

"Huh?"

"Where the hell do you think the armor on those Humvees in Iraq comes from?"

"Uh, er, well, I don't mind my taxes going for armor, but I don't like seeing it go to those big salaries the politicians get."

"What the FUCK are you talking about?" I said. "Bush is the highest paid politician in Government."

"Well yeah," he said, "four hundred thousand dollars a year, for what?"

"For leading the most powerful nation on Earth," I answered, "when the CEO of any fortune 500 company gets four hundred *million* a year."

His face went white, and he left. Everybody started buying me drinks, and I got wasted.

I never saw the guy again.

I ain't gonna do it no more. Write, I mean.

Aug 26, 2005

298

I'm dreaming of a secular Christmas

I'm dreaming of a secular Christmas
In this modern secular day
With a secular tree with secular lights
And a Santa in a secular sleigh

I'm dreaming of a secular Christmas
With lots of secular snow
With a secular wreath and some secular lights
And some secular mistletoe

No baby in a manger
No wise men at his bed
No thought of Jesus Christ at all
Just get him out of your head

I'm dreaming of a secular Christmas
With lots of secular snow
With a secular Santa in a secular sleigh
And a secular HO HO HO!

No baby in a manger
No wise men at his bed
No thought of Jesus Christ at all
Just get him out of your head

I'm dreaming of a secular Christmas
Have a Happy Holiday!
Don't forget the secular eggnog
Just forget just whose birthday...

Dec 3, 2005

Don't try to outweird me, three eyes!

"Don't try to outwierd me, three eyes, I get stranger things than you with my breakfast" – Zaphod Beeblebrox

I think I was born nearsighted. I can remember thinking as a small child that I could see air. I never told anyone this, because after all, none of the superheros in my comic books ever admitted *their* super powers.

I found out different when I had my eyes checked. I remember my first pair of glasses, how clear and shiny (and bent and distorted) everything was.

I also remember being called "four-eyes" in school.

My eyes were *bad*; 20/400. That's incredibly bad; it means that what a normally sighted person could see at 400 feet I could see at 20. If your eyes can't be corrected to better than 20/200 you're legally blind. I wore Coke bottle glasses to correct my 20/400 vision. Of course, since this is slashdot I'm pretty sure a majority of you wear coke bottle glasses as well.

When I was a young man, I tried contact lenses. I couldn't wear them, it felt like there was glass in my eyes.

Contacts were made of glass back then. Yep, I'm gettin' old.

But glasses were such a *bitch*. If it's raining, you can't see. If you're mowing the lawn in the hot sun, sweat covers your glasses and you can't see. If you walk inside on a cold winter day your glasses fog up and you can't see. They get dirty and you can't see.

If you get hit in the face with a baseball you can't see.

By my mid 40s I noticed I had to pull my glasses down my nose to read.

One evening I walked downtown in a drizzle, looking forward to a drink or three and listening to some live music. I got downtown, went in the bar and sat down. I grabbed a bar napkin and started wiping the rain off the lenses.

300

One of them popped out of the frame, skittered across the bar, and went underneath a 3,000 pound cooler.

Damn!

I tried to work the next day; no good. One lens wouldn't cut it. I knew they had eyeglasses at Walmart and figured they'd be faster than anybody else, so I took a bus down there. Drive? You wanted me to DRIVE like that??

They did an examination, and said they could have a pair of glasses in three days.

THREE DAYS??? Jesus H. Christ! I can't go without glasses for three days!!!!!

"Would you like to try contacts? you could get contacts today!"

Just try 'em? Why not, sure.

The lady showed me how to put them in and take them out. After fumbling for a few minutes I got one in my eye – and it didn't hurt! And I could **SEE!!!** WOW!!! No more glasses!

Well, not quite... I couldn't pull contact lenses down my nose to focus to read. You see, in middle age the eye's focusing lens, back behind the iris, gets hard. The muscles still work theoretically, but there's nothing for them to move to focus, as the lens is too hard.

I needed reading glasses on top of my contacts. Now I was *six-eyes!* Damn!

What a shitty century. My country was attacked; my President was a fucking moron hell-bent on making gasoline ten dollars a gallon and to hell with the country; my beloved uncle and grandmother died (not in the attack. My uncle died of lung cancer 25 years after he stopped smoking, and my grandmother fell and broke her hip at age 99); my wife left me and my teenaged daughters for another man; all of what they (not I) called "rock and roll" sucked ass; the record companies were suing their customers; the Democrats and Republicans seemed to become two arms of the same fascist party; they passed the "Patriot" Act (which should have been called the "Cowardly Government Is Scared Shitless Act"), the DMCA and

301

the Bono act; without my ex-wife's added income my van was repossessed and my house foreclosed, and I declared bankruptcy. And I got another God damned eye infection!

Shit!

So I went to Urgent Care and saw a doctor (I'd already canned my family doctor for taking me off the Paxil I was prescribed for "Adjustment Disorder with Depressed Mood" right in the middle of getting my house foreclosed). The doc gave me some eye drops.

They didn't work; the eye was redder and hurt even more. I went back to the doctor, who referred me to a specialist, who gave me some *steroid* drops. The eye stopped hurting.

A couple weeks after stopping the drops I noticed my vision in that eye was getting worse. When I ran out of contacts I went back to Walmart for more. I'd been wearing them a few years by then.

The doctor examined my eyes and said my left eye, the one that had been afflicted with the infection, had a cataract. I thought I was too young for cataracts, not even 55.

"It's a young man's cataract; you get this kind from steroids."

Steroids? Like the *steroid eye drops???*

"Don't worry, just go to the Prairie Eye Center and see Doctor Yae if it gets much worse. She'll fix it and your insurance will cover it. Meanwhile I'll up your lens strength."

That was last January, by April I could barely see at all out of that eye. So I went to see Dr. Yae (whose name I may be misspelling).

"You have a cataract," she said.

She told me about the procedure, and said I should know about this new technology just approved by the FDA in 2003 called the CrystaLens.

Since 1949 (I looked it up) they have been replacing cataracts, which are actually an occluded lens, with an IOL, or Inter Occular Lens. It's a plastic lens that replaces the eye's natural focusing lens. Besides curing the cataract by replacing it with an artificial lens it also cured nearsightedness and astigmatism in patients like me who were so afflicted. You still needed reading glasses, of course, but no matter since everybody's lens gets too hard to focus before they're old enough for cataracts, anyway.

The CrystaLens lets you focus!

Before the surgery, I amused myself by grossing people out with graphic descriptions of what I was going to let them do to me. "They stick a needle in your eye, turn the lens to mush with ultrasound, and suck it out through the needle. Then they stick a piece of plastic in. My mom says it's a piece of cake." She had the old fashioned IOLs inserted a few years ago.

"I guess that's what I get for saying 'cross my heart and hope to die' when I was a kid!"

The eye's lens is covered in a kind of bag, the "lens capsule". When they insert an IOL they put it inside the capsule, which is still attached to the focusing muscles. The CrystaLens is hinged, allowing the muscles to move it forward and backward.

But it costs $1,900 more than the traditional implant, and this part comes out of my pocket. I normally eat at restaurants, but started eating TV dinners and ham sandwiches instead. And pretty much stopped drinking.

The area bars, in effect, paid for the part insurance wouldn't.

Now, I'm leaving a lot out here, they have to measure your eyeball, you have to get a physical exam to make sure you're okay to get a needle stuck in your eye and stuff, but the day of the surgery came around and I had barely paid the bill; it must be in advance, as they can't repossess your eye. My daughter drove me to the hospital for the outpatient procedure.

Most of the day was spent waiting. I waited for my blood pressure to be taken, weighed, etc.

Then waited for pre-op, where they dosed my eye with what seemed like gallons of eye drops that hurt like hell, and stuck an IV needle in my wrist. Then waited for the actual operation.

Doctor McCoy would have been jealous of the technology at a modern hospital; we've gone WAY past what the science fiction writers of the '60s could imagine.

They tied my arms down. "So you don't try to help the doctor." They put a thing over my face.

I distinctly remember freaking out when they stuck the needle in. But my memories of the actual surgery are very, very dim; I do remember the only pain was in pre-op when they dosed me.

They finally took the thing off my face and untied my hands, and wheeled me into the recovery room. *I could read the clock on the wall! With no corrective lenses at all!* I'd never experienced this before!

They released me, and told me I was legally intoxicated for 24 hours and to not make any important decisions, sign any documents, operate dangerous machinery or drive. "If you get caught driving they'll put you in jail" I was warned.

The next day my daughter took me to the Eye Institute, where my eyesight was measured at 20/20. Now, the drops they put in your eye paralyze the focusing muscles, but in a week when I went back I was already starting to focus. My eye was now 20/16, meaning I can see at 20 feet what a normally sighted person can see at 16 feet. I'm now better than 20/20!

I was instructed to read at least ten minutes per day, without reading glasses, to build up the atrophied muscles I'd not used in ten years.

On a good day in good light I can now read the date on a dime! Outdoors, with a contact lens in my right eye, my vision is pretty much the same in each eye. Inside if I close the eye with the CrystaLens, everything gets fuzzy. And the more I read, the better my eye gets.

There is no lens needed for my left eye now. Dr. Yae

says I'll need the other eye done in a year or two, until then I wear a contact in that eye.

Finally, something about this century that doesn't suck!

So just call me three-eyes. For the next year or two, anyway.

Oct 26, 2007

Taking a "hydrogen bomb" to school

It's been a boring week. I love it!

However, a pleasant life for me makes for boring reading for you. So I think I'll take a newspaper article and walk down memory lane with it. I submitted "Student charged for bringing tool into high school" (news articles about it are in the Chicago Tribune and Belleville News Democrat) to slashdot this morning. This is similar to a story I submitted last year, "Student Arrested for Writing Essay".

Jees but kids today have it rough. I once made an F on a paper because the incompetent teacher thought I made up the word "hierarchy", and got an A on a different paper because it was over the incompetent teacher's head. I bet teachers hate nerds. But at any rate, I never got arrested for writing a paper, but I did almost get expelled for a science project.

The student in the linked newspaper articles is

...an honor student at Grayslake Central High School, a choir singer, as well as a former football player who spends half the day training to be a firefighter.

That exemplary record now includes something new: A police ticket for reckless conduct given last week after school officials discovered a a multi-tool flashlight in a jacket he left in the cafeteria.

The tools include a 2-inch blade, screwdriver, pliers and other gadgets prohibited under school policy

When I was in seventh grade, I needed a floating balloon for something or other, I don't remember what, but it was some geeky project or some such nonsense. It wasn't for school, only for my own personal curiosity and amusement.

I often took these nerdy things to school to amuse my fellow students and annoy my incompetent teachers. The previous year I had built a "dufus detector" out of a soda can, small light, battery, magnetic switch, a ring, and a magnet. I'd cut up the soda can and made a housing out of it, and wired up the light, battery, and switch, and glued a magnet to a ring. Place the ring correctly and the light on the box would light up. I had loads of fun with it until it pegged the teacher as a dufus and she took it away.

Another one was a prototype for what was later to become a real computer program, *Artificial Insanity* (which I'm going to translate to javascript some time). It was a computer that wasn't really; it was a box again fashioned out of a can, only it held a roll of paper with generic answers to questions on it, like a "Magic Eight Ball". You would ask the question and the next sheet out was your answer. The other kids ate it up until it, too was confiscated.

I made a real computer out of two potentiometers, a voltmeter, a battery, and a switch. Well, actually it was more of an electric slide rule, but it really did compute. If I remember correctly, I turned that one in to a science teacher and got an A on it before it was confiscated.

So I have something in mind that floats, I don't remember what but I've always been a weirdo with a strange sense of humor. I had no idea where to get helium, so I schlepped down to the library and researched.

Helium was quickly ruled out as "no way in hell can a 7th grader do that" so I switched my research to hydrogen, and found two feasible methods of production. One was electrolysis, but I would have had to construct an airtight container with two chambers and... well, it would be too much work and if it had a leak between the anode and cathode where the oxygen could mix with the hydrogen it could explode.

The chemical solution was much simpler. It seems that if you eat zinc with acid, hydrogen is produced. So all I had to do was fill a coke bottle (they were made of very thick glass back then) with galvanized roofing nails, then fill it with vinegar, and put a balloon on the top.

The next morning saw a full balloon on top of the coke

bottle. I took it off, tied its neck, let it go and it floated... straight down to the floor, as if it was filled with normal air.

Wanting to test that it really was hydrogen, I figured I'd see how flammable it was; if it was very flammable it probably was hydrogen (and the book had said...). So I put another balloon on the bottle and left it for ten minutes, just enough for a golf ball sized balloon. I tied that, put it on the end of a coat hanger, turned on the stove, reached out and

WOOMP! A big fireball a yard wide! Okay, this was at least flammable. *Very* flammable. I decided to ask my science teacher about it. I took the full balloon to school, and asked the science teacher why a balloon full of hydrogen might not float.

"Well," he said, "if the hydrogen was impure it might not float. Why do you ask?"

"Because," I said, "I have a balloon full of hydrogen in my locker and..."

"You have WHAT?!?!?!???!!!!"

I was whisked out of class and to the principal's office, leaving the other kids to gossip about what that crazy nerd mcgrew had done this time. It was obviously a little more serious than a dufus detector.

At the office they were talking expulsion.

"So," I said, "you're going to punish a student for being curious and doing a science experiment? And you wonder why kids hate school?"

Somehow I talked my way out of any punishment at all! I did, however, have to take my balloon full of hydrogen outside and break it. This was one project the teachers were afraid to confiscate. Today they'd probably have the bomb squad there and I'd be in guantanamo, or at least the county jail.

The kids talked about how "mcgrew brought a hydrogen bomb to school and almost blew the school up" the rest of the year.

Jan 16, 2008

The Bleeding Eyeball

it's an orangy sky
always it's some other guy
it's just a fuckin' lullaby
-The Cars

You're not going to believe this, but in the middle of a very long losing streak I turned down sex with an attractive woman on Saturday and said "no" to two hookers on Monday.

I was puttering around the house, washing clothes and dishes and drinking coffee and listening to MP3s when the phone rang. It was Crazy Debbie. What was I doing? I said I was straightening up the house and drinking coffee. "You by yourself?" I replied in the affirmative, having gotten rid of both Amy and Tami. She said she was going to Felbers, the tavern I couldn't remember the name of in another journal, next door to Floyd the Barber. Would I join her for a beer?

Why not?

Debbie's a good looking woman. That is, she would be if it weren't for the crazy hair and the way she doesn't know how to apply makeup properly.

She wasn't wearing any makeup. And she was buying me beer.

And I drank too much of it. We wound up in my living room passing a joint. Then somehow my hand was in her pants.

I was going to get lucky. And then... I'm not sure exactly what happened, but I got a bad case of the willies and took her home, and didn't have the sex she so very obviously wanted me to give her.

I'm not sure what it was that scared me off, but something I can't quite put my finger on told me if I had sex with this woman my already increasingly unpleasant life was going to take a very unpleasant turn for the worse. I took her home.

What was really weird was that she freaked me out so much I didn't even feel horny any more, even though I didn't have sex and hadn't had any for quite some time. I'm still trying to figure it out.

The rest of the day is hazy in my mind; I had a couple of shots somewhere that I can't remember, and I'm told by two people I was at JW's that afternoon.

I don't remember being there. That scares me; I think I'll stop drinking, at least for a while.

I owed "Ralph" ten bucks and as I was paying him, it seemed I was twenty bucks poorer than I should have been and couldn't figure out where it went. Later I remembered that I'd been at a new pizza place with Crazy Debbie.

I went and shot a game of pool with Linda. I think it was at the Blue Grouch but I'm not sure, I was fucking *wasted*.

Then, my hazy memory tells me I was drinking with Tami at my house, and she told me later we did some unintentional four wheeling in a muddy field in the ghetto after having a flying car for a couple of seconds. They told me I'd have a flying car in the twenty first century! I don't remember that, either. The car seems to be none the worse for the incident.

Sunday I slept late. Very late. I went to Farley's and drank a single beer, JW's for another single beer and talked with Mike for a while, and wound up at home that evening. Sunday was uneventful.

Monday was President's Day and I didn't have to work. I was looking forward to another day of sleeping late.

Like Arthur Dent on Thursdays, I don't do Mondays very well. This one started with someone banging on the door at the crack of dawn.

"Who is it?"

She said her name – it was Bighead, the skinniest woman I ever met with the smallest tits I've ever seen. And the last time I'd seen her she'd stolen fifteen bucks from me.

"Go away!"

"Open the door!"

"Go away! You sold the best friend you could have ever had for fifteen bucks."

"No."

"Go away!"

"What are you going to do, have your girlfriends beat my ass?"

"They wanted to, I saved you from an ass beating."

"Open the door!"

"No!!"

"Open the door!"

I ignored her and eventually she went away.

Later, coffeed up and in a good mood, my day was ruined when "Kathy" (not her real name, of course) called with an offer that would would have made me twenty dollars richer. She wanted to use my house as a whorehouse.

This hurt. Here I hadn't been laid in like forever and a woman wanted to fuck another man in my house. I turned her offer down and went to Farley's, where the day got marginally better – they had free food. Walleye, pasta salad, potatoes, cake, I don't know what else.

Later I dropped by Ralph's, and his girlfriend's daughter "Missey" was there. She's a kid, only nineteen, two years younger than my youngest daughter. She pulled me aside into the bedroom and closed the door.

"Somebody said you wanted to try ecstasy? My guy's in jail but I can get you some when he gets out." I admit I am curious; I don't think they had ecstasy back in my days as a drug-addled young hippie in the late '70s. Guys? Tell me?

Linda and I made plans to go shoot some pool, and I sat and watched the evening news with Ralph. Halfway through the news I saw a snake. It wasn't Bighead, and it wasn't the DTs.

I knew this snake. It was the black snow snake.

My left eyeball was bleeding internally, with snakelike

311

objects inside it and a shower of black snow that got thicker and thicker.

My good eye. The eye with the implant that makes me, by dictionary definition, a cyborg. The eye I spent a shitload of money on. The eye that's better than 20/20.

I hurried home to put a contact lens in the other eye, which is about 20/400 without the lens. I hadn't been wearing the contact lens, relying on the eye with the implant that makes my friend Tom call me the "six thousand dollar man", a play on the six million dollar man from the old TV show.

A year ago last December I suffered a torn retina. I found a very good specialist who welded it mostly back together with a laser, but the implant I have in that eye is on struts so it can focus, unlike older implants. He couldn't reach the whole tear with the laser beam so he had to finish the treatment with an older method, which involves supercooling a metal probe with liquid nitrogen and holding it to the sclera, the white of the eye, opposite the tear.

If I'd been strapped to a chair at Guantanamo when they did that I'd have confessed to anything.

The place where the tear had been has let loose bleeding inside my eyeball several times since then, the last time being last June or July. The symptoms of the bleeding are the same as that of a torn retina, so of course whenever that happened I hightailed it to Dr. Odin, my retina specialist. He was on vacation, so the office referred me to another specialist at one of the local hospitals where the guy was training an intern.

"And there's where a cryotherapy was done... oh, that's right on a major nerve. Man, that really had to hurt!"

I've never in my life heard more of an understatement. Women bitch about the pain of childbirth; well, let Dr. Odin stick that supercooled metal probe on a major nerve on *their* eyeball and see how resistant to pain they are!

I met "Larry" and "Ralph" and "Missey" and Linda at the Blue Grouch, where Linda kicked my ass on the pool table royally. I was used to using the cybernetic eye, and now was using the other eye instead, with a contact lens in it. I think I got one ball in. Linda was very pleased with herself!

I've not been wearing the contact; the eye with the contact lens bled internally once, a couple of months ago, and I kind of stopped bothering to put the contact in. I've thought about changing my sig as a result, but once again I'm three eyes, even though one of them isn't working. Kind of like one of Zaphod's heads in the BBC TV version of The Hitchhiker's Guide to the Galaxy. The one that looks like it's made of paper maché.

Speaking of aliens, as I was driving home from the Blue Grouch to get an early bedtime, Tami called. Her alien husband had left her again and she needed a friend. As I was going to need a driver to get home from the eye doctor the next day, I picked her up, bought her a half pint of whiskey and listened to her whine about her husband, before letting her crash on the couch. I fell asleep in the other room to the sound of her crying.

At work Tuesday the first thing I did, of course, was get on the phone to Dr. Odin's office. True to the last few days, nothing was going my way at all. The doctor was in Decatur, and they had me come in around nine. The doctor I saw couldn't see anything inside my eyeball, which didn't surprise me one bit since I couldn't see anything outside of it.

Last night Tami talked to her Peruvian husband, who'd been thrown out of his girlfriend's house. Knowing that asshat she probably caught him fucking a different woman. Tami sold him a key to their apartment for drinking money.

I went back in this morning to see Dr. Odin, and sat down next to a not bad looking, garrulous woman who delighted in striking up a conversation with me. Of course, the conversation only lasted about two minutes since they got me right in to see the doctor, who did a sonogram on my eye. It appears the retina is intact, and my vision should clear back up in a month or so. I go back to see him next month.

I cooked some omelettes for Tami and myself and took her back to her apartment after the dilation eyedrops wore off.

I forgot to mention that the doctor said that I face the possibility of further eye surgery, a Vitrectomy, if the eye continues its periodic bleeding.

Do NOT look that up on Wikipedia if you are squeamish! It leads to the article on vitrectomy, and has a very ugly nasty photo of an eyeball undergoing the procedure.

The good outweighed the bad, however. First, as the bleeding episodes seem to be more and more rare he may not have to do the surgery, and second, it would stop the bleeding (and periodic blindness) for good as well as completely eliminating the "floaters" in that eye.

Feb 20, 2008

Dork Side of the Moon

The lunatic is in my head
The lunatic is in my head
You raise the blade, you make the change
You re-arrange me 'til I'm sane
You lock the door
And throw away the key
There's someone in my head but it's not me.

And if the dam breaks open many years too soon
And if there is no room upon the hill
And if your head asplodes with dark forebodings, too
I'll see you on the dork side of the moon – Pink Floyd

Tami was in tears. Again.

This was getting old. I'd spent way too much time Tuesday night letting her cry on my shoulder, and got to bed past my bedtime after pawning her off on someone else. And my own life hasn't been too great lately either; I went blind in my good eye Monday night. I'm starting to get some sight back in it, thank you, but it's going to be a while before it's useful again.

I've spent way too much time lately letting Tami cry on my shoulder. It wasn't just getting old, it was getting lame and feeble. Now she was on the phone again right before I got off work, wanting to hang out. By "hang out" what she meant was that she wanted me to buy some alcohol and drink it with her.

"I may be able to later, but I told 'Ralph' I'd drop by." Actually I'd told "Mary Jane" I'd drop by, not Ralph, as she said she had some pot for sale. "It's hydro," she'd said, "with *red hairs*. When it has red hairs…"

"I know," I interrupted. "I've been smoking pot since before you were born. I can only afford twenty bucks worth." So I was on my way to buy a few buds of killer hydro. Tami could wait. All night maybe, if the pot was as good as Mary said

315

and I was having fun.

So I drove over to see Mary Jane after work. She had the reefer, and the bag looked small and she wanted an extra five bucks for it. I went ahead and bought it anyway.

"Want to go shoot some pool?" I asked "Linda".

This isn't the Linda that just got out of prison that I'm usually shooting pool with. This is a different woman. I'm just calling her "Linda" to confuse you. Like these journals aren't confusing enough.

But life's confusing like that, too. Amy works with a cab driver named Tammy, there's a different Tammy that tends bar at Farley's on Sunday, and then there's Tami, AKA "Lucifer" by her alien husband. It can get comical when Tami and Tammy are at Farley's on a slow Sunday afternoon when Tammy (the other Tammy) is tending bar.

About the ex-prisoner Linda, she seems to have made good on her pledge not to sell pussy or smoke pot. And she got a legitimate job, too!

So at any rate, "Linda" said yeah, she'd shoot some pool. Mary went along too. But first they wanted me to give them some taxi service. Mary had family pictures at Walgreen's, and wanted to take them to her relative on north Eighth street.

I haven't known Mary Jane very long, but the relative is a friend of mine I met through "Ralph". She's a medium height plump blonde. Almost too plump, but she's shapely and very attractive – except for her eyes. She'd be really attractive if she didn't wear makeup. She uses way too much eye shadow which gives her sort of a "crazy-eyed" look. "Julia" is like that, too.

At any rate, Mary Jane wanted to take these pictures to her. Sure, why not? We also had to stop by the grocery store... Women!

I'd forgotten completely about the predicted eclipse of the moon until I saw the thing, big and fat, hovering above the horizon. "Hey," I said, "we're supposed to have an eclipse tonight."

"We are?" Linda asked. Mary Jane just gave me a funny look. She's young, barely drinking age.

We finally got to the bar we were going to shoot pool in, and before we could get the balls racked, Lance walked out of the rest room.

As I mentioned, all the names in this particular journal have been changed to protect the guilty. Except Lance. Lance is this fellow's real name. And he's not well liked.

Ralph and I used to be drinking buddies with him. The three of us are veterans of various wars, Ralph in WWII on a Navy ship, me in the Air Force during Vietnam but nobody ever shot at me, and Lance in the first Gulf War in the Marines. Lance has been shot at, and at various times various people have wished that the people shooting at him had been better shots.

One night at a cookout at Ralph's last summer, Lance thought I had been putting my dick in a woman he wanted to put his dick in. She and I were going to make a beer run, and as she was getting in the car and I came around the corner of the house toward it, Lance walked around the corner from the other direction and sucker punched me square in the face, knocking me on my ass and nearly breaking my elbow when I hit the ground.

I jumped up and dialed 911. Stupid young people, don't fuck with me because I fight like an old man. I'll be out of the hospital before you're out of jail and my lawyer will take half of everything you've got and give me the other half.

Lance was lucky he had no belongings worth taking.

The woman jumped out of the car screaming at him and told him to leave. He left and she turned on me, cursing me for calling the cops. "There's a warrant out for me!" she exclaimed. I gave her a ride home, and as I was on my way back to Ralph's the police called – they'd picked Lance up and had him in a squad car. Did I want to meet them at Ralph's or my home? I was on my way to Ralph's with the beer anyway.

The woman he thought I was fucking had talked me out

of pressing charges, and besides, not only did he not have anything worth taking I remembered what religion I was and decided to act accordingly. I told the deputy I wasn't pressing charges, and he let Lance out of the car and removed the handcuffs. Lance apologized profusely, thanked me for not having him locked up and shook my hand.

The next week Tami, AKA "the psycho bitch from hell", went off on Lance on the phone. Tami had never liked Lance.

Actually nobody liked Lance, but all felt sorry for him and tolerated him. The man badly needs psychiatric help.

"Fuck off and die" Tami had told him.

So he left a message on her answering machine pretending to be me. "Hi, lover, this is Steve" the message started, and he continued, saying how much he'd enjoyed the sex with her and was looking forward to it again. Nobody was fooled; it was unmistakably Lance. Tami's alien husband, who thinks I'm fucking her anyway (I'm not), seemed to want Lance's blood.

Nobody had much more to do with him after that, especially me, and including the woman he wanted to fuck that he thought I was fucking that triggered the violent outburst against me the week earlier. Ralph's caretakers were scared of similar violence against Ralph; after all, Lance had no hesitation in violently ambushing a man old enough to be his father and quite a bit smaller than himself. There was no reason to think he'd be more thoughtful with the truly geriatric. It wasn't hard convincing Ralph; the episode with the answering machine pissed Ralph off, too. Ralph and I are friends.

So here comes Lance walking up like a long lost brother, apologizing yet again.

Mary Jane and Linda kept trying to pick a fight with him so he'd get thrown out of the bar, and finally succeeded in getting him to angrily leave. "I'm going to..." I forgot who he said he was going to visit, but he doesn't drive, riding his bicycle everywhere. So he wouldn't be going far, as it was well below freezing outside and there was snow on the ground.

I went out in the beer garden with Mary, she to smoke and me to look at the moon. It had gone from full to crescent. When we went back in I decided to waste some money and contribute to the evil RIAA, just this once, because there was an RIAA album that fit the situation perfectly.

I hate those damned internet jukeboxes. I'm no fan of jukeboxes anyway, and always let some other fool put money in them. But the new internet jukeboxes cost twice as much as a normal old fashioned CD jukebox, and if it has to download a song it takes a whole dollar, and it doesn't sound as good as a CD jukebox. But at least I should be able to hear a song from an album that was in the top 100 for twenty years.

I put my dollar in and searched for *Dark Side of the Moon*. The only song from the album was "Money". Fitting.

Fucking dickweeds. One more reason to hate the RIAA! And congress; that album should have been in the public domain long ago, which is why there's only a fair-use snippet at the beginning and end of this instead of the entire lyric; there is no way to contact whoever holds the copyright.

So I played the old Patti Page song "Crazy" which should have been in the public domain when "Dark Side of the Moon" was recorded, and "Dirty Deeds Done Dirt Cheap". As the second song started, Linda broke and put the yellow ball in. "I should have played *Big Balls*" I said.

Lance came back in. "He wasn't home."

I went outside again, and Mary Jane followed me out, butt in hand. I'm glad I'm not a butthead any more. Giving those things up was the hardest thing I've ever done.

The moon was totaled. It wasn't like the eclipse I'd seen in '75. That one the moon had turned red, this time it was kind of an orangish yellow. "Wow!" said Mary Jane.

Her phone rang, and she started having an animated discussion with whoever was on the other end. I went back inside. "Your turn" Linda said; we were still shooting pool. I took my shot and missed badly. I'm not used to using my right eye. Well, that's as good an excuse for sucking as any, I suppose.

Mary came back in fuming. I had two balls on the table, Linda only had the eight, and she dropped it in the called pocket, followed by the cue ball. I'd won the game. "That fucking bitch!" Mary steamed.

"Who?" asked Linda.

"My relative, damn her. She ripped that poor old man off again..."

"What?!" exclaimed Lance. "I bet it wasn't her. I bet it was that fucking boyfriend of hers. I KNOW it was him! That cocksucking motherfucker!"

"Shut up, Lance," Linda told him.

"No! I'm going to kill that God damned son of a bitch!"

They eventually calmed him down, and I went home to bed, having already gone past my normal bed time for the eclipse and with an alarm clock slated to annoyingly wake me up the next day.

Friday's State Journal-Register brought News about Wednesday night:

Accused of death threat

Lance S. Carter, 37, of the 1300 block of Ledlie Avenue is accused of barging into a home and threatening to kill a man.

The victim told police that he and a woman were in a home in the 900 block of North Eighth Street about 11 p.m. Wednesday when Carter barged in through the front door and began yelling at him while holding a large kitchen knife. The victim picked up a 2-by-4 to defend himself, pushing Carter out the door.

Carter allegedly threw the knife on the street when he saw police coming.

Mary Jane said they'd charged him with attempted murder, assault with a deadly weapon, home invasion, and breaking and entering. She heard they found "drug paraphernalia" on the dork as well, but that was a third-hand rumor. She said he'd pleaded guilty to something or other, she didn't know what, and that his sentencing hearing is on March fifth.

That's the day I go back to see Dr. Odin about my eye.

All that is now
All that is gone
All that's to come,
And everything under the sun is in tune
But the sun is eclipsed by the moon.

Errata: there was no dork side of the moon. As a matter of fact it was all dork.

Feb 25, 2008

Vitrectomy

Laser beam in my dream, laser beam in my dream, laser beam in my dream, I can't get on, I can't get off, laser beam's like a sawed off dream -Steve Cash, Ozark Mountain Daredevils

"DO NOT LOOK INTO THE LASER WITH YOUR REMAINING EYE!" – tired old Slashdot joke

Tami's alien husband joined the National Guard, and left her homeless while he was in basic training. Swell guy, eh? So I let her crash at my place. It turned out to be a better deal for me than for her! Because I'd seen the snake. I knew this snake. It wasn't bighead (although she played a part in the previous journal).

A visit with Dr. Odin was scheduled on a Friday, and I went. It seemed the eye was almost cleared up – but Dr. Odin was worried. The retina might be detaching, but he wasn't sure. "I'm going to be out of town, but if you lose any peripheral vision or see a gray curtain descending, be sure to come in to the office. I have an alternate in case you need surgery."

He sent me over to Dr. Yeh to laser my bloodstained CrystaLens implant before sending me home.

That Sunday it seemed I lost some peripheral vision at the top of my field of vision. I went in to work the next day, and left for the eye doctor as soon as they opened. I saw Dr. Ekon, an optometrist, who thought I did indeed have a detached retina. So he sent me to St. John's Pavilion at St. John's Hospital, a Catholic hospital here in town, to see Dr. Dodwell.

The doctor had good and bad news. The bad news was that I did indeed have a detached retina. "But if I had to have one myself, yours is where I'd want it." He said he thought it would wait for Dr. Odin, but if I saw a gray curtain "then you're my problem."

It did indeed wait for Dr. Odin the next Monday, who scheduled surgery at St. John's for Thursday. But first he said I had to have a physical exam to make sure my heart and lungs were good enough to get anesthetized and have needles stuck in my eyeball.

He asked if I wanted a local anesthetic or a general anesthetic. "I have a choice?" I asked. "Yes," he answered.

"Knock me out!"

I scheduled an appointment with Doctor Smelter for Wednesday.

For my birthday I got a physical exam. First the nurse took my temperature and blood pressure. Then the doctor looked in my ears, listened to my chest with his stethoscope, poked around my abdomen, and decided to find out if he could see the detached retina. He shut out the light and shined his instrument in my eye.

From his response, I think he's a slashdotter.

"I think your cataract implant is loose. It's moving around in there!"

"It's supposed to do that," I replied. "It is?" he exclaimed.

"Yeah," I said, "it's a new kind. You can focus with it. I've got better than 20/20 vision at all distances. I don't even need reading glasses!"

"Really? Wow! Well anyway I couldn't see anything. Did Dr. Odin dilate your eye?"

"Well, yeah."

"Oh, well there you go" he said.

The nurse wished me a happy birthday and I went home. As I'd been instructed not to eat or drink anything after midnight, I decided to take a couple of hours off that afternoon. I collected Tami to be my designated driver.

There is a tradition in most Springfield bars of giving you a free drink on your birthday. There is also a Springfield tradition of hopping from bar to bar getting shitfaced drunk on your birthday for free. I cashed a check on the way home, and had the teller give me some of those new dollar coins to mess with bartenders with; they look kind of like bronze quarters. My guess is they'll go over about as well as the Susan B Anthony dollars they issued back in the seventies. Kids, go to your bank and get some of these dollars, I hear the Anthony dollars are worth more than a buck each now.

The first place we went was Felber's, and the bartender poured me a giant glass of beer and a normal twelve ounce glass for Tami. I tipped the bartender with one of the bronze coins.

"So what did you get for your birthday?" the bartender asked.

"A physical exam. Tomorrow's birthday present is getting needles stuck in my eye!"

"Ouch!" she said. I explained about the detached retina and its subsequent need for a vitrectomy.

Some time short of midnight we got home, and I staggered to the kitchen to drink a gallon or so of water before bed. The surgery was scheduled for ten o'clock the next morning, and as I planned on going in to work for two hours before the surgery I set the alarm and got the coffeepot ready. No, I wasn't thinking straight, there would be no coffee until after the surgery.

The alarm went off and I blearily stumbled into the kitchen, and as I reached for the switch on the coffeepot I remembered – no food or drink. Damn. I'm a caffeine addict and can't function without my coffee. So I set the alarm on my phone and went back to sleep.

Sans my "third eye" I had Tami drive me to the hospital. We didn't have to wait long for them to call my name, unlike when I had the cataract surgery. My blood pressure and temperature were taken again, questions asked (allergies, did I eat or drink after midnight, etc.) and was given a hospital gown and told to wash my face with some strange liquid soap that looked like Mercurochrome, and to put a dot over the eye to be operated on so they wouldn't poke needles in the wrong eye and my initials on my neck so they wouldn't confuse me with a different patient who might be there for an enucleation or brain surgery or something. Yeah, this really restored my confidence...

I then met my anesthetist, whose name I can't remember. She was a gorgeous, thin black woman who could have easily been a supermodel, and she unfortunately talked me into a local anesthetic. She pointed out that for general I would have to have a breathing tube inserted, there would be a whole lot more postoperative pain as there wouldn't be as much anesthesia in the eye itself, etc.

I regretted that decision!

They would dose my eye with drops, then cover my face. Then do it again. And again. Slashdot would mod them "redundant".

"Would it be okay if I prayed for you?"

I uncovered my face and there was an angel standing next to the gurney. No, on second look it wasn't an angel, just an old woman dressed in white, a Nun. "Yes," I said, "thank you."

They stuck electrodes on my chest and a needle in my arm and wheeled me into the operating room, where I was knocked out for a short time. I came to with my face covered, instruments apparently already inside my eyeball, unlike the cataract surgery. I was told it would take between an hour and a half and two hours.

The first part of the operation was easy. So easy, in fact, that I fell asleep a few times and they had to wake me up.

The later part, however, was pure torture. I have arthritis in my spine, and my neck started hurting. Then it started hurting BAD. "Hold still" the doctor said, and I discovered to my horror that I was strapped to the table with my head bolted down.

By the time the surgery was finished I was in agony

from my arthritis, although the eye didn't hurt a bit.

In post-op they asked what kind of juice I wanted. I told them I'd rather have water, and they brought a glass of ice water, followed by some grape juice. They then gave me the post-op instructions: two kinds of eyedrops four times a day, one kind twice a day, and a tube of ointment for if there was any itching or irritation in the eye.

And I was instructed that I had to keep my head down at all times until the doctor said otherwise. I could only look up ten minutes out of each hour. They put a plastic bracelet on my arm, with instructions that it was to remain there until the doctor removed it. *Warning: Gas bubble in eye Use of nitrous oxide or change in atmospheric pressure may cause an increase in IOP* [inter ocular pressure] *resulting in blindness. Consult the optometrist on the other side of this bracelet before treatment.*

Leadfoot Tami had run out of gasoline going here and there, and had been hassled by the police, and was in a foul mood when she picked me up. I would have none of it – I was still in arthritic agony, and had been sternly instructed "no aspirin, Ibuprofen, or Naproxin." And I was jonesing for a cup of coffee. Cup? No, hell, I was jonesing for a whole damned pot! I had her drive me to the D&J Cafe on Laurel street near MacArthur for breakfast and COFFEE! COFFEE! MUST HAVE COFFEE!!!!

After breakfast (at maybe two in the afternoon) we were both in better spirits, although my neck and back were still in pain. I spent the rest of the day at the dining room table with my head down, and laying down when the pain in my neck and back got too excruciating. Tami was impressed – she saw from the expression on my face and by how pale I was that I was in terrible pain, and said I was the first man she'd ever known that didn't turn into a little girl when he was sick or in pain. But what good would complaining do?

I'd get up to get a glass of water or something, "I can get that for you!" she'd say. But I needed to get up once in a while.

I wanted to go to Felber's for a beer; their drafts are only a buck, JW's beer is a buck and a quarter. "I don't think you should go drinking so soon after surgery!"

"Damn it, woman, the doctor told me no aspirin but he didn't say no beer! I'm going to Felber's and you can come along if you want or you can stay here!"

She regaled the lady bartender with tales of my stoicism, which I didn't understand at all, and understood even less when the bartender, a woman who looks maybe ten years older than me, agreed with Tami that most men turn into little girls when they get sick or hurt. This puzzles me, as I've seen *Die Hard* and all the war movies and action flicks where the guys limp along with a bullet in their leg and broken glass in their feet and still manage to beat the shit out of the bad guys.

The next morning I was to see Dr. Odin again. The retina looked good, but the pressure in the eye was thirty-five. Thirty five what I don't know, but it's supposed to be between ten and twenty. He gave me a giant orange pill and told me to come in the next morning, a Saturday. I spent most of the day at the table with my head down, part of the day in bed (on my right side as instructed, although my right shoulder has problems of its own, having been dislocated back in 1976 in a head-on car wreck and not wearing seat belts) and yes, at Felbers, where I showed everybody the picture of a vitrectomy from Wikipedia.

Saturday morning we drove to the doctor. Pressure in the eye was still 27, and he gave me a prescription for fourteen orange pills, which I can't remember the name of. I sent Tami to Walgreens to drop it off. She said they told her the co-pay would be four dollars.

Then we went to Felber's.

About six-thirty we went back to Walgreens to pick up the prescription, and the drugstore was open, the camera department was open, everything at the pharmacy was open except the God damned pharmacy! WHAT THE FUCK?! It's supposed to be a goddamned drug store, and I can buy anything there except DRUGS! I demanded to see the manager, who informed me that the pharmacy was closed – at six thirty on a Saturday evening, because it wasn't profitable.

"Yeah? Well how fucking profitable is it going to be for Walgreens when I go blind and SUE YOUR GODDAMNED ASSES???"

My pain had left me with a bad disposition and I was in no mood to put up with any corporate bullshit. God damned money worshiping FOOLS!

He said the pharmacy was open at the Walgreens at MacArthur, so I drove down there. They filled the prescription. "That will be forty four dollars."

"Wow, that's a lot for fourteen pills, how much is the co-pay?"

"That is the co-pay! The medication is sixty seven dollars."

"WHAT? I don't have forty four dollars on me right now! I'm going to go blind!"

She said she'd see if there was a generic alternative. I sat down and waited. Tami had stayed in the car, seeing that I was already going to explode after the Sixth street Walgreens' pharmacy was closed on a Saturday evening and not wanting to be caught up in it when the police came because I'd have murdered all those people with my teeth.

The lady walked up and sat down next to me with a bag in her hand. "We couldn't find a generic and we couldn't get hold of your doctor."

I felt like crying.

"But I can see your pressure is high and I don't want you going blind. Here, I'm not going to charge you." All I could do was thank her, take the drugs and leave.

I saw the doctor again Monday morning, and the pressure was down to a safe 11.5. Tami was a godsend; cooking, cleaning, doing laundry, everything a housewife does except sex, but a lot of married guys I know get less sex than I do. Which lately has been none at all.

The week was still hell.

I ran out of the Vigamox drops and remembering the episode with the pills decided to call all the pharmacies in the area for the lowest price. The highest priced places informed me that my co-pay was the same no matter what the insurance paid, so I went to Walgreens.

"Are you going to come back for them?" the pharmacist asked.

"Hell no!" I said. "I'll wait." Theirs was the highest price of anyone's, eighty seven dollars. But it wasn't as bad on my end. The tiny bottle of eyedrops cost me twenty two dollars. Retail price in Canada is twenty five. Tell me again how the free market is the best under all circumstances? Or how it even applies to health care at all?

I went back to Dr. Odin yesterday, who informed me that I don't have to keep my head down any more, although I still have to sleep on my right side.

Anyone who saw the smile on my face yesterday probably thought I'd just gotten laid.

Apr 15, 2008

Seven of Nine, or Dors Venabili?

A few weeks ago I went to Felber's and got a beer and took it outside, in the back, where there's a picnic table and some lawn chairs. The weather was beautiful. Kathy was out there, and Mike and Debbie, and a few other people, including a tall, thin, attractive blonde with a nice figure and a pretty face who looked to be around my age.

I'm not normally attracted to tall women but there was something about this one. Maybe it was the reading glasses on a chain around her neck that made her look like a librarian, as I've always loved books and libraries. Or maybe it was the way she looked at me. I said Hi. "I haven't seen you around here before," I added. "I'm Steve."

"Hi, I'm Kathy," she said, and held out her hand. "I'm not in town much, I live in..."

I forgot where she said she lived, one of the little towns within fifteen miles of Springfield.

"Another Kathy!" I said. "When I say 'Kathy' how will you guys know which one I'm talking to?" I said, grinning. Actually, the blonde Kathy's name was spelled "Kathie". But I didn't know that then.

"I'll be Kathy one and she can be Kathy two," blonde Kathy said.

"Huh uh," brunette Kathy retorted. "I knew him first, I'm Kathy one!"

"Kathy One" went in to get more beer for her and Debbie and I chatted with "Kathy Two" for a while. Being the nerd I am, "Kathy One" and "Kathy Two" made me think of Seven of Nine. And of course being a cyborg myself, with the device implanted in my left eye, it made sense.

Seven of Nine made me think of the actress who played it, Jeri Ryan. Thinking of Jeri Ryan now makes me think of our President Elect and how he got there.

If it wasn't for the fact that a Borg's husband was a sex maniac, Barack Obama might never have become Senator and our first black President. I wrote about it back in 2004 when Obama was running for Senate, in a K5 diary called "The election is coming".

Ryan and Seven of Nine's messy divorce (and sex parties, including wanting to watch his wife have sex with other men, according to the newspapers) was a horrible scandal to the uptight Republicans, and candidate Ryan no longer was Candidate Ryan. The Republicans had no candidate. They wound up running a black ultraneocon named Alan Keyes from Maryland, who had never set foot in Illinois before yet had the gall to badmouth Hillary Clinton for running for Senate in New York, even though she'd obtained residence there.

Obama beat the fellow by a landslide. The rest is history.

Uh, I guess that was history, too.

But I digress. I've been broke as hell this week; it's mortgage week, and after paying the mortgage and grocery shopping at Walmart, I didn't even have any drinking money left, let alone Supersizeme money. I've been taking sandwiches to work and snacking on crackers and peanut butter.

Thank God for George Washington Carver, who invented the stuff.

But Linda sold some of her furniture that she's been keeping in my garage, and at least paid *some* of the rent she's behind on. So I had ten bucks. I figured I'd go to the Shell station and put five in the gas tank and to Felber's and put the other five in my bladder.

As I was driving down sixth street I saw Mike's Lincoln parked outside JW's, so I pulled in behind it. I hadn't seen Mike in a while.

I owe him money. But Mike's a good friend I've known almost two decades.

He was playing one of the illegal gambling machines

331

that are in every bar in Illinois, and drinking tequila as he is wont to do. I ordered a draft beer as I always do, because I can seldom afford anything more expensive.

He is indeed not doing well; I'm paying him back next payday. He'll need it.

He bought me a couple of beers. He left, and so did I. I got the gasoline and went to Felber's. Kathy, the blonde Kathy, Kathy Two, was there. We talked, and before my beer was done she bought ME another!

I'm not used to this, folks. Usually it's me that's buying, especially with women. Seldom does a woman buy ME a drink!

I made a dinner date with her for next payday. Fingers crossed...

We got to talking about family and kids and so forth, and she's had a bit of tragedy lately. Her grandmother just died, as did the guy she'd been living with. She's staying with her mother, who she doesn't get along with.

I told her about Linda renting a room. "Do you sleep together?" she asked. I replied in the negative, and she looked dubious.

"If we were sleeping together would I be collecting rent?"

As I said, she'd had some hard times and we talked about heartbreak and heartache and lost love and the story of an evening after Evil-X left when my youngest daughter caught me crying in the kitchen and asked "what's wrong, Dad?"

"My wife left me," I sobbed.

"That's nothing, my MOM left me!"

I told Kathy "she really put me in my place with that."

"I can't cry," she said. "Never could."

Borg, or android?

Nov 06, 2008

Stormy Weather

I got drunk and made out with a married fat chick who was mad at her boyfriend Friday night.

And Charlie's back.

She's been back for a few weeks now. "Come get me. PLEASE come get me," she'd begged.

We'd had some sort of argument, and I'd told her to "get the fuck out of my house." She refused and I called the police. "Can you please get this parasite out of my house?"

When Ralph had gotten sick and his daughters made her leave his house, she asked to crash at mine "for a few days" and just sort of moved in; a squatter. I called her a squatter to the cops.

"There's nothing we can do," they told me. "She put your address on her driver's license and has her mail coming there. You have to go down to the courthouse to get a thirty day eviction notice."

So there's an answer to any of you who may be homeless – just put in a change of address at the post office to somewhere where someone might let you visit for ten minutes, put it on your driver's license and you have residence for at least thirty days.

She went to Stuart's two days later. I thought I was rid of her.

Stuart accused her of stealing from his late mother's house, and she didn't want anything more to do with him. About the only kind of person Charlie hates more than a prostitute is a thief, and he'd called her a thief. That would have been worse than calling her a whore.

Then Tami called Friday. I can't figure out why Charlie has anything to do with "Lucy Furr", because Tami's a thief and Charlie knows it. Maybe it's because the two of them both hate hookers. I won't let Tami in my house anymore without someone else there to keep an eye on her.

"I really need a friend, can I come over?"

She'd had a terrible day. Her alien husband, who was in the Illinois National Guard and deployed in Afghanistan, wasn't sending the support checks the military had ordered him to send her. She'd gotten thrown out of the Bedbug Inn (named "Lincoln Lodge" of course) and had broken up with her boyfriend.

It seems lately that every time one of my lady friends breaks up with her significant other, she winds up with me. I can't get a girlfriend of my own, but it seems I've got everybody else's. If it isn't Annie (who'd moved to Chicago for a while but was back, and happily on her own now) it was Amy. Now it was Tami, it seems.

"I guess," I said. Charlie was there to make sure she didn't steal anything. I picked her up at lunch, and she had tears in her eyes and a bottle in her hand. By the time I got off work she was drunk and crying. I sat on the couch next to her, wiping her tears away and hugging her and rubbing her back.

Alan dropped by before I'd finished a beer.

Tami and Alan don't get along too well. Alan knew "Snake" and scared the hell out of her with some parlor trick involving a hammer, a nail, and ketchup. "You're Lucifer!" she'd told him, horrified. So it was fitting that the two people I know who both have the nickname of "Lucifer" don't like each other much.

And Alan had bragged that he could have any woman, which set Tami off. When he came in she sat her fat ass in my lap and put her arms around me. "Me and Steve got married today," she joked, drunkenly trying to make Alan jealous.

He left with Charlie after a few beers, and Tami had cheered up. No longer crying, she was still in my lap with her arms around my neck. I got up to get more beer, and sat on the couch. Tami sat next to me, close. We wound up making out.

My dick got hard. And then Charlie came back home.

334

"Cockblocker!" Tami said to Charlie, accusingly but with an evil grin. I got up and moved over to the table, embarrassed that I'd been caught in a compromising position with the fat woman. Although I was still fully clothed, my woodie kind of gave things away.

My phone rang; it was Julie, who I hadn't seen in six months or more. She gave me her new landline number and I promised to call. She didn't say, but I'd bet money she's fighting with her boyfriend, if she still has one.

"The One" had been playing on the TV. I'd missed most of the movie, but it was Charlie's tape and I'd seen it before. After a bit more drinking, Charlie sacked out on the couch, Tami crashed on the cushions, and I went to bed.

Saturday morning came after noon, and the now sober fat lady wasn't so amorous. Phew!

The three of us sat on the porch in the nice weather, watched a couple of movies, and generally had a pleasant Saturday. I was in bed asleep before nine, leaving the girls in the living room with the TV. Sunday morning Tami was gone. There was a note on the kitchen table.

"Went to Jessie's. Call if you need me for anything." Jessie is the boyfriend, and obviously they'd kissed and made up.

Charlie was more than asleep; she was unconscious. I couldn't wake her up. Even her phone ringing didn't wake her up. I watched *This Week*, then put in a Deep Space Nine tape. When *This Week* was on there were notices on the screen about some tornado watches, but they were in counties quite a bit south. Charlie farted in her sleep, then woke up and went to the bathroom. "Your phone was ringing when you were asleep," I told her.

She called the number back. "It was Alan", she said. "He wants you to give him a ride to get some beer. He's on his way down now."

A few minutes later he showed up, and I gave him a ride to get his beer and rolling tobacco. While I sat in the car waiting for him, my daughter Leila called. "We're under a severe thunderstorm watch," she said.

Alan came out of the store and we went to his house so I could show him (again) how to make his VCR work. I can't figure out why someone as intelligent as Alan is so stymied by technology.

The tornado siren went off. Luckily his house is a lot closer to it than mine is and you can actually hear it there. It took a minute for me to figure out what the sound was.

"Tornado!" I said. "We have to get to my house, you don't have a basement."

"I ain't scared of no tornado," he said.

"Yeah, well I didn't used to be until I was in one. Come on, we have to go."

When the tornadoes hit Springfield in March 2006 (and the pictures at Wikipedia don't do it justice) I wasn't the least bit worried. I'd been through a hurricane before.

In either 1971 or 1972, I don't remember exactly when it was, Hurricane David (I *think* it was David), a mild hurricane with winds of maybe 80 mph, went through Delaware, with its eye passing right over Dover AFB, where I was stationed. I can't find a Wikipedia reference, probably because a more severe hurricane had the same name in 1978. I stood at the barrack's upstairs door's window watching the storm. And what a storm it was! Junk flying through the air, rain going sideways, young trees bending sideways and old trees breaking. It was a sight! I'd never seen a storm like it before.

Then, like someone had flipped a switch, the rain and the wind stopped suddenly and the sun came out, with a gentle breeze blowing. I stepped out on the upstairs porch and lit a cigarette. It was a beautiful day – for maybe twenty minutes or so. Then what looked like a gray wall came toward me from the east, and as suddenly as the storm had stopped it started again, with the wind blowing the opposite direction.

As I stood and watched the storm, I amazedly watched a car inching through the screaming wind and streaming water, stopping in front of the barracks. Two guys got out, fought their way through the wind and up the wooden stairs. They opened the door and it disappeared, along with most of the porch's railing.

By the time the hurricane was over there was an inch of water in the barracks – upstairs. They later condemned it and a few other buildings that had been badly damaged.

So on March 12, 2006 I wasn't the least bit scared. Marilyn was terrified.

She'd invited me over for dinner that night, again. I'd been eating dinner at her house a lot, and had been spending quite a bit of time with her after she'd broken up with Tom and I'd taken her to Gallager's, about the most expensive (and worth every penny) restaurant in Springfield.

It stormed violently all evening, with almost continuous thunder. If you'd been outside with a waterproof book you could have read it by the lightning flashes. Then a weather alert came on her television, with the weatherman saying a tornado had been spotted and to "take shelter immediately" as the tornado sirens screamed. The old sirens were *loud*; if they went off, you knew it. We went to her basement. Then the power went out and the sirens stopped.

Patty hadn't yet moved to Cincinnati, but Paul had asked me if he could marry her. I'll tell you, I was greatly impressed by the gesture. Paul's a really good kid and I couldn't think of anyone else I'd rather have marrying my daughter. They were at Target shopping, and left to go to his apartment.

The tornado hit Target two minutes after they left, tearing its roof off and terrifying everyone in the store. Unaware, they calmly drove home in the storm – with the tornado right on their heels. It hit moments after they got inside. It left both their cars and the apartment building alone.

Steve, the handyman in the apartment I lived in, lived upstairs from me and was watching the storm from his balcony, and saw the tornado. He banged on everyone's door

337

and got them downstairs in the big janitor's closet in the basement, outside my apartment door. He was worried about me, as I didn't answer when he banged on mine. The tornado hit the neighborhood.

I was in Marilyn's dark basement, with the only light coming from her flashlight and a battery powered television. She was hanging on to me for dear life, terrified. She'd been through a tornado before. I wasn't a bit scared. I'd been through a hurricane before!

Marilyn lived on fourth street about four houses down from the railroad track. "There's a train?" she asked, amazedly. "Trains run in this kind of weather?"

"No, they don't," I said.

"Oh SHIT!" she screamed, terrified. "It's a tornado!"

Then we heard a jet engine sitting on her roof. When you hear the train, there's a tornado coming. When you hear the jet, the tornado's on top of you.

The noise was deafening; thunder mixed with all sorts of unidentifiable sounds. She was hanging on to me so tightly I thought she'd break my ribs.

The storm subsided, the TV man called the all clear and we went back upstairs. There was a knock on the door as she was lighting candles; her neighbor. "Are you all right?" he asked, worried. Marilyn assured him we were safe, and we went outside in the dark.

It was pitch black, with no light at all except flashlights. Tree limbs and trash and debris were everywhere. Despite her protests, I drove home, worried about my daughter's cats. Both my daughters were as worried about me as I was of them, and both called me.

Trees and limbs blocked almost every street, but I somehow made it home. My car was unscathed, and it appeared that everything in the apartment, including the cats, was, too. People were milling around with flashlights, dumbfounded. The sound of fire, police, and ambulance sirens was everywhere. I used my phone as a flashlight and made my way downstairs to my apartment, and went to bed.

The sight the next morning was incredible. The big tree outside my west window looked like a weed someone had stomped on. The house trailer on the other side of the parking lot looked like a box of crackers someone had crushed in anger. Trash was everywhere, a sea of yellow and pink insulation. Corrugated steel and high voltage electrical transformers and other debris was in treetops. There were dead birds everywhere. Knowing all the streets were blocked with trees and limbs, I decided to walk in search of hot coffee.

Devastation was all around. If Osama Bin Laden had seen it he would have given up, knowing that nothing any terrorists could do could come anywhere near the damage the tornadoes (it turned out there were two of them) had done. Roofs were missing everywhere. One roof I saw was impaled by another roof. A cinder block wall had five inch long wooden splinters stuck into the concrete. Giant trees were uprooted. Utility poles were snapped off in the middle, with the tops hanging by the wires, where the wires were still standing. Most weren't. Wires and transformers laid in yards and streets and everywhere. One commercial building had large, twisted girders showing.

The air was filled with the sound of sirens and chain saws.

Both Third Base and Doc's lounge, where I thought I might find coffee, were closed. The walk-in beer cooler at Third Base had been ripped from the building. I walked on, jaw hanging in disbelief at the destruction, thinking maybe JW's might have coffee. I walked by Marilyn's on the way, and she was outside, also in shock and disbelief. The destruction had spared her property, too, although none of her neighbors were as lucky.

Inside JW's people were drinking by candle light. The entire electrical infrastructure from Jerome, where Target and the Barrelhead had lost their roofs and almost every sign was gone, past JW's and on to the east side, would be out of power for the week it took to rebuild. They had no electricity so they had no coffee, so I walked on to George Rank's. Its east door was missing, its south door's awning was half down. They had been busy when the tornado struck, but luckily had a basement to take cover in.

"No power," they said. "You can have a beer."

"Thanks," I replied, "But I'm looking for coffee."

The Track Shack had no power either. Neither did McDonald's. I finally found a lit sign at the Sunrise Cafe, where I finally got coffee before trudging back through the destruction to my apartment. I hadn't been scared when the tornado had hit, but I should have been!

People with only landline phones were without communication for days. There was no cable, no internet. My cell phone worked through it all, even though I couldn't call long distance.

So Sunday morning here I was at Alan's and the new sirens that I can't even hear at my house went off. It was sprinkling, and there was a wall of gray to the west. We drove down the alley to my house, and I didn't even bother putting my seat belt on. Charlie was laying on the couch watching TV. "Get in the basement!" I ordered.

"Don't tell me what to do!"

"Suit yourself, dumbass," I said, and herded the cats downstairs after Allen. They didn't want to go. Ever tried to herd cats? Especially to where they don't want to be?

Charlie came flying down the stairs. "Holy shit!" she exclaimed. "It's raining buckets!" The wind howled and thunder roared and lightning flashed – for maybe a minute, then it was over. We went upstairs, and the sun was shining on the flooded street. The tornado had touched down somewhere where there were no people and everything was spared. I took Alan home and drank a beer with him.

Later that afternoon Tami called, wanting a ride to the grocery store. I got to her boyfriend's to pick her up, and she handed me something wrapped in kleenex. "Here", she said. "I

stole some of that asshole Jessie's pot for you."
Mar 10, 2009

Sickness, pain, and death. And Star Trek

Everybody's been sick with the flu, Charlie doesn't have a belly button any more, and there's a dead woman living in my basement.

Tami's mother's ashes are stored with Tami's stuff down there.

Saturday morning the doorbell rang at five in the morning. "Who's there?" I demanded; Charlie was asleep on a pallet on the floor. Nobody responded; maybe it was Tami's mom. I went grumpily back to bed.

I couldn't get back to sleep. So I got up and started the coffeepot about five thirty or six.

Charlie woke up about nine; I'd already eaten breakfast and started the dishwasher. She complained of stomach pains.

I put *Braveheart* in the DVD player. About the time the British soldier tried to rape Wallace's wife, Charlie got up to go to the bathroom and doubled over in pain. "It hurts from my neck down," she said. I wanted to take her to the hospital, but she would have none of it.

An hour later she said "you win, lets go to the hospital, I can't breathe!"

Shit, she was having a heart attack. I hurriedly put my shoes on. "Call an ambulance," she said.

I dialed 911 and asked for an ambulance. "I think my friend is having a heart attack," I urgently told the dispatcher. The fire truck showed up within a minute and a half, as the fire house is right down the street from my house.

Yes, in Springfield, whenever you call an ambulance, a fire truck shows up. "Sure is handy having a firehouse down the street," I said to one of the firemen.

They carried their gear in – oxygen, heart monitor, defibrillator. They hooked her up checking vital signs, and the ambulance came maybe five or ten minutes later. They put her on a gurney, and I told her I'd meet her at the hospital.

I got there before the ambulance did. Yes, I care about Charlie.

I went back to the treatment room in ER with them, where they had her hooked to Star Trek machines kind of like the ones Dr. McCoy had, only Bones didn't have wires and tubes hooked to *his* patients. "Damn it, Jim," I can imagine him saying if his patients had wires and tubes in them, "I'm a doctor, not an engineer!"

Amy called, and I told her about Charlie. She said she'd have Connor drop her off at the hospital.

By then the Star Trek machines had told the medical people that Charlie wasn't having a heart attack, and they suspected a gall bladder problem. Amy, who was once a nurse at that very hospital, showed up and said she, too, thought it was a gall bladder because she'd had a gall bladder operation before and the symptoms were exactly the same.

She went out to my car to roll a cigarette, as you can't smoke on the hospital grounds, and while she was out there they came to take Charlie, who was still in severe pain despite the drugs that the nurse said were four times as powerful as morphine, to get an ultrasound of her gall bladder. We were in the ultrasound room for quite a while as the technician tried to get a good picture. Amy was in the treatment room when we got back.

"Where were you guys? I've been here an hour!" She exclaimed. I told her, and I said something about being hungry. She said she was hungry, too, and "I need a drink!"

Of course she needed a drink. She *is* Amy, after all. I told Charlie we'd be back, and we went to get some lunch. We picked up burritos at a convenience store and went to my house, where I had beer; Amy would of course rather have cheap rotgut whiskey but beer would have to do.

We ate our burritos and drank a beer and she said she wanted to see Tami about some sort of business deal. We went to Tami's boyfriend's house, where Tami gave me a ham and some reefer she'd stolen from her boyfriend. She must like me, which is scary, seeing as how she *is* Lucy Furr.

We told her about Charlie, so she went with us to visit her in the ER. She was there about half an hour and she and Amy left with Jim, a friend of ours who's about my dad's age. I went back to see Charlie again.

A few hours later they said that her gall bladder was okay and they were going to do a CT scan. While they were doing that I went to Felber's for a beer, and down the street to Alan's to give him the news about Charlie. She called and said they were going to operate, so I went straight back to the hospital. He went with me, and he was of course drunk, as usual.

Don't go to the hospital drunk.

As we were driving there, Amy called from Jim's and said "come get me". I told her I couldn't, "they're going to operate on Charlie."

The doctor came with their plans for her and asked her if it was okay for us to be there. It was, of course. "She's my next ex-wife," Alan said. "She lives with me," I told the doctor, who got a puzzled look over the remarks. He explained what they were doing, what they were looking for and what could possibly happen, from a keyhole incision to possibly a long incision to even worse, depending on what they found. The "worst" would have been cancer. This troubled me greatly, as I'd just lost Linda to cancer in February. I stayed quiet, listening to the doctor, but Alan kept drunkenly interrupting and misunderstanding, as he was drunk and talking too much to pay attention.

"Get him out of here," Charlie ordered. "Come on, Alan," I said. I walked him outside where he could smoke. He was crying like a baby. "My little buddy!" he sobbed. "Oh God... poor little Charlie!"

I got him calmed down somewhat. We went back in as they had her prepped for surgery, and followed the gurney to the OR. As it would be a while I called Jim's to see if Amy was still there and wanted a ride. "No", he said, "she walked down to her friend's house." That would be Plumber's, so we went by there. "Yeah, she was here but she left to go back to Connor's." Alan and I went back to Alan's house, where he got a half dozen beers and a half pint of brandy. We went back to the hospital to wait for her to get out of surgery.

Alan got lost somewhere walking around the grounds, and I didn't see him until the next morning.

I fell asleep waiting for Charlie's surgery to get done. The phone woke me up, they told me what room she was in and I went up to see... a Borg.

She was laid out with cables and tubes and wires going every which way, a mask over her mouth and and plastic bag coming from her nose. Machinery was tracing lines and displaying numbers and beeping, my now-assimilated friend laying there looking every bit the Star Trek Borg. She couldn't speak, barely could move. I sat with her for maybe an hour, and went home to bed. It was about one thirty in the morning.

I woke up about nine and started drinking coffee. Alan called, asking how Charlie was and would I hook his DVD and VCR up for him.

I ate some ham and eggs, rolled a joint out of the pot Tami had stolen for me from her boyfriend, and left for Alan's. I hooked his gear up for him and said I was headed to the hospital. He didn't want to go; either he needed to drink or he was afraid to go up there, or maybe both. I still didn't know what they'd done to Charlie, how bad she was, or what was wrong with her.

She was asleep when I got up there, so I pulled up a chair and just sat with her. She stirred and woke up after I was there for fifteen minutes or so. She could talk, barely, in a croaking voice.

She'd had a hole in her intestine, so now she had a nine inch gaping, open gash in her belly stuffed with gauze and covered with a bandage. She was understandably bitchy; it was obvious she was in terrible pain, which the morphine

345

dispenser tubed into her arm with the button for her to press when she needed drugs not helping her a lot.

I drank a lot of coffee.

Late that afternoon I was hungry, and left for Felber's, where they were having a pot luck dinner and Easter egg hunt.

This wasn't an Easter egg hunt for kids – the eggs had beer, shots, mixed drinks, six packs, etc. It was pretty much fun, and I found my three egg limit. Inside were a bottle of beer, a mixed drink, and a six pack. John called asking for a ride, and he gave me enough reefer to roll another joint. I'd only smoked half the one I'd rolled in the morning.

I went to Alan's with the news about Charlie. "Do you want the good news or the bad news first?" I asked. "Oh God, she's gonna die!" he said.

"No, that's the good news. She's gonna be okay. But she ain't okay now, she's in really bad shape." I described her condition, and fortified against seeing Charlie the Borg he went up there with me.

She'd wanted me to bring a hair brush and a notebook and stuff, and berated me for forgetting it. Scornfully scolded me. I left and got her stuff, and rather than thanking me when I got back berated me more.

Around eight I said I needed to go home as I had work the next morning. "You can't," she said. "You have to be here when they change my dressing, 'cause you're gonna have to do it when I get out of here."

"Okay," I sighed, getting tired of her scorn and abuse. I'd spent the whole weekend at the hospital with her and she'd spent the whole time treating me like a red haired stepchild. You would have thought we were married she treated me so bad.

About twenty past eight Alan said he was going down for a cigarette. "He's chicken", Charlie said. "He doesn't want to see it."

The doctor came in to change the dressing. Charlie opened a Velcro corset she had around her abdomen, revealing a very large bandage, which the doctor carefully took off. Charlie bitched at me about being too close.

Under the bandage was an open eight inch long gash, pointed at the top a couple inches below her breast and round at the bottom where her belly button used to be, open more than a half inch wide. Alan looked pale. When the doctor was done repacking gauze back into the wound and explaining everything, I told her I'd have to go as it was bedtime and I hadn't had dinner yet. "Wait a minute" she said, "I need to talk to you."

She laid there for five more minutes and I repeated that I hadn't had dinner and I had to get up in the morning so I was going. She went off, calling me a selfish, uncaring, impatient asshole. I tried to talk and she wouldn't let me, saying "go on, just get out of here".

"Okay" I said, and put on my coat. She said "Oh, you're just leaving, are you?"

I took my coat back off and sat back down.

"Go on, just leave," she said.

"I've had enough of this shit!" I'm afraid I got a little loud. "I've been here for you at this damned hospital all weekend and you've done nothing but abuse me. Nobody else's been here for you but you don't treat them like that!"

"Just go!" she demanded.

I went to leave. "Wait a minute" Alan said.

"Nope, I'm leaving. If you want a ride you better come on."

He tried calling as I was halfway home. I didn't answer. I went home, ate, smoked my roach and watched a little DS9 before going to bed.

The phone kept waking me up, but I left it in my pocket and didn't get up to answer it. When I got up it said there were nine missed calls, one new number - the hospital.

Alan called as I was drinking coffee, making sure I was okay. He'd seen how I'd been treated and how upset I finally let her get me. When I got to work there was a message from

Charlie on my answering machine. "You son of a bitch, you can't even answer your goddamned phone!"

It's going to take months for her to heal.

Still pissed off and needing a break I didn't go up to the hospital the next day, but watched TV at home instead. Tuesday I visited for a short while, and was up there for at least two hours a night the rest of the week. I bought minutes for her phone, a red rose, and other stuff, but the nicer I was to her the more hateful she was to me. She'd been hateful to everyone.

Patty called and said she was visiting for the next two months. Charlie got out of the hospital and moved in with John and Jennifer. Tami's at Alan's, and finally I got some peace.

It's going to be a pleasant summer.

May 02, 2009

Coincidentally, the "first" Star Trek movie came out a week later. In it, McCoy says "Damn it, Jim, I'm a doctor, not an engineer!"

Nov 11, 2014

July 20, 1969

In 1969 I was a seventeen year old nerd in high school, using my slide rule to cheat in math class. I was probably the only one in the school who even had a clue how a slide rule worked, let alone owned one.

Most of my teen aged friends were amateur musicians, and I'd fix their broken amplifiers for them. Guitar fuzzboxes were relatively new, and they were expensive, costing well over a hundred dollars in an age where a gallon of milk or gasoline cost not much more than a quarter and a high-end TV set, including oak cabinet, was around $500. I'd take ten dollar transistor radios, usually used and often broken, and hack cheap fuzzboxes out of them and sell them to my noisy friends for chump change.

I also worked at a drive-in theater, and the nights that I had to work in the ticket booth were boring nights, once people stopped coming in and the movie started. I couldn't keep enough library books checked out to keep me occupied, and Cahokia didn't have a very good library, anyway. So I bought a little twelve inch black and white Panasonic TV for the ticket booth. It also came in handy on the nights I didn't work, because we only had one TV in the house (the norm back then) and my younger sister and I would argue about what to watch, and our parents would wind up shutting it off. So now I had my own TV.

The whole world was anticipating Aldrin, Griffin, and Armstrong's trip to the moon. I don't remember what night of the week it was on, but I did have to work. In the summer the drive-in was always busy unless it was raining, which it wasn't.

My boss' name was George, and he and his his brother owned a string of theaters and restaurants. George was a good guy, a short, fat, second generation Greek with a great sense of bawdy humor. But he hated TV – TV was the theater's enemy,

349

the competition that in his mind kept food out of his overerprivileged childrens' mouths. Despite this, tonight I was taking my TV to work and not to the ticket booth; Jim was selling tickets that night.

I pulled up and parked my mothers' car by the concession stand and walked in with my little television.

"What the fuck do you think you're doing with that thing?" George demanded.

"I'm watching Neil Armstrong and Buzz Aldrin land on the moon."

"No, you're not. We're going to be busy tonight and I'm not having a TV set in my concession stand."

"Sorry, George," I told him, "but the first moon landing is only going to happen once. We're incredibly privileged to be alive right now. You can fire me and I'll go home, or I can watch it here. But I'm watching it!" Bill the projectionist came in, cursing himself for not bringing a television, and he saw mine. "All right!" he exclaimed. George gave him a hard time, and they argued about it for a while. I was ready to go home.

George relented, and he was wrong about it being a busy night, as we only had one carload of people; everyone else was at home watching the moon landing. George was one of the few people I knew that didn't care about it. My grandmother was sure that the moon landing was going to end in disaster, as God would surely not let us leave the planet and go to heaven to land on the moon. Everyone knew how dangerous it was, and how after tonight the world would be a completely different planet than it was the day before. Human beings were going to step onto the surface of another world and walk around.

I doubt those born afterwards can imagine what it was like. This was one time history was being made, everybody knew it, and everybody was going to watch it happen on live TV.

Except George.

"Where in the hell is everybody?" George kept demanding, worrying and fretting.

Bill said "They're all at home watching history being made, you dumbfuck," before going into the projection booth do do his nightly maintenance, which included splicing films where they were broken, firing up the arc lights inside the projectors, and getting the projectors synced. Each movie came on six to eight reels of film, and there was a mark at the top right of the screen that flashed momentarily to tell the projectionist to switch projectors. To the viewer, it was seamless if the projectionist was competent. You can still see the reel change marks on old movies you see on DVD if you know where to look.

The way a drive-in worked, there were short steel poles at every other parking spot, with two speakers hanging on them. You would park your car, and take the speaker, which had a wire going into the pole, and hang it from your car's window by its hook.

There was a reel to reel tape in the projection booth that played the same tape every single night over those speakers. The sun started setting, and that Godawful song from the movie M*A*S*H that I had to listen to every night I worked the concession stand played. "And suicide is painless, it brings on many changes..." What a stupid song, I thought to myself for the seemingly millionth time. I wished they'd get a new tape.

George was cursing the government for sending men to the moon. "What a fucking waste of tax money!" Of course, what had him really pissed was the business it was costing him.

The sun set and the movie started. I don't even remember what movie was playing that night. I watched TV most of the time, and there was only one show on – the moon show, on every channel, except of course every channel had a different moon show, up to the point where they were starting the landing. Bill almost missed one of the reel changes because he was out there watching with me.

As the lander was touching down, all of us were watching in awe, even George. The lone carload's occupants came in to the concession stand. "Is there a TV in here anywhere?"

We all watched the moon landing; me, George, Bill, the other kids who worked there, and our lone carload of customers, on my little twelve inch black and white TV set.

That's one small step for Neil, one giant leap for a young nerd watching it on TV at work.

Jul 20, 2009

Note the date, 40 years after the landing. When it was first posted, someone commented that the movie "M*A*S*H" didn't come out until 1970, which is true. The answer is that the tape played more songs from movies still in production than songs from movies that were currently showing in theaters.

Nov 13, 2014

Misery in Missouri – the birth of a poem

I think I almost died yesterday.

It was almost ninety and very humid. The weeds in the back yard were waist high. I changed the oil in the lawnmower, replaced the rusted spark plug that had come with the mower when I bought it ten years ago, and started cutting.

Halfway through and I was sweating profusely. Sweat was dripping off of me, my hair and clothes were soaked, but for some reason I didn't think of the danger – I was hot, but so what? I finished the lawn, washed my face, poured a glass of ice water and sat on the couch, and that's when it hit me. I was weak, disoriented, and realized I was suffering from heat exhaustion and had been very, very close to a heat stroke. Had I passed out while I was mowing I'd never have gotten up; I live alone, and there would have been nobody to find me and get me to medical care. Unconscious in the yard, I would have laid there until my body temperature reached criticality.

I realized this as I sat on my couch, sweating out what I was drinking in. I'd had two heat strokes in the past, back when I was a younger man. Once I'd seen it coming and gotten to an air conditioned public place before I passed out, and was taken to a hospital. The second time was at Disney, working in the hot sun when I'd collapsed on the asphalt. So I knew the danger, and had disregarded it. And here I thought it was only young people who were stupid like that.

Feeling a little better I thought "a beer would go down real good right now", and headed to Felber's. My phone rang after I got there; it was Kathie, wondering what I was doing later. "Not sure," I said. "I'm up at Felber's now." She was at the park with her kids and grandkids and said that maybe we could do something later.

"Sure," I said, "If I'm not too drunk to come get you."

I took my draft outside to the beer garden, where

someone was passing a bowl around. The pot made me feel a lot better, but the beer wasn't agreeing with me. I went back inside the bar; maybe the second beer would go down better. It didn't. I said something to Kathy, the bartender, whose name is thankfully spelled differently than Kathie's so the journal is less confusing than reality, about almost dying.

"At least I don't live in Joplin," I said.

I went back home for more water, and called Kathie. "I doubt I'll be drunk," I told her. "The beer wasn't going down good."

"Why don't you come out here with us?" she said. I said "sure" and went out there. The park is right behind her apartment, which is handy for her I guess, as she doesn't drive. There were maybe a half dozen kids ranging from diapers to near adolescence, Kathie, five other women, and a very drunk, very gay man. VERY gay. Obviously gay; this guy made Kenny from *My Name Is Earl* look like a testosterone fueled macho heterosexual. His name was, coincidentally, Kenny.

This guy was the stereotypical limp-wristed gay. Every mannerism screamed "flamer". I don't think I've ever met anyone like him before.

Kathie's friend Cynthia was as drunk as Kenny, and wouldn't stop hitting on me. It had nothing to do with me per se, except that I was male; she hit on every man that walked by. I probably don't have to say that she wasn't the least bit attractive. Both she and Kenny lived in Kathie's apartment building.

They ran out of lemonade, and Kathie asked if I'd give Ken a ride to the restaurant he worked in so he could pick up his paycheck; she was broke until Tuesday and he owed her money. "Sure," I said, and gave Kenny a ride.

God but he was annoying. The damned queer couldn't keep his hands off of me. He bitched and moaned about his problems, which included having AIDS, being a drug addict, and having to face his boss when he was drunk. "At least you don't live in Joplin," I told him. He stuck his head out the window and puked all over the passenger side of my car. At least he had his head outside. At least I don't live in Joplin...

He wanted to be dropped off at the apartment across the street from Kathie's apartment. "Tell them I got a phone call and you dropped me at Two Brothers and I'll be back in a few minutes."

I lied and told him "sure"; I wasn't going to lie to cover up an addict's shenanigans, and went back to the park and told the girls. They were pissed, especially Kathie. "That son of a bitch is going to smoke his fucking paycheck! Take me over there so I can get my money before he smokes it. No, wait, we'll take my dog home and you can wait for me there. I'll tell him I saw another one of his crackhead friends who told me where he was."

She came back and we went back to Felber's, where I got a pizza and salted the hell out of my pieces. The sweating had apparently drained my electrolytes and the salty pizza made me feel even better. I'd only had two beers and a couple of tokes hours earlier, but I started to realize that I was impaired, not by pot or alcohol, but from heat.

I took her home around eight thirty, walked her to her apartment and we had a passionate goodbye kiss. "I'm sorry for the way I act sometimes, but I have feelings for you and... well, I don't know why I get like that" she said.

"You're scared," I said.

"Yeah," she replied, "I guess I am."

This morning I was listening to WQNA on one of their eclectic allkindsofmusic kicks (which I thoroughly enjoy) and following a rock song, a country song I'd never heard came on – and words completely different than what the redneck was singing came into my head unbidden. By the time I got the computer fired up the tune and most of the words had gone, but I managed to rebuild it.

A preacher held up his hand
And said "judgment day is on the land"
He was wrong except for me
And misery in Missouri

Everyone thinks it's swell
That Bin Laden's dead in hell
His violence could never do
What happens when a storm comes through

Everybody cried,
So many died
I thought Joplin was the place for me...
Misery in Missouri

I lost my home
And everything I own
I lost the baby that was born to me
Misery in Missouri.

Half the town is gone
I feel so damned alone
I lost my family
Misery in Missouri.

Thank God you don't live in Joplin. It's been on my mind a lot lately; as regular readers know, I've been through a tornado but it was a strong F2, it's impossible for me to imagine what an F5 must be like. If you have any spare change, please send it to the Red Cross or any of the other relief organizations that are helping those poor unfortunate people.

Every day is judgment day. Live accordingly. Today may be your last day on Earth.

May 30, 2011

357

Simpleton

My daddy told me when I was young
Come sit beside me, my stupid son
And listen closely to what I say
And it'll help you some dark, rainy day.

Just be a simple, be a simpleton
Go out and get stoned, and have lots of fun
Just be a simple, be a simpleton
Oh, won't you do this, if you can, for me son?

Don't take your time, just live real fast
Troubles will come and kick your ass
Go find a woman and you'll find love
And don't forget son, wrap it in a glove

And be a simple, be a simpleton
Go out and get laid, and have lots of fun
Just be a simple, be a simpleton
Oh, won't you do this, if you can, for me son?

Get your money at the rich man's door
Take your lust to a twenty dollar whore
And you can do this, oh baby, if you try
All that I want for you my son is to stay high

And be a simple, be a simpleton
Go out and get drunk, and have lots of fun
Just be a simple, be a simpleton
Oh, won't you do this, if you can, for me son?

Boy, don't you worry you'll sure catch hell
Avoid the cops and the courts as well
And you can do this, oh baby, if you try
All that I want for you my son is to be stoned and high

And be a simple, be a simpleton
Go out and get stoned, and have lots of fun
Just be a simple, be a simpleton
Oh, won't you do this, if you can, for me son?
Oct 10, 2011

The best things in life are free

There IS a free lunch, and money does indeed grow on trees.

Earlier this summer as I was sitting on my front porch, drinking a beer and watching traffic go by, I noticed the color red in the tree in my front yard. Curious, I inspected more closely and it was full of red fruit – nectarines. I've lived there three years, and it never had fruit before.

I didn't even know it was a fruit tree. The thing was full of fruit. I've been eating them all summer long now, they're delicious. And cost absolutely nothing whatever. I've also been giving a whole lot of them away, for free... but I could sell them if I wanted. The money would have grown on my tree! My neighbor made some excellent preserves from them, and gave me a jar. Free preserves from free fruit!

This past spring I bought a "Big Boy" tomato plant for five bucks. Those tomatoes would have been incredibly cheap, less than a penny each, but not free. Alas, lack of something as free as FOSS and something I pay for killed killed it – city water and a lack of rain. Tomato plants don't much like city water, and we've had no rain at all to speak of. I got one tomato off of it, thanks to the lack of free rain, and it was the size of a billiard ball. That was the most expensive tomato I ate in my life, thanks to the lack of something that's free.

FOSS people shouldn't say "free as in beer," they should say "free as in rain." Rain enjoys the ultimate freedom. It goes where it wants, and it costs no one anything. But when the rain decides it wants to take a vacation in Europe, you have a drought here. Lack of the free rain here in the US is going to cost everyone else in the world, because the corn crop – actually most crops – are decimated. They estimate we're going to get way less than half of what is normal. And the price of corn affects the price of all your food. ADM's slogan is accurate; the US is indeed "breadbasket to the world" (despite the fact that we grow little wheat in Illinois, most of that comes from Kansas). Corn is in everything. It, rapeseed, or soybeans are what your cooking oil is made of, and all of those crops are doing terrible. The sugar in your soft drinks comes from corn. Almost all animal feed comes from corn, affecting the price of meat. All processed foods will go up for at least a year.

So no matter where in the world you live, the price of your meat, cooking oil, and many other foodstuffs is going up, all because of the lack of something that is free – and that's a free something you cannot live without. Much like air, which is also free.

If you don't think money grows on trees you must not own a commercial orchard, because all their money grows on trees. Most of Illinois' money grows on cornstalks and bean poles and things like that. Paper companies' money all grows on trees. Well, mostly on trees, you need more than wood to make paper. But timber companies' money grows on trees.

Anyone who disparages something because it costs nothing isn't seeing reality clearly. "You get what you pay for" and "Linux is only free if your time is worthless" are incredibly stupid sentiments. If you buy Aleve or any other name-brand analgesic, you're paying three times what someone buying generic is, and you get exactly the same relief, because it's exactly the same drug. If you buy Green Giant corn for $1.50 per can, you're getting an inferior product to the generic on the same shelf that costs sixty cents, because Green Giant doesn't taste as good – they add high fructose corn syrup, making your corn taste like it was starting to rot and ferment.

As to Linux and your time, that used to be accurate, but no more. Installing it takes very little time (far less time than installing Windows) and will save you *lots* of time once it's installed. No more patch Tuesdays with reboots; patching Linux takes a single click and you're done. No reboots unless you're upgrading the entire OS. What takes ten to fifteen clicks in Windows takes one or two in Linux – provided, of course, you choose your distro wisely. You can't just pick a random distro and judge Linux as a platform, because all Linuxes are different, some in small ways and some in huge ways.

Not only are the best things in life free, but the two things you absolutely cannot live without, air and water, are free. The third thing you absolutely cannot do without is food, which requires free rain and which you can grow for free.

The best things in life are not only free, but in many cases, like water and Linux, the free commodity is superior to the one you pay for. Oh, and those free nectarines are the best tasting ones I've ever eaten, but then, all the others I've eaten were commercially grown and sold in a store. Home grown, free food is always superior to the stuff you buy in the grocery store.

You can keep that pile of gold. I don't need it, Mr. Midas.

Aug 09, 2012

John thinks I'm a space alien

"Hi, Steve, how ya doin'?" Ruthie said as she got a mug out of the freezer.

"Hi, Ruthie. Pretty good, except I don't think I'll ever get that book finished. I keep finding mistakes," I said as I sat down next to Crazy John and pulled out my wallet. Ruthie handed me the beer she'd just poured.

"Computer's battery died so I thought I'd get a beer or two while it was charging," I said.

Crazy John really is insane; he suffers from schizophrenia and its delusions. They tell me he used to be really intelligent, but one night he was beaten, robbed, and thrown in a dumpster and left for dead. He was never the same afterwards.

John's passion is his main delusion – that he was once abducted by space aliens and that space aliens have infiltrated our world. I try to debunk the poor fellow's insane ramblings with scientific facts. I've explained how Einstein had worked out relativity and the cosmic constant, that the faster you go the slower time goes and there's no way to go faster than light, obviously not mentioning space warping which some theorize might someday get us past that hurdle. He talks of Area 51 and I respond with how unlikely that even if there were space aliens, they wouldn't be the least bit humanoid. In fact, that's where the idea behind *Little Green Men* in the book *Nobots* came from -- talking with Crazy John.

He gave me a pointed look, and by that I mean he actually pointed at me. "I know who you are!" he said sternly.

I was amused. "Of course you do, John, I've been drinking with you for years!" pretending to not know what he was talking about. He changed the subject. Sort of.

"Where did that face on Mars come from?" he asked.

I groaned; not this nonsense again. "It's a trick of the

363

light and where the position of the camera is, John. Other photos of the same rock show that it doesn't really look anything like a human face. It's the same with the Martian bunny rabbit."

"What bunny rabbit?"

"There's a rock one of the robot rovers took a picture of that, from the angle it's taken, looks just like a rodent. There are a lot of other things like that."

I tried to explain the concept of Pareidolia to him, pointing out so-called images of the virgin Mary made from rust running down overpasses and things, but he would have none of it and simply changed the subject again. "There is one thing that will go faster than light," he said. "Human telepathy!"

I rolled my eyes. "Show me some proof of telepathy's existence, John. If you can show me someone who can read my mind or even some biology that shows it's possible I'll believe it. But I've seen no documentation of anyone actually being able to do it."

I finished the mug and put it and another buck and a quarter on the bar, and Ruthie poured another beer. John got a weird look on his face and wandered off.

Good, I'd had enough crazy for one day.

Ruthie shook her head sadly. "Poor guy," she said.

Jun 12, 2013

Where's my damned tablet?

I'd like to know why in the hell nobody is selling a tablet, or maybe an app for existing tablets, that will let me watch over the air TV on it?

All of the necessary hardware is there. Wi-fi and bluetooth are radios. Some cell pones can pick up FM music stations, and have been able to do so and have done so for years.

The FM radio band sits between channels six and seven on the VHF television band. If it can hear radio, it can see TV.

The technology is there, why isn't the commercial device to be found? Offer a tablet I can watch TV without the internet and I'll buy one. Maybe two.

March 16, 2015

Are printed books' days numbered?

In his 1951 short story *The Fun They Had*, Isaac Asimov has a boy who finds something really weird in the attic – a printed book. In this future, all reading was done on screens.

When e-books like the Nook and Kindle came out, there were always women sitting outside the building I worked in, on break on a nice spring day reading their Nooks and Kindles. It looked like the future to me, Asimov's story come true. I prefer printed books, but thought that it was because I'm old, and I was thirty before I read anything but TV and movie credits on a screen.

And then I started writing books. My youngest daughter Patty is going to school at Cincinnati University (as a proud dad I have to add that she's Phi Beta Kappa and working full time! I'm not just proud, I'm in awe of her) and when she came home on break and I handed her a hardbound copy of *Nobots* she said "My dad wrote a book! And it's a REAL book!"

So somehow, even young people like Patty value printed books over e-books.

My audience is mostly nerds, since few non-nerds know of me or my writing, so I figured that the free e-book would far surpass sales of the printed books. Instead, few people are downloading the e-books. More download the PDFs, and more people buy the printed books than PDFs and ebooks combined.

Most people just read the HTML online, maybe that's a testament to my m4d sk1llz at HTML (yeah, right).

Five years ago I was convinced ink was on the way out, but there's a book that was printed long before the first computer was ever turned on that says "the news of my death has been greatly exaggerated".

March 20, 2015

A suggestion to mobile browser makers and the W3C

There are an awful lot of pages on my web site, and I've been busy making them all "mobile-friendly". Most of them are little or no problem making them look good on all platforms, but there are three that are especially problematic.

I jumped this hurdle (well, sort of stumbled past it) by making two of each of the pages with a link to the mobile page from the index.

Ideally, I could just check to see if it was a phone or not and redirect phones to the mobile page, but there's no way to make this 100% successful. Each brand of phone has a different user agent, and there are a lot of phone browsers you can install. On top of that, is it an Android phone or an Android tablet? With the minimum typeface size and viewport set, those pages are fine on the PC version but the phone version looks like crap.

Apple should have thought of this when they made the first iPhone, and Google should have thought of this when developing Android. The answer is simple, but it can only be implemented by browser makers and perhaps the W3C.

From the beginning of the World Wide Web, browsers looked for index.html, the default front page in any directory. This worked fine before smart phones, but no longer.

Phone browsers should look first for mobile.html, and if it exists display that, and display index.html if it isn't there. Tablets and computers would behave as they always have.

It doesn't have to be mobile.html, it could be any name as long as everyone agreed that it was the standard, like they did with index.html.

Maintaining a web site would be much easier if they did

this. What do you guys think?
Thursday May 14, 2015

I finally did find find workarounds for the three pages that need a mobile-only version. At first I just had a link at the top of the page, but this morning did a little googling and found a very short javascript program, about four lines long, that looks at the browser's screen resolution. This won't work if the phone's javascript is shut off, and I've only tested it on my own phone, so I need to leave the links in.
Saturday March 12, 2016

Futurists...

I just uploaded the last item in *Yesterday's Tomorrows*, a futurist essay by "the father of science fiction," Hugo Gernsback. In his essay, written in 1926, he describes the year 1976. Those of you who believe the guys who say the singularity is near or that death will be conquered within your lifetime should read it.

Futurists! Where in the hell is my flying car? Why are there no bases on the moon, like the futurists said in the 1960s we'd have by now? Why did no one see digital photography coming? Or phones in your pockets? Or the internet?

Gernsback sold electronic components, some of which he designed himself, yet didn't seem to understand "electricity, the mysterious fluid". He thought we'd be able to control the weather with it, and even more nonsensical things. He seemed steeped in the cult of Tesla, who had promised wireless delivery of electricity.

Coincidentally, Soylent News just mentioned a story about transplanting porcine hearts into humans, and the company's co-founder is a futurist. Of course, I left a comment about futurists.

I go into it in detail about futurism both in the book's foreword and the introduction to the Gernsback essay.

August 14, 2015

369

"My God! It's full of fail!" -David Bowman

What a mess.

Yesterday when I turned my computer on, an old Acer Aspire One, the "Upgrade to Windows 10!" nag screen popped up. Okay, what the hell, I'll try it, since Microsoft says going back is easy.

It took four hours to download and another hour for "preparing to upgrade Windows" to finish, and I was given a choice – upgrade now, or schedule for later? I scheduled it for nine last night, since I wanted to use the computer for, you know, computing.

At nine I told it to go ahead. I probably went to bed around ten, and the computer screen was still black with a "working..." graphic.

This morning it said it was ready. It rebooted, and took a full half hour to reach the desktop, which was simply butt-ugly and primitive looking. The kids doing the designing at Microsoft really suck at what they do.

Before it got to the password box there was quite a bit of user-hostile Microsoft spyware to opt out of. That, and the extreme slowness and butt-ugliness is all I could see that was changed. All of the changes seemed completely cosmetic. I found no additional features or usefulness at all.

My shortcut to Firefox on the task bar was gone. Microsoft Word and Excel were gone as well, although Open Office was still there. I went through the start menu's "other programs" or whatever it's called, and those applications were just *gone*.

Microsoft is just evil.

I have the flashblock extension installed, with a few sites whitelisted. Since KSHE changed their stream provider, I can't hear it on Firefox, so I set it to run IE on startup with the KSHE player as its home page. It took a full fifteen minutes before any music came out.

The new IE is called something else, I forgot what, but fortunately they didn't change the icon much or I'd never have found it. What is wrong with those people?

And I have never seen a slower computer, and my first one back in 1982 had a CPU that was over a thousand times slower than my notebook. The computer was simply unusable and extremely hard to navigate.

I was really glad I have my passwords written down, and it looked like I was going to lose all my bookmarks. I downloaded Firefox, and decided to go back to W7 before installing. I worried I'd have to buy Word, since the magazines all insist on it and Microsoft had apparently uninstalled it. Oh, magazines. I got my first rejection letter yesterday. I'll post it tomorrow.

Windows Ten is the worst operating system I've ever used. Of course, I understand that W8 was worse.

I went to uninstall it and it said I'd have to plug it in to uninstall – and it was fully charged. I figured it would take all day, so I plugged it in and set it going. Then doing something I never do, I went to facebook on my phone, and I hate typing on a phone.

Surprisingly, it only took an hour, and after it booted it seems to be like it was before the "upgrade". Firefox, Word, and Excel were back.

September 15, 2015

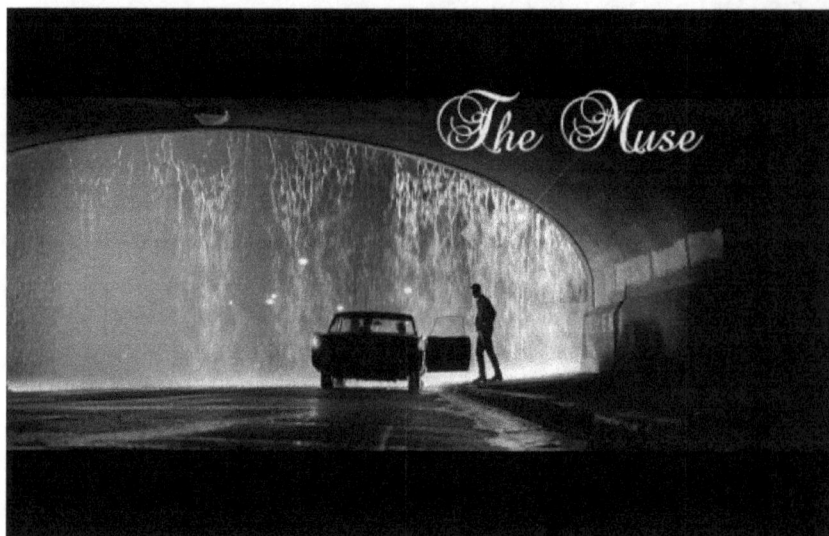

The Muse

I received a strange note, made of cut up magazines pasted to paper and slipped under my door. It read "Your muse has been kidnapped. If you want her back, meet under the Facebook Street Bridge after dark. Bring your wallet, passport, and an umbrella."

Crap, my muse was gone? I looked, and sure enough it was missing. It's really important to me, so I got my passport, made sure my wallet was in my pocket, and took an umbrella, even though the weatherman said there was no chance of rain. I went to the bridge around sunset and waited.

The weatherman was wrong. As I waited under the bridge it started pouring. A little after dark a black limousine pulled up, and the rear door opened. "Get in," a woman's voice said. I did.

A mean looking short haired blonde in the front passenger seat was pointing a very large black handgun at me. "You're not Neo," the skinny dark haired girl in the back said accusingly.

"Me?" I replied, scared to death. Or scared of death, maybe. "No, I'm mcgrew, I don't know any Neo. I'm missing some property and someone said to wait under this bridge and I could get it back."

"Oh," said the blonde, putting the gun away. "Morpheus said to give you this," and handed my muse to me!

I put my muse in my jacket and started to open the door. The blonde had her gun out again. "Fifty bucks, asshole!"

I gave her two twenties and a ten. "Why was I told to bring a passport?" I asked. The dark haired skinny girl laughed. "Morpheous was just fucking with you. Now get out!"

I still can't figure out what that was all about...

November 3, 2015

Where's My Fridge?

I plan to buy a house next spring, so I'll almost certainly need a new refrigerator. There's a problem: they don't make the fridge I want, and never have. I can't figure out why.

Refrigerators today are quite different than antique ones, using a different coolant because of the ozone layer, better insulation, the use of rare earth magnets in the motors, and other improvements.

But they're still incredibly wasteful.

The fridge I want has two vents outside, much like dryer vents but insulated. There is an electronic outside thermometer, one in the refrigerator, and one inside the freezer.

When the temperature outside is above seventy Fahrenheit, the heat taken from the fridge is vented outside, so the air conditioner doesn't have to work harder to cool the hot air refrigerators let out inside the house.

Under seventy the air is vented into, rather than outside, the house. If the heat is on, it doesn't work as hard.

But most of all is winter. It's ludicrous that we pump

the heat from our freezers with a lot of energy expenditure, while freezing air is right outside that could come in the intake hose and freeze and cool your food. At freezing, this fridge doesn't need the compressor at all and compressors take a lot of energy to operate.

I don't know why nobody is selling those things.

November 07, 2015

1950s
TV

A year or so ago, an executive from an electronics company (Apple, if I remember correctly) spoke of the lack of innovation in television sets since the 1950s, and my reaction was "He's either stupid or thinks I am."

In the 1950s, televisions had knobs on the set for changing channels and adjusting the volume. Remote controls were brand new, expensive, limited in capability, and used ultrasound rather than infrared.

The screens were vacuum tubes, and most were monochrome. Color television was brand new, and it was nearly 1960 before any stations started broadcasting in color. Rather than being rectangular, color screens were almost round; even black and white sets' screens weren't true rectangles.

They had no transistors, let alone integrated circuits; the IC had yet to be invented, and transistors were only used by the military. They were a brand-new invention. TVs didn't have the "no user-serviceable parts" warning on the back. When the TV wouldn't come on, as happened every year or three, the problem was almost always a burned out vacuum tube. One would open the back of the set and turn it on. Any tubes that weren't lit were pulled and taken to the drug store or dime store for replacement. If that didn't fix the problem you called an expert TV repairman.

The signal was analog, and often or usually suffered from static in the sound, and ghosts and snow in the picture.

There was no cable, and of course no satellite television since nothing built by humans had ever gone into space.

However, there is one thing about television that hasn't changed a single iota: daytime TV programming.

In the 1950s most folks were well paid, and a single paycheck could easily pay for a family's expenses. Most women, especially mothers, stayed home. As a result, daytime TV was filled with female centered programming like soap operas, game shows, and the like. Usually there were cartoons in the late afternoon for the kids.

Today the rich have managed to get wages down so low that everyone has to have a job. The demographics of daytime television have radically changed as a result. Now, rather than housewives (of which few are left, and we now have house husbands as well), who can watch daytime TV? Folks home from work sick, both men and women, folks in the hospital, the unemployed, and retired people.

Yet daytime TV is still as female centered as it was when I was five. Soap operas, talk shows with female hosts and female guests discussing topics that would only appeal to women, and game shows.

What's wrong with the idiots running our corporations these days?

November 29, 2015

What a mess!

I was watching the morning news the other day, and opened the computer to record KSHE's "Lone Klassic"... and it was in Linux. What the hell? Apparently I should have shut it off the night before, because Microsoft had apparently installed an update and then rudely and maliciously rebooted the computer. It was in Linux because kubuntu is the default OS in GRUB. So I rebooted again, selected Windows, and the little thing came up and... just sat there. Ten minutes later I still had a black screen.

I pulled the battery and tried again. Ten minutes later and I still had a black screen. So when I'd yanked the battery again and restarted it, I selected "Windows Recovery" from GRUB. An Acer screen came up with selections for reinstalling Windows. The first wiped the hard drive, the second kept your files. I picked that one; there were data on the hard drive I hadn't backed up in a few days, including a new story I'd started the night before and was on a roll with.

Twenty minutes later the first progress bar said "1%".

I'd decided a long time ago to get a DVD burner for the old Dell, until about three weeks ago when I'd taken it apart to install the video card and hard drive from the old HP that had computed its last. There were no slots that would fit the card (older computer than I thought, I guess) and the drive ribbon was a single drive ribbon. I probably have a spare double drive ribbon in the basement, but since the card wouldn't work in the Dell, there really wasn't any point. I'd decided then to get an old laptop that already had a DVD burner. So this was the time, because I had writing to do and the install was going to take all day and half the night.

I drove to the pawn shop and bought an HP laptop with Windows 7 and a DVD burner. It's a lot bigger than I like a laptop to be, but the smaller, cheaper one with a DVD burner ran Windows 8, and I didn't want to deal with that garbage. Windows 7 is still the least annoying and least problematic of all of MS's OSes.

Of course I had to download Windows Defender and Firefox with IE, install Firefox, uninstall Norton and McAfee and Bing Bar and all the other effluent that comes with a new computer, reconfigure everything, and download and install Open Office and all the other programs I need.

Meanwhile, the Windows reinstall on the Acer had hung. Damn, I was going to lose everything I'd written the day before, since Windows had surely overwritten GRUB. I got lucky; it hadn't. So I went into Linux to copy everything to thumb drives, since I still can't get it on my network (time to try a new distro). I even found some movies I thought I'd permanently deleted by mistake months ago!

After I saved the data on thumb drives I rebooted again, and went back into Windows restore and let it wipe the drive. That was the next morning, and it took all day. By then I had the new laptop running pretty smoothly and was writing again. The next day was mostly spent getting the old Acer back to normal. I was amazed and pleased that it had destroyed neither Grub nor Linux.

I'd lost a few passwords and haven't yet reset them all, and lost all my bookmarks.

That new computer is too big, but it's a lot faster than the Acer.

So I turn the TV on this morning and it wouldn't pick up channel 49. Flipped through the stations, and all of them had really screwy colors. I have my fingers crossed that it's the converter and not the TV, since the converter had fallen off the shelf last night. I hope it is, because they're not expensive and TVs are. I'll find out when I play a DVD.

December 12, 2015

It was indeed the converter; it had been running too long. The next time it was on it was normal.

March 18, 2016

The Color of God

My dad was color blind, and he hated that term. "I can see colors," he would say, "Just not the same ones as you."

He was one of the five percent of males with the red/green color blindness, as was his brother Bill. They couldn't tell the difference between red and green at all.

When I was small, stop signs in Illinois were yellow. Dad was mad as hell when they changed all of them to red, because the red stop sign stands out against a green background for most people, but for someone with this type of color deficiency the sign becomes practically invisible when there are green plants around.

He got a ticket for running a red light once in Arizona. For you and me, green means go, red means stop. To him, the light on the top means stop and the light on the bottom means go. They had installed the traffic light upside down! He still had to pay the ticket, even though it was the city's fault that he ran the light.

Now, imagine not color deficiency like my dad had, but a true color blindness, where a truly color blind person could see no color at all, only shades of gray.

Imagine a world where half of the people were truly color blind and could only see gray. How could you describe "red" to such a person? I don't think it's possible; one needs a referent, and there would be none.

People who could see color would know for sure that

color exists, even though they couldn't explain color to someone who couldn't see color. But what would a color blind person believe? Probably half, who have half of the people they know able to see color and half who don't telling them that color exists, and they would believe that they were lacking in this useless ability.

A very large percentage of the color blind population would believe that those who believe in color were fools or insane.

"Prove that your 'color' is real!"

"I can't."

"Then it doesn't exist."

Now, imagine that God exists. Guess what? He does. I can no more prove that He exists than I can prove that the color red exists. I can prove that the frequency 4×10^{14} Hz exists, but I can't prove that I can perceive that frequency as the color red, which is what you want me to prove.

Half of us know God. We don't just believe, we *know*. We can see his handiwork everywhere, feel his love. Half of us can't, so must either believe me or think I'm full of bovine excrement.

Such is the color of God.

January 23, 2016

KDE! What Have You Done?!

Note: Typed this out last year but never got around to posting it.

I've been meaning to install Linux on this notebook for quite some time, and finally got around to it Friday.

I started using Linux back in 2002 with Mandrake, and I loved it. They later renamed it Mandriva, and I kept using it. Then I found out that they were disbanding and patches would stop coming, so I switched to kubuntu, which is Ubuntu with a KDE desktop instead of that God-awful Gnome desktop. It ran happily on an old HP tower for years until the old tower had a severe hardware failure. I still need to take its hard drive and video card out and install them in the old Dell, which isn't on my network because it's running XP.

My first notebook I had like this one was stolen in a burglary five or six years ago. It was the same model as this, and it ran kubuntu very well, far better than its native Windows. With Windows I had to run a program from the ISP to get wi-fi working on it, but it just worked fine on kubuntu without my having to do anything.

So Friday I put it on this notebook dual-boot, since I need Microsoft Word even though I hate Microsoft Word. Knowing it would take a while I plugged in its power, and plugged it into the network for more speed. It took ten minutes to get my part of the installation done, and I watched the news as Linux installed.

I booted it up when it was done, and egad, KDE! What have you done?! Yes, it's a beautiful desktop, but it isn't the same KDE I've been using for almost fifteen years.

What the hell, you stupid wet behind the ears software designers, are you NUTS? Look, you dumbasses, changing an interface all around for no good reason is just brain-dead stupid. *I don't want to learn a brand new God damned interface* unless it's instantly recognizable as an improvement, and this is about the same stupid move Microsoft made with Windows Eight. Look, you morons, if I wanted to learn a new interface I'd install Gnome or something.

Next I wanted to hear music, so I needed on the internet. I tried to connect to my server but simply couldn't get on with the wi-fi. Strangely, I was able to connect with someone else's unsecured wi-fi. It had gotten on the internet easily with the network cable plugged in.

Someone had said that Libre Office could read and write .doc files well, so I tried it. First I opened an Open Office document, and the font face was some cartoonish sans serif font instead of Gentium Book Basic.

Then I opened a .doc file, and it opened, although instead of Courier it had a different sans serif face.

I wanted to get at some files on my external hard drive, so I plugged the network cable in. It indicated a connection, and I could get on the internet through the router, but the external drive didn't show up.

I doubt that it's the OS's fault, though, since it wouldn't let me connect with my own wi-fi but was fine with someone else's. I'm pretty sure it's that damned modem-router that the cable company makes me rent. I'd change ISPs if I weren't planning to move next Spring.

At any rate, KDE now sucks. Someone said XCFE was good, I'll have to try it.

Posted March 16, 2016

MY GENERATION
(Peter Townshend)
21st Century

DECCA

31877
(116,675)

THE WHO
Vocal With Instrumental
Accompaniment
PRODUCED BY SHEL TALMY
RECORDED IN ENGLAND

Devon Music,
Inc. (BMI)
(3:15)

People try to put us d-down
Hard for us to get around
Things kids say sound awful c-c-cold
'cause I didn't die before I got old

This is my generation
This is my generation, baby

Why don't you all f-fade away
I can't dig what kids all s-s-say
I'm not trying to cause a big s-s-sensation
I'm just talkin' 'bout my g-g-g-generation

This is my generation
This is my generation, baby

Why don't you all fu-fu-fu go away
Forgot what I was going to say
I'm not trying to cause a b-big s-s-sensation
I'm just talkin' 'bout my g-g-generation

This is my generation
This is my generation, baby

People try to put us d-down
Hard for us to g-g-get around
Things they say sound awful c-c-cold
I didn't die before I got old

This is my generation
This is my generation, baby
April 2, 2016

385

Useful Dead Technologies Redux

Ten years ago I wrote a humorous article titled "Useful Dead Technologies" about technologies that are no longer used that I sorely miss, like furnaces that still worked when the power went out, or things made of durable steel instead of today's fragile and short-lived plastics.

A couple of the things on the list have improved since then. Shoelaces, for instance. Ten years ago I wrote:

"Shoelaces have been designed for hundreds of years to keep your shoes on your feet. No longer. Today's shoelaces are designed with one purpose in mind – to annoy you.

"What are they making shoelaces out of now? *Nylon!* Good old frictionless nylon 'because of its strength'. One wonders if today's engineers even need a college degree, as it seems that some things, like today's shoelaces, were designed by 'special ed' students.

"Because now, not only are they made of a friction-free material, they're round rather than flat, further eroding their ability to stay tied."

Since then, they've been making them of both cotton and nylon woven together, with all the friction of cotton and the strength of nylon.

And they're flat again.

Another item was knobs on car radios. At the beginning of the century they had buttons for tuning and volume, so you

386

couldn't turn it up or down without taking your eyes off the road. It was dangerous. Thankfully, they've gone back to knobs, even though they're digital rather than potentiometers.

The radio in my car now really annoys me, because the morons who designed it stupidly put the volume knob right above the tuning knob rather than the time-tested volume on the left side of the radio and tuning on the right. Often when I try to adjust the volume, I'll grab the wrong knob.

I also miss the way presets worked back in the analog age. They were simple to operate: to set a preset to a station, you tuned the radio to that station, pulled out on the button, and pushed it back in. These days you simply cannot tune a station to a preset while you're driving, at least unless you're a suicidal maniac. What's worse, every radio has a different way of tuning a preset button, and many are impossible to figure out without an owner's manual.

The worst thing about that radio is I can't change the time on the clock. The car came with a manual, but they put three different models of radio in those cars, and the manual lists all of them. But each of the three says to push a button that simply isn't on the radio!

And I just discovered by watching a commercial where they were trying to sell new cars – the morons took the knobs away again, and now it's even worse than the buttons. Now they have touch screens. *There's no way possible to change the station or volume without taking your eyes off the road!*

I'm all for hiring the handicapped, but I wish they wouldn't hire idiots to be engineers. Touch screens for automobile controls are brain-dead stupid.

The following items haven't all become extinct in the last decade, I simply didn't think of them when I wrote the first article. Here are some more.

Thermostats that don't need batteries

In the twentieth century, thermostats were simple yet clever devices: a mercury switch on the end of two dissimilar metals. The metal would bend one way or the other depending on temperature. When the metal reached a certain shape, the mercury would roll down the inside of the switch and close the circuit.

Shortly before the turn of the century they came out with programmable thermostats, and they were indeed superior despite the one disadvantage of needing a battery; perhaps it could be done, but I don't see how you could have a programmable thermostat without one. But they could be set to turn themselves down at bedtime, then warm the house back up before you arose in the morning. More comfort, lower heating costs.

Fast forward to a couple of years ago when the landlord had a new furnace installed in my house. With the new furnace came a new thermostat. The old thermostat was programmable, the new one isn't.

But it's digital and still needs batteries.

At first I thought they had to be digital because mercury has been shown to be toxic, but on second thought you could simply have a copper ball replacing the mercury. Such a switch would be easy to engineer.

Folks, digital thermostats have been in use for a couple of decades now. Why aren't new homes designed to have a low voltage DC supply to thermostats so batteries wouldn't be needed?

Sticky Menus

When GUIs first came out they were a great improvement over the old CLIs. Easy to use and hard to screw up. Click on a menu heading and the menu drops down. Nothing happened until you clicked somewhere. If you clicked on an empty space the menu closed. Click on a different menu and that menu opened.

So some moron had the bright idea that if you had the file menu open and simply mouse over the edit menu, File closes and Edit opens.

This incredibly stupid change drives me nuts, especially in Firefox and GIMP. I have nested bookmarks in Firefox, and after clicking a folder I have to slowly and carefully slide the cursor over, making sure the cursor never goes over a different folder, as the folder I want will close and the one I don't opens.

GIMP drives me nuts, too, especially trying to select the "rectangle select" from the "selection" menu, as the "filters" menu will open when I'm trying to navigate to "rectangle select".

Folks, losing sticky menus was an incredibly stupid, productivity killing thing. BRING THEM BACK!

Rectangular cabinets

Stuff used to have cabinets made of wood. The better stuff had rounded corners, because they were safer.

Every large CRT TV I ever owned was rectangular, before 2002 when I bought a forty two inch Sony Trinitron. It takes up a huge amount of floor space, and you can't set anything on it because it's stupidly shaped. My DVD and VCR and converter box should be able to sit on it, but nothing can.

The rectangular shape is far from extinct, but more and more things seem to be eschewing it.

Useful user manuals

Some would criticize me for this one, saying user manuals always sucked, and they would have a valid point. When I was young, user manuals were complete – and completely unreadable to many if not most people. I had trouble making heads or tails out of more than one, and I could read at a post-doctoral level at age twelve.

DOS 6.2 came in a box with two floppies and a thick user manual. Windows 95 came with a very thin manual. I don't remember what XP's was like, but the manual for this old Acer laptop was really thin.

Then my phone. Honestly, come on, now. A smart

phone is a complex, sophisticated piece of equipment but its user manual is three by five inches and a dozen pages?

The worst was the "Seagate Personal Cloud", which is really a network hard drive. Tiny pamphlet with pictures and few words. Look, folks, pictures are good for illustration but lousy for information. I spent twenty useless minutes studying the thing, then finally just plugged it in and turned it on. It didn't even need a manual!

I did find a detailed, very good manual for it online. Its printed manual should have added its URL.

Automobile hoods and trunks that didn't need props

Before the 1970s, to open a hood you opened the hood latch, and springs opened the hood and held it open. It was an ingenious design where it didn't spring open right away, you lifted it a little first. Trunks worked the same way. It didn't matter if it was a Volkswagen, a little Plymouth Valiant, or a big luxury Cadillac.

Then the Arab oil embargo hit in 1974 and the price of gasoline doubled in a matter of months. People started replacing their American gas guzzlers with compact Japanese cars that had far better mileage.

The more weight a vehicle carries, the worse its mileage is. Part of the raising of gas mileage was replacing the heavy steel with a lighter material when possible, and those springs and the rest of the steel assembly for them were jettisoned, replaced with that stupid hood prop.

Soon American auto makers started following suit. I don't know if big sedans and luxury cars ever went to hood props, but I know my '67 Mustang had no hood prop, nor did my '74 LeMans. My '76 Vega did, though, as did every other car I owned afterwards until I bought an '02 Concorde. Rather than springs or a hood prop, it had lightweight hydraulic struts for both the front and back.

It was far better than a hood prop, but not as good as the spring mechanism. Those springs lasted forever, but the struts fail in a few years and you wind up propping up your hood and trunk with a stick. Either that or shell out for new ones.

Bumper Jacks

All cars and trucks used to have bumpers, and there was a slot on each end of each bumper. The slots were for flat tires. If you had a flat, you got the jack out of the car, hooked it into the slot, and jacked it up with its handle like you were pumping water out of a hand operated well pump. This was easy on the back, as you were standing up. It took very little effort to jack up the vehicle.

Now they all have scissors jacks, and I hate them. You have to get down on your hands and knees to slide it under the car, and jack it up by cranking it. It always takes skin off of your knuckles and takes twice the effort and three times the time.

Yes, the new jacks take up far less space, but the trade-offs simply weren't worth it.

I miss the full sized spares, too. If you had a flat, you changed the tire, got the flat tire fixed, and simply put that one in the trunk instead of having to change the "doughnut" to put your real tire on.

At least we have fix-a-flat now.

May 5, 2016

The Old Sayings Are Wrong

There's No Such Thing as a Free Lunch

Taken literally, this is patently false, as anyone with a grandmother knows. You may say "well, Grandma paid for it so it isn't free." But it is free – to you.

I have a fruit tree in my front yard, and all its fruit is completely free.

What this old saying means is "never trust a salesman". If a salesman offers to buy your lunch, it will cost you.

From a physicist's perspective, it means you can't break the three laws of thermodynamics; you can never get more energy out of a system than you put in.

You get what you pay for

This is another salesman lie, with the sales lady getting you to believe that the higher priced item is always better than the cheap item. But you *don't* always get what you pay for. Often the less expensive item is equal or superior, with over-the-counter drugs being an excellent example. Aleve costs three times what generic naproxin does, yet is the exact same drug.

And of course there are swindlers. If someone sells you a counterfeit Rolex at a real Rolex price, or a diamond ring with a zirconium stone, you have been swindled and certainly didn't get what you paid for.

You usually pay for what you get, but often you pay far less than you otherwise did. Just yesterday I saw a "going out of business" sign at a Radio Shack, and since I needed a new soldering iron I went in. The iron and solder were a third what I would have paid had I not procrastinated, and I got a TV antenna for five bucks. I got a lot more than I paid for.

Get what you pay for? Usually, but sometimes you get more than you paid for and sometimes a high priced item turns out to be utter junk.

What goes up must come down

This was true until July of 1969, when astronauts left man-made objects on the moon. They're not likely to ever come back down.

There are robots rolling around Mars. These, too, are unlikely to ever come down.

Then there are the Voyager spacecraft, which are now outside the entire solar system. It's a certainty that these machines will never return to Earth.

Money doesn't grow on trees

Of course it does, orchards grow lots of money. Not only does it grow on trees, it grows on corn stalks, tomato plants, soybean bushes...

A picture is worth a thousand words

If it is, then draw me a picture that says "a picture's worth a thousand words." Pictures can be aids in communication, and a picture is better than a description, but it's impossible to teach using only pictures.

However, it is true in a monetary sense, in that a thousand word magazine article will garner a commercial writer less than the artist who made the cover art did.

What doesn't kill me makes me stronger

Nietzsche was an idiot. Just ask any brain-damaged quadriplegic if he's stronger than he was before the accident.

Oh, and also, God isn't dead, Nietzsche is.

You can never be too rich or too thin

Whoever started this stupid meme was a gold plated idiot. Of course you can be too thin. Bulimia and anorexia have killed people.

The "too rich" is subjective. I'd say if you have more

money than anyone could spend in a lifetime when there are hungry people, you're too rich. How can someone like that live with themselves?

Lightning never strikes the same place twice

It amazes me how gullible most people are, believing everything anyone tells them. They even believe stuff that was proven untrue centuries ago, as in this saying. It was believed for at least hundreds of years and likely longer until Ben Franklin disproved it with his kite and his invention of the lightning rod. If lightning never strikes the same place twice, lightning rods wouldn't work.

Only the good die young

Well, they showed you a statue, told you to pray
They built you a temple and locked you away
Aw, but they never told you the price that you pay
For things that you might have done
Only the good die young
That's what I said
Only the good die young – Billy Joel

I've heard this nonsense all my life, and can't understand why people actually believe that tripe. Yes, some good young people do die way before their time.

But if *only* the good die young, then why are so many inner-city young men killed in gun battles with rival gangs? Good people never die in gang battles unless they're not a part of the fight and simply get caught in the crossfire.

Why do so many young people get drunk and die in their cars when they wrap them around trees? Good people don't drive when they're drunk.

And if you're Christian, remember that Jesus said "none are good, except God." Only the *very* young; the small children who die innocent are good. But bad young people die all the time.

June 1, 2016

They say that Santa's coming,
He comes 'round every year.
He comes he'll meet a shotgun slug
'cause he ain't welcome here.

Five years ago this Christmas
The fatass came around
With jingle bells and ho ho hos
And looking like a clown.

He came in for a landing
As I let out a yawn
My house is pretty little
So he landed on the lawn.

I didn't have the time to yell
As he came through the fog;
He came in fast and and came down hard
And landed on my dog.

He looked around all furtive like
As I reached for my gun,

Then grabbed the reins, yelled "giddie up,"
And took off on the run.

And so, that fatassed bastard
Better stay away from here
'cause ever since he killed my dog
I have no Christmas cheer.
December 1, 2016

Complete
Springfield Fragfest
Table of Contents

Page 74
Nacho joined the game

Page 75
Quake 2 mod sank like a rock
W2K frags Q3A

Page 76
Team frags Murray

Page 77
Yello joined the game
Tikki joined the game

Page 78
Quick updates frag Sunday

Page 81
Tikki joins the game

Page 82
Yello frags pinball guy
Mr. Hanky melted
Matt and bill can't escape, uh, what's that thing, durn when I
was younger my memory was better...

Page 83
Tikki can't escape Planet Quake's BFG
`eNtiTy frags Tikki
Yello can't escape Phone company's GFB

Page 84
Napalm melted
Gestalt died

Page 85
Yello joined the game
Nacho frags Dallas
Dallas melted
Hulka frags visitors

Page 86
Flamethrower frags Elephant

Page 87
Moon frags Blue
Page 88
Qidz can't escape Level's BFG

Page 89
Nooze can't escape drought's blaster
Everybody frags ticket

Page 94
Ticket frags slowpoke

Page 96
Ticket does a back flip into the lava

Page 98
Arcadia melted

Page 100
Smurf frags particle accelerator

Page 101
Arcadia died
crash joined the game

Page 103
Hell Hole died

Page 107
Arcadia did a back flip into the lava

Page 108
Nacho joined the game
Arcadia died

Page 109
World Peace tripped on its own grenadine

Page 110
Yello joined the game
Beach house and Spew can't escape ticket's grenade

Page 111
Ticket tries to escape Smurf's shotgun

Page 112
Mail frags fragfest
BitchX joined the game

Page 113
Smurf should have used a smaller gun

Page 114
E3 frags Nacho
BitchX tripped on his own grenade

Page 115
Yello swallowed Granny's rocket

Page 116
Green and orange with purple polka dot h4x0rz swallow U.S. government page's grenade

Page 117
Ticket tries to escape mail's grenade

Page 118
Tikki tripped on his own grenade

Page 119
Fragfest tries to escape Blue H4x0r's rocket
Beach House ate Tikki's Rocket

Page 120
Yello joined the game
Desiato joined the game
Mad Scientist and Sued tries to escape ticket's super shotgun

Page 122
Golf Course tries to escape Dopey's BFD

Page 124
Fragfest frags ticket
H4x0rz frags H4x0rz
GL Setup tried to avoid download's shotgun

Page 125
List can't escape Drive's rocket
Clan Undergrounds frags l33t
Yello melted

Page 126
Pulse frags ticket
Old Folks frag Tea

Page 127
Yello joined the game
Ticket disconnected